These Were People Once

These Were People Once
The Online Trade in Human Remains, and Why It Matters

Damien Huffer and Shawn Graham

berghahn
NEW YORK · OXFORD
www.berghahnbooks.com

First published in 2023 by

Berghahn Books

www.berghahnbooks.com

Library of Congress Cataloging-in-Publication Data

Names: Huffer, Damien, author. | Graham, Shawn, author.
Title: These Were People Once: The Online Trade in Human Remains, and Why It
  Matters / Damien Huffer and Shawn Graham.
Other titles: Online Trade in Human Remains, and Why It Matters
Description: New York: Berghahn, 2023. | Includes bibliographical references.
Identifiers: LCCN 2023017767 (print) | LCCN 2023017768 (ebook) | ISBN
  9781805390862 (hardback) | ISBN 9781805390879 (ebook)
Subjects: LCSH: Human remains (Archaeology)—Collectors and collecting. | Dead—
  Collectors and collecting | Sale of organs, tissues, etc. —Moral and ethical aspects.
Classification: LCC CC79.5.H85 H84 2023 (print) | LCC CC79.5.H85 (ebook) |
  DDC 930.1—dc23/eng/20230602
LC record available at https://lccn.loc.gov/2023017767
LC ebook record available at https://lccn.loc.gov/2023017768

British Library Cataloguing in Publication Data

A catalogue record for this book is available from the British Library

ISBN 978-1-80539-086-2 hardback
ISBN 978-1-80539-363-4 epub
ISBN 978-1-80539-087-9 web pdf

https://doi.org/10.3167/9781805390862

Contents

Figures

Tables

Preface

They Sell *What* Online?

Studying the online trade in human remains was never part of the plan. For Damien, it stemmed from blogging he did from 2010 to 2012 about his graduate student research when studying for his PhD at the Australian National University. His blog, *It Surfaced Down Under!*, was where he shared his interpretations of the latest news about the antiquities trade in Southeast Asia and the Southern Hemisphere, highlighting and calling out galleries known to be actively participating in the trade in the Southern Hemisphere, as well as commenting on news of the day. One day, a particularly rapacious dealer based out of Melbourne was brought to Damien's attention—a man actively selling a wide variety of antiquities both big and small and authentic (or alleged to be so). He was also selling several items made from human remains. Via his website he advertised various fragments of forearms (ulnae and radii), fingers, and even two lower legs (tibiae and fibulae), still encased in soil. The corroded bronze bangles on the forearms showed that these individuals were buried over 2,500 years ago, most likely in what is today northwest Cambodia. Because Damien was beginning to make a name for himself in local circles, the authorities had reached out to him as an expert on human remains and on the antiquities trade. They brought him to the evidence room in the Canberra offices of the Cultural Property Division of the Australian government's Department of Environment, Water, Heritage, and the Arts. As he stood there with the field agents, one of them remarked, "Fair warning, what you'll see in there is more horrific than how it looked online."

The images that Damien had seen online had made the remains look almost . . . artistic. But on the cold evidence tables, they looked like evidence from a crime scene. They *were* evidence from a crime scene. What is more, these were *people*, once. Now, disarticulated, robbed from their resting place, the remains were relegated to anonymous things, fragments, stripped of their humanity, their dignity. This dealer knew the law and knew how to avoid being shut down completely. He had been previously arrested (in Cairo in 2008), and in 2005 he had been forced to forfeit items to the Australian Federal Police, in both cases for attempting to smuggle Egyptian artifacts, mummies, and sarcophagi into Australia (Milovanovic 2008). Once again, he wriggled free, returning to his gallery and resuming his sales of "rare and exotic" items (Chappell and Huffer 2013. He is active to this day, but so far he has not risked including human remains in the online catalog again.

From there, more and more of Damien's research involved studying the online places and mechanisms for trading human remains. Shawn followed Damien's work on Twitter out of a shared interest in the threat posed by the antiquities trade. We first met in person at an archaeology conference in 2015 when Damien presented his research on the human remains trade online, which was happening on sites like eBay and Instagram (Huffer and Chappell 2014). Shawn was in the audience and remarked to the effect, "That was very interesting, but did you know you can do this on a much larger scale? What do you think you'd find if you could look at thousands of posts at once? What if you could get the computer to do the looking for you?" For both of us, how we came to study the online trade in human remains, and to work together, was in a way a function of how social media algorithms work. We were embedded in the same mechanisms that powered the trade. We realized that archaeologists were missing something very important that was happening, and so we began our partnership.

If you know where to look, who to follow, and what phrases to search, it is ridiculously easy to buy human remains online. Vendors and collectors can be found all over Instagram, Facebook, e-commerce platforms of all sorts, and "regular" webstores. For the last several years, we have been trying to understand *why* people do this, *where* and *from whom* do the remains come or belong to, and *how extensive* is this trade. Damien is a bioarchaeologist (one who studies primarily ancient or historic-period human remains to understand how lives were lived in the past). Shawn is a digital archaeologist (one who uses digital technologies to ask new questions of the past, and who also thinks about how archaeological methods shed light on our digitally mediated present). In this book we pull together the answers we have found so far to those different questions by remixing, updating, expanding, and backfilling the gaps in our existing publications into a single, coherent narrative. This book will show that the human remains trade continues to thrive, causing harm to descendent communities and prohibiting what we can ever hope to know about humanity's shared past.

As coauthors, we have tried to remove as much technical jargon from our respective disciplines to make this book as accessible as possible (we imagine our ideal reader to be an undergraduate student or generally savvy member of the public who has not encountered these issues before). There is a glossary at the end of the book that will define terms and point to useful online sources for further information. At times, we do have to draw on our own disciplinary language working with this information or in these fields to get our points across.

We imagine that you might be interested in understanding the broader context that surrounds the trade in human remains. Everyone knows that one can buy all kinds of wondrous and bizarre things online. In the last few years, the number of e-commerce websites (in multiple languages) available for bidding, clicking "buy it now," or selling your own creations, services, or that used microwave that has been sitting in your garage for eons, has exploded. Increasingly large numbers of globalized citizens take this situation for granted. And yet, what is much less seen, understood, or (fortunately) acted upon, relatively speaking, is that these same e-commerce and social media platforms allowed at one time, or in some instances still do, for the sale of a very wide variety of illicit or questionable activities, at a variety of scales. This ranges from one-off individual transactions for, say, a pretty variety of parakeet you have always wanted, to persistent transnational organized criminal networks for wildlife, drugs, "fighting" dogs and other domestic animals, human trafficking for sex or labor, drug cartel recruiting, and the illicit (and so-called "licit") antiquities trade, among many other problems (e.g., Paul, Miles, and Huffer 2020; Xu, Cai, and Mackey 2020; Garcia 2021; Montrose, Kogan, and Oxley 2021).

These days, the persistence of the use of the internet for illicit activities continues even sometimes against the best efforts of certain platforms to fight misuse of their product. And here, we are talking primarily about e-commerce platforms. Factor social media into the mix, and the landscape has changed entirely, allowing various categories of e-crime and the scope of trafficking networks moving each category of material to flourish. In some cases, such as the human remains trade, the rise of social media platforms as go-to locations for both licit and illicit transactions—the exploitation of built-in features of these platforms for purposes perhaps never intended by the original designers—has actually created markets for products that would have otherwise received minimal attention.

The number one question that we have both been asked when giving talks to students and colleagues alike is: "You can buy that?!" The very existence of human remains for sale, whether loose bones, hair, whole skulls, organs in jars, fetuses, cremated ashes, or a wide variety of items or artwork made from or with human remains, is, we have found, a shocking revelation to most. And that is just the shock that can be elicited from realizing that such a market exists, never mind the immediate follow up questions of why?!, how?!, and who would actually want this?!

In our research to date, and in this book, we attempt to tackle these questions to the best of our ability. To set the scene, in Chapter 1 we will explore some of the routes through which the dead cease to be treated as people and become, after death, mere "things" to be traded. The trade in cadavers for anatomical specimens is one vector; another is as research specimens to fuel eugenics, social Darwinism, and the scientific racism of the late nineteenth and early twentieth centuries. We will present stories of specific individuals who were "otherized," turned into things for entertainment or were displayed or used as educational materials. Indigenous communities and allied scholars have in the last few decades sought to restore names, identities, and a sense of humanity to these disenfranchised people. This kind of collective response to encountering the "thing-ification" of ancestral remains stands in stark contrast to how much of the human remains trade operates explicitly or implicitly. Chosen from among hundreds of possible similar case studies, the life histories of the individuals we discuss in relation to the early days of the human remains trade is contextualized by an overview of key events or players that shaped early Western markets for human remains and the attitudes, the desire, the economic underpinnings, and the connection of early collectors to the birth of anatomy and physical (biological) anthropology as disciplines. We will outline how we conduct our research, and the ethics that go along with it.

In Chapter 2, we continue to look to the past to set the stage for the present. We take as examples two areas of human remains collecting with long histories that remain active today: mummies and reliquaries, as well as the related phenomenon of making contemporary "art" from human remains. We trace some of the themes that unite these earlier phenomena with the more modern social media dimension. We discuss how e-commerce and social media platforms have become primary locations for illicit trafficking, and what collecting looked like before and in the early days of the internet. This means we have to dip into the history of the US Communications Decency Act §230, the foundation of so much of our online lives. As we show, this legislation shields many forms of illicit trafficking and their practitioners online, and the intricacies of how human remains are advertised for sale. We then explore the language of online postings, whether these are made with an attempt to sell, or an attempt to "entertain," within the context of why our earliest research focused on Instagram and the ethical protocols for studying illicit trafficking on social media "at scale." Through scraping thousands of posts, and using various techniques of close and distant reading, we explain how it is possible to draw out the patterns that characterize the way people talk about the human remains that have passed into their possession. Not everything that is posted for sale has a price tag attached—many vendors are canny enough to take such discussions offline or into private messages—but still, there are enough price mentions that we can get a sense of the size of this trade. Such numbers are necessarily an underestimate of course, but the broad patterns of change year over year suggest that the trade is accelerating. We can also get a sense of the overall shape of the trade, on some platforms, by stitching together the network of who follows whom; the shape of that network also has implications for how ideas about the "proper" way to "appreciate" or consume the dead circulate in these spheres. We explore how buyers and sellers find each other both online and off, and how the current, and potentially forthcoming, tools provided by social media and e-commerce platforms make this increasingly easy.

In Chapter 3, we turn attention to how human remains, as pieces of once-living individuals now (usually) disarticulated, commodified, and "fetishized" into "curios," "specimens," "trophies," "oddities," and the like, are "looked at": that is, how they are viewed by those who collect, how aesthetics and "taste" trends are formed and disseminated, and how researchers like us also develop and use a variety of techniques to try to understand the visual effect/affect of these posts. We look at how collecting community tastes can be formed through online interactions with the bioarchaeological research community itself (where the latter chooses to engage with the former). We also take a slightly different approach to the question of taste formation among collectors and their online audiences by summarizing our recent work on the community formed around one particular TikTok personality and the "pushback" by archaeological professionals and concerned viewers that this platform's mechanics allows (Graham, Huffer, and Simons 2022). We introduce and use a neural network approach to see if we can map influence from one collector to another (and so, building up a network of influence that sits on top of the network of followers discussed in Chapter 2). This includes discussion of something of the longer history of how "Western" culture has consumed bodies and why. We try to understand what owning human remains does for collectors and vendors.

In Chapter 4, we ask the big question that everyone wants to know the answer to: is this *really* legal? The answer is complex and depends on many factors, including knowing the actual origin or cultural group to which the human remains belong. But we can approach the question from another direction and ask, *are vendors telling the truth*? Can anything be said about the cultural origin of human remains that are only known from a single photograph or video that emerges for a while on social media, then disappears again, usually once a purchase is made? This was one of the original motivating questions for our "Bone Trade Project" research. To begin to delve into this, we turn to neural network approaches that are built to identify human faces from a single photograph (and discuss the ethical issues that such an approach raises). Through a carefully designed pilot-level experiment drawing on key principles of forensic anthropology that underpin so-called ancestry (read: population) estimation and facial reconstruction (areas still important to law enforcement faced with missing person or John/Jane/Trans Doe cases), we use computer vision to see if broad groupings (formed on patterns of differences rather than similarities) can be determined via reference to examples from published forensic case reports, the bioarchaeological literature, and the same museum collections whose problematic origins were discussed to some extent in earlier chapters (Graham, Huffer, and Blackadar 2020). We do not think that it is possible to say anything about the large-scale origins of human remains circulating online to date, with the exception of individual examples that sometimes surface that clearly show a burial being looted, or bones naturally or culturally modified in very specific ways too difficult to "fake," or with the clear inclusion in the sale of specific documentation indicative of provenance, showing former museum accession numbers, or other such clues that can be investigated by civilians or law enforcement. However, we do think that we can demonstrate that what vendors claim about the remains is sometimes false. With that being the case, we argue that many more laws might be applicable than usually thought.

In Chapter 5, we sum everything up and tackle the biggest question of all—why does it all matter? What have we learned in our several years studying this phenomenon to date and where do we see the research headed? We want to leave readers thinking about what the continued and evolving existence of this once-niche, now growing, submarket means for threats to global cultural heritage, the evolving legal landscape of e-commerce and social media platforms, questions of online privacy when illicit or questionable activities are occurring, the damage that "puff-pieces" in news venues lauding a collector as a kooky or interesting individual do, and global society's ultimate responsibility to do right by the dead. Finally, a series of appendices will walk you through some of the technical tasks related to our work—from scraping to image analysis to some text analysis. We conclude the volume with advice on what the reader can do about this—and related—trades if you inadvertently encounter sales "in the wild" on your daily surfing.

Acknowledgments

Many people have traveled alongside us as we've tried to understand this trade. We are enormously grateful for their help, insight, encouragement, and good humor: Cristina Wood, Emma Gillies, Alex Lane, Jeff Blackadar, Cassandra McKenney, Scott Coleman, Kavita Mistry, Susan Lamb, Donna Yates, Katie Paul, Amr Al-Azm, Kathleen Miles, Gretchen Peters, Sam Hardy, Kim Martin, Tom Brughmans, Christine Halling, Ryan Seidemann, Cameron Walter, Judith Winters, and Tony Guerreiro, David Keller, Robert Fromkin, Caroline Greenway, and Alison Reid and TikTok user Archaeothot. Thank you all!

We'd like to particularly thank Katherine Davidson who read through and offered perceptive comments on our initial drafts, challenging us, pushing us to be better, and also Jaime Simons who helped sort out the catalog of pertinent laws; and Steph Halmhofer and Quinn Dombrowski who took our code for a spin. We are also grateful to the entire team at Berghahn Books for seeing this project come together, and to the anonymous peer reviewers of both the original articles and this expanded volume who pushed us in such productive ways.

Damien would especially like to acknowledge the unflagging love, support, and encouragement provided by his parents, his mother- and father-in-law, and most of all, his partner.

Shawn would like to thank his family for bearing with him and listening to him talk at length about all of this. He is also reminded of his classmate from his undergraduate Introduction to Human Osteology class, who dropped the class because of the aura of the remains they were working with. He did not get it then, but he understands better now.

We have been working and publishing on the trade in human remains for some time. This research is supported in part by funding from the Social Sciences and Humanities Research Council of Canada.

In this present volume we have drawn new research and new writing together with several of our open access publications (listed below), suitably reworked, overhauled, and remixed for thematic unity, to tell the story of our research and what we have found.

Huffer, Damien, and Shawn Graham. 2017. "The Insta-Dead: The Rhetoric of the Human Remains Trade on Instagram." *Internet Archaeology* 45(2). https://doi.org/10.11141/ia.45.5

Huffer, Damien, and Shawn Graham. 2018. "Fleshing Out the Bones: Studying the Human Remains Trade with Tensorflow and Inception." *Journal of Computer Applications in Archaeology* 1(1): 55–63.

Huffer, Damien, Cristina Wood, and Shawn Graham. 2019. "What the Machine Saw: Some Questions on the Ethics of Computer Vision and Machine Learning to Investigate Human Remains Trafficking." *Internet Archaeology* 52. https://doi.org/10.11141/ia.52.5.

Graham, Shawn, Damien Huffer, and Jeff Blackadar. 2020. "Towards a Digital Sensorial Archaeology as an Experiment in Distant Viewing of the Trade in Human Remains on Instagram." *Heritage* 3(2): 208–27. https://doi.org/10.3390/heritage3020013.

Graham, Shawn, Alex Lane, Damien Huffer, and Andreas Angourakis. 2020. "Towards a Method for Discerning Sources of Supply within the Human Remains Trade via Patterns of Visual Dissimilarity and Computer Vision." *Journal of Computer Applications in Archaeology* 3(1): 253–68. https://doi.org/10.5334/jcaa.59.

Graham, Shawn, Damien Huffer, and Jaime Simons. 2022. "When TikTok Discovered the Human Remains Trade: A Case Study." *Open Archaeology* 8(1): 196–219. https://doi.org/10.1515/opar-2022-0235.

1

The Lives behind the Photos

Every photo of human remains for sale online represents a single piece of evidence of a life lived. In most cases, it is also the only piece of evidence that the person whose mortal remains have been disassembled and sold was once alive.

Introduction

Last week (in late 2021), as we were writing this, we reported a Facebook page to Facebook's self-regulation machinery. A few days later, we received the response: the page does not contravene Facebook's policies. The page in question? It sells human skulls.

Dwell on that. Meta's main platforms of Facebook and Instagram, like all other platforms, make money from providing the infrastructure to facilitate the sale of human remains.

The prevalence and general lack of regulation of social media and e-commerce platforms worldwide has allowed numerous illicit markets to flourish, including those for antiquities and human remains. Much discussion and public outreach has, and continues, to focus on the damage done to the archaeological record in general from large-scale looting, the destruction of monumental sites, the subsequent trafficking and sale of artifacts, and who profits from it (see Mackenzie et al. 2020). Relatively little has been written from the perspective of osteologists and forensic anthropologists regarding the damage done by the human remains trade to osteoarchaeologists' efforts to understand lives lived through contextualized data from the skeleton itself. Or indeed: the continuing damage to descendant communities whose ancestors are bought and sold as things.

We know that social media was being used to facilitate buying and selling human remains as early as twenty years ago. The initial investigation of the mere existence of a trade in human remains online can be seen in Huxley and Finnegan's (2004) research. They found that crania of potential medico-legal importance were actively for sale on eBay ca. 2002–3. Further exposure of this traffic on (the US site) of the world's most popular e-commerce platform continued to put pressure on eBay (Halling and Seidemann 2016) and eventually contributed to a more-or-less complete ban on human remains and the products made from them (Vergano 2016). More recent work has begun to demonstrate that this specific category of trafficking is global and includes auction houses and brick-and-mortar stores with websites (Huffer and Chappell 2014). Since the eBay ban, the trade online has migrated primarily to social media platforms such as Instagram and Facebook (Huffer, Chappell et al. 2019; Huffer and Charlton 2019).

We have been researching this trade in human remains especially as it intersects with social media and the web. We are trying to understand how the trade works, why people do it, and where the people bought and sold might have come from, in an effort to restore some dignity to the dead. The trade represents loss of archaeological knowledge and loss to descendant communities whose ancestral human remains are looted to feed this market. The trade represents an assault on the dignity of descendant communities whose cultural heritage (e.g., a tradition of modifying or decorating the crania or bones of the deceased) is commodified.

Discussion of the implications behind each post is contextualized by an overview of research detailing the damage caused to osteoarchaeological knowledge and forensic crime scene integrity when looting or deliberate disturbance is detected. Our goal is to illustrate the repercussions of this trade that are often obscured by the shock of what is being sold. It is only appropriate, then, that this volume will end with our suggestions to the public for what to do if they encounter suspicious (i.e., still covered in dirt, stained, fragmentary) human remains for sale on or offline.

While cemetery looting to obtain antiquities is certainly not new (Atwood 2007; Kinkopf and Beck 2016), the number, frequency, and diversity of cemetery sites looted today to feed ever-expanding markets made more accessible through the use of social media and e-commerce, makes the threat all the more real. However, the speed and sincerity with which archaeologists, forensic anthropologists, general law enforcement, and the public now respond to discoveries of recent or in-progress cemetery looting or vandalism has markedly increased as authorities and the public become aware of both the realities of looting on the ground, and more recently, the existence of the human remains trade (J. Hanson 2011; Kersel and Hill 2019; Halling and Seidemann 2016). At the same time, archaeological survey, salvage excavation, and retrospective statistical analysis methods have improved so that archaeologists can now piece together the extent and severity of damage done by looting even after the fact (e.g., Kinkopf and Beck 2016; Parcak et al. 2016; Fradley and Sheldrick 2017; Lasaponara, Danese, and Masini 2012). But looting isn't the only crime here. To understand what the trade means today, we have to back up a little bit and consider how these human beings became objects of study, and then *objets d'art*, and then mere "curios" or "oddities." At each stage of this process, different operations of power serve to eliminate their humanity.

These Were People Once

The Story of Abraham Ulrikab

An Inuk living in the Moravian missionary settlement of Hebron, Labrador in the late nineteenth century, Abraham Ulrikab was a devout Christian. He was a painter and could play the violin. He was literate and kept a diary in Inuktitut. He could speak German and English (Chartier et al. 2021). In the autumn of 1880, Ulrikab and his family were invited by the Norwegian ethnologist Adrian Jacobsen, on behalf of Carl Hagenbeck, owner of Hagenbeck's Zoo in Hamburg, to travel to Germany. The Hebron missionaries discouraged them but recorded that the promised daily earnings were difficult to refuse, especially since Ulrikab and his family owed significant debts to the missionary store (Lutz 2005). His diary records the decision-making process and reveals a desire to visit Europe "and the [Moravian] communities there" (Lutz 2005). Abraham, thirty-five, along with his wife Ulrike, twenty-four, and daughters, Sara, four, and baby Maria, agreed to board Jacobsen's ship and travel to Europe to enroll themselves in a Völkerschau—human zoo—tour. They also convinced Ulrike's nephew Tobias to join them, and they also helped Jacobsen to recruit three Inuit in Nakvak who had refused to be Christianized (Lutz 2005).

Jacobsen neglected to have the eight travelers immunized when they arrived, and they fell ill within weeks. Less than four months later, all had died of smallpox (Rivet 2014). With the help of his diary, and that of Jacobsen's, researchers have been able to locate the travelers' remains (Rivet 2014). After their deaths, the skeletons of Abraham, Ulrike, Maria, Tobias, and Tigianniak from Nakvak were mounted and kept by the Musée National d'Histoire Naturelle. Tigianniak's wife Paingu and daughter Nuggasak died before reaching Paris, and Paingu's skullcap is also in the Paris collection (Rivet 2014). Sara's body was kept by a collection in Berlin (Rivet 2014). The translation of Ulrikab's diary, and further research with European institutions and Nunatsiavut communities in Labrador, has led to the initiation of a repatriation process (Rivet 2014, 2018). Though the Inuit have not yet been returned home (a *New York Times* article from November 2022 implies their remains are still in the Musée de l'Homme, see Franchi 2022), the story and fate of Ulrikab, his family, and his fellow travelers prompts us to ask: how many other Abrahams are out there?

The Story of Mangi Meli

Chief Mangi Meli was killed on 2 March 1900 by colonial German officials in what is now Tanzania. He and nineteen others were hanged for resisting the German occupation of their lands in the district surrounding the Kilimanjaro region (Silayo and Meriki 2022; see also the 2018 film and associated video installation and photography exhibition *Mangi Meli Remains*, https://flinnworks .de/en/project/mangi-meli-remains for an artful telling of the story). For approximately fifty years, Mangi Meli's grandson, Isaria Meli, has been leading efforts to locate what happened to Mangi Meli's head after his body was decapitated (BBC 2018a, 2018b). At the time of Meli's execution, Felix von Luschen was Director of the Africa and Oceania Department of the Königliches Museum für Völkerkunde (the Royal Museum of Ethnology, founded in 1873; from 1957 onward the Stiftung Preußischer Kulturbesitz, Prussian Cultural Heritage foundation or SPK). Von Luschen had written to German officials in their colonies to provide him with ethnographic specimens (the taking of African body parts by Europeans was motivated not only by "scientific" reasons but was part of a broader apparatus for establishing European power in Africa; Webb 2015). This was probably the channel through which Mangi Meli's skull was *sent* to Berlin—but the exact path is unknown, and it's not at all certain that Meli's skull *arrived*. Like nearly 5,500 other skulls that were sent to Berlin at the beginning of the twentieth century, the precise sequence of whose possession the skulls passed through as they were forwarded on to Berlin is not known, nor is the exact number sent (see BBC 2018b).

Now ninety years old, Isaria contributed his DNA in 2011 as evidence to aid research into the origins and identities of the 5,500 skulls held by the Prussian Cultural Heritage Foundation (SPK). Two hundred of these skulls are labeled "Dschagga/Wadschagga," the German spelling of Mangi Meli's ethnic group, the Chagga. Six skulls in that collection were identified as having been collected and recorded by Lt. Col. Moritz Merker, second in command at Moshi when Mangi Meli was executed (BBC News 2018a, 2018b), but there is no associated name with any of those skulls. Results of aDNA testing (ancient DNA) of those six skulls suggested that Mangi Meli's was not among them (SPK 2019) and so the search continues. Collections such as those held by the SPK and other museums would have changed hands many times. Sometimes skulls were removed or added, sometimes original documents were lost, labels fell off, or writing faded. The story of Mangi Meli's fate and how part of his body entered colonial circulation as a "spoil of war" continues to haunt both the Tanzanian and German national consciousness (Uliwa 2019; Iken 2021).

Stories such as Mangi Meli's illustrate two important facts about the human remains trade today and in the past: colonial-era record keeping strips humanity from the remains; deep archival research coupled with scientific testing *might* successfully return a name to remains, but it is not guaranteed. Secondly, colonial-era mismanagement of human remains (and other trophies of colonialism) and their transportation to the intended institutional contexts seems a likely path into private collections. Perhaps we might also add a third important fact: having disappeared into the apparatus of European colonialism, Mangi Meli's life remains unfinished. In the village of Old Moshi itself, the tree from which Mangi Meli was hanged remains standing and serves as a meeting place, but the still-missing head has meant that the cycle of Chagga burial rites was never able to be completed (Mayallah 2020).

The Story of the Spirit Eye Cave

In Texas (and throughout the US Southwest) there are places where landowners will let you dig for archaeological materials, for a price. One such location is called Spirit Eye Cave, and recreational diggers and a succession of landowners exploited and turned over the site from the 1950s to the 1990s. In a remarkable piece of archival detective work and interviews with some of the participants, archaeologist Bryon Schroeder and collaborator Xoxi Nayapiltzin have detailed the sequence of digging events that robbed this important site.

Schroeder writes,

> It took months of unanswered calls, hours of driving, several visits, circuitous conversations, multiple missed connections, and a follow-up detailed letter explaining the reason for the persistence. The result of these efforts was the hesitant admission on the other end of the phone that they still held Native American ancestral human remains that were stored in the attic. We set a date when I could visit. When I arrived, after some small talk, the woman led me to a large wall and removed one of the dozens of sepia-toned portraits. After putting a key in a hidden lock, the wall swung open. Behind it, surrounded by dozens of perishable artifacts, corncobs, and fake pictographs in a replica cave built under the staircase were the Native American ancestral remains for which I had been searching. They had been disinterred from an occupied cave system in a remote region of Far West Texas near the US-Mexico border, where the private possession of Indigenous ancestral human remains is common. (Schroeder and Nayapiltzin 2022: 26)

Schroeder and Nayapiltzin had identified from the notes of a local historical society, the records of a student newspaper, and other sources that at least four burials had been removed from Spirit Eye Cave. Some of the remains were put on display in local storefronts (Schroeder and Nayapiltzin 2022: 29). One was supposedly donated to the Smithsonian, though no records exist to support this. Burial #3 was in the possession of a private house museum. And one (Burial #4) was offered for sale in a classified advertisement in *The Shotgun* magazine. Correspondence between the buyer and seller was in the archive of the El Paso Archaeological Society. In 1998 the buyer was raided by the California Department of Fish and Wildlife for dealing in protected wildlife. The agents found the human remains, and the coroner transferred the remains to the Texas Office of the State Archaeologist (they are now currently in the University of Texas at Austin). Schroeder obtained a sample from Burial #4, and he was permitted to take a small sample from the Burial #3 remains for further mtDNA (mitochondrial DNA) testing, while the final disposition of those remains are negotiated (observing the relevant NAGPRA procedures and protocols).

Since mitochondrial DNA is passed matrilineally, the test identifies which matrilineal groups the two individuals come from—in this case haplotype B2a4a1. As it happened, Nayapiltzin who is Mexican also has that haplotype. Here we have a case where human remains were looted, sold, recovered, and now, have family again. Xoxi Nayapiltzin writes,

> Recently, I learned that two ancient burials—dated approximately 710 and 860 years old and located just 55 miles from my birthplace—were sampled for mtDNA. They were classified as being of the B2a4a1 family; that is, they are my direct maternal ancestors. Modern science now confirms what the wind, the mountains, *xegoy* (*Larrea tridentata*), *xíkuri* (*Lophophora williamsii*), and *wikókuri* (*Phrynosoma cornutum*) continually tell me: we, my family, belong to this land. It would seem that this was good news. But sadly, there was the most horrifying news a grandchild can receive: two of my ancestral grandmothers had been removed from their burial grounds! One is now in an unrelated person's attic and the other in an institutional laboratory. They do not belong there. They belong in Mother Earth with their family in our homeland.
>
> No natural person would unearth their relatives, nor should any other human being. Sadly, the trans-Atlantic immigrants to our homelands did not recognize us as fellow human beings and relegated our human remains to artifacts, and now many of our relatives are in a plastic bag in a cardboard box sitting on a shelf. Worse, some have been exhibited like curios in museums, private houses, and even storefronts. They belong in Mother Earth with their families in their homelands.
> [. . .]
> What about the thousands of graves disturbed before and outside the purview of NAGPRA? Where are they now? And when will those human remains rest in peace? (Nayapiltzin, epilogue to Schroeder and Naypiltzin 2022: 36)

The Story That Sells the Skeleton

Contrast the stories above—the result of patient historical research, diligent reporting, and descendant community engagement—against the story told by vendors of human remains:

This beauty came into my possession recently, a human skull with an axe wound. No healing here so would've been cause of death. (Instagram dealer, March 2022)
—I just love it when things have some sort of story. (Commenter)

This is a skull from the Congo region. This is a genuine piece and not a piece created for the tourist trade. Known as ancestor skulls, this would've been a village elder skull, which was then kept and decorated. The earring type things that you can see hanging off of the zygomatic arches are known as "Manilla" which are a form of money, usually made of bronze or copper, which were used in West Africa. They were produced in large numbers in a wide range of designs, sizes, and weights. Originating before the colonial period, perhaps as the result of trade with the Portuguese empire. Manillas continued to serve as money and decorative objects until the late 1940s and are still sometimes used as decoration. In popular culture, they are particularly associated with the Atlantic slave trade. (Instagram dealer, February 2022)

A baby skull with severe cleft lip. A cleft lip is an opening or split in the upper lip that occurs when developing facial structures in an unborn baby don't close completely. This piece was prepared by a German medical professor and kept in his personal collection for many years. Foetal [sic] and baby specimens can always be a touchy subject. But what should be remembered is that specimens used in the medical field have and will continue to help medical professionals learn how to care for those still fortunate enough to be alive. If we buried or cremated all human remains, we would not have the medical understanding that we do to look after the living. (Instagram dealer, January 2022)
—Would love to see this beautiful skull in person. (Commenter)

This beautiful piece is a stunning example of the body's ability to heal after operations. The hole in the skull has been taken out for a medical procedure and then stitched back in. You can see where the bone has then healed over. (Instagram dealer, January 2022)

This is a real human skull headdress created and worn by the Ekoi people. Ekoi people, also known as Ejagham, are an ethnic group in the extreme south of Nigeria and extending eastward into the southwest region of Cameroon . . . . (Instagram dealer, January 2022)

Real human skull, this skull comes from Haiti and was part of a vodou altar. The skull has been burnt and has a small scrap of fabric inside the nasal cavity. (Instagram dealer, December 2021)

Examination of the posts themselves and their associated comments and discussion reveals that it seems the *adventure* story that can be told about these remains is part of the "cachet" generating the monetary value exchanged. But the story is not one of lives lived, and they are not stories tied to named indi-

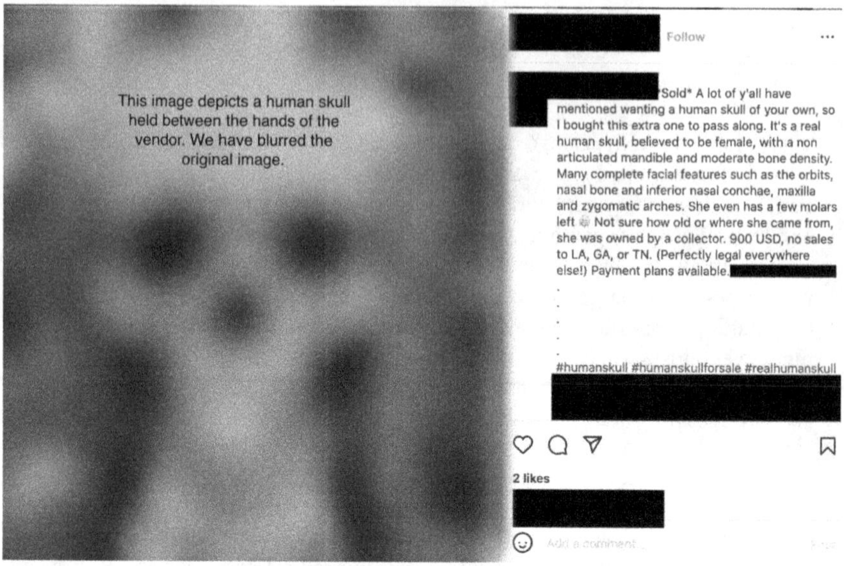

This image depicts a human skull held between the hands of the vendor. We have blurred the original image.

Follow ···

"Sold* A lot of y'all have mentioned wanting a human skull of your own, so I bought this extra one to pass along. It's a real human skull, believed to be female, with a non articulated mandible and moderate bone density. Many complete facial features such as the orbits, nasal bone and inferior nasal conchae, maxilla and zygomatic arches. She even has a few molars left 😬 Not sure how old or where she came from, she was owned by a collector. 900 USD, no sales to LA, GA, or TN. (Perfectly legal everywhere else!) Payment plans available.

#humanskull #humanskullforsale #realhumanskull

2 likes

Figure 1.1. Screenshot of a vendor's post on Instagram. Note the framing of the language of the post. Source: Instagram.

viduals. Instead, the focal point is the "artistic expression," the "beauty" of the *thing*. The exotic. The anonymity is part of the point because it allows the collector to project their fantasies. A heroic collector tells this story of the transformation of human remains into commodities, and a constant search for the allegedly old, authentic, rare, and macabre.

The contrast between the "actual" story and the collector's "stock" narrative is why we presented the tragic case of Abraham Ulrikab. It is to highlight the colonial violence at the heart of these collections of human remains, many of which have (one way or another) been released into the market, a violence that depends crucially on ways of looking, of consuming, of constructing, an exotic "other." It is a literal dehumanizing: a named individual becomes a mere thing. Ulrikab's story is not unique—other stories that spring to mind include the way that Sarah Baartman was put on display while living, and her body dissected and displayed after death by George Cuvier within the Musée de l'Homme in Paris; the story of White Fox, a Pawnee who died in Sweden and whose remains were eventually repatriated in 1996 (Jibréus 2014); and the thousands of skulls collected under the auspices of colonial governments in Africa (Tharoor 2016), which include such leaders of uprisings as Chief Songea Mbano (Gross 2018) and Mangi Meli himself. Our own academic careers (at least the aspect related to our investigation of the online human remains trade) are tied to this exploitation, even if we try to maintain ethical standards of best practice.

Archaeologists and osteologists must follow numerous codes of best practice and ethical guidelines when proposing or conducting new research (Scarre
and Scarre 2006; Zimmerman, Vitelli, and Hollowell 2003; Alfonso and Powell
2007; Márquez-Grant and Squires 2018). This includes professional curators
of human remains and the researchers and students who seek access to human remains collections (e.g., Márquez-Grant and Fibiger 2011). However,
collectors and dealers on the private market are not so bound, regardless of
whether they seek archaeological or ethnographic remains, and irrespective of
the circumstances leading to those remains surfacing on the (online or offline)
private market (see Williams 2019 for a discussion of the auction of early Medieval remains and artifacts).

Collectors can tell very good stories about why they are doing what they
are doing and what makes it appropriate, creating a pronounced us-vs.-them
dichotomy between how collectors and scholars can use social media for commerce, research, or even community representation (e.g., Huffer 2018).

"From a Former Medical Collection"

One story in particular is told over and over again, in many variants: "From
a former medical collection." This is the osteological equivalent of a common
phrase that an antiquities dealer might use: "From the collection of an anonymous Swiss collector." Let's unpack this.

This story has its roots in the emergence of modern medicine and training
over the eighteenth and nineteenth centuries in European and North American
contexts. The teaching of anatomy and pathology required the use of specimens. The problem was, where could one obtain such human remains legally?
The solution to this problem was usually a variant of "from people no one cares
about," or rather, ones who could not be buried in consecrated ground (and
thus the responsibility for their mortal remains could not be transferred to the
church). Human remains were not considered property under common law.
A person was ultimately owned by God and was, while alive, merely the curator of the vessel, as it were, that contained their soul. Once dead, there was a
limited right by next-of-kin to see to the disposition of the body, but once buried, no further rights existed. Thus, the bodies of people who died indigent or
similarly outside-the-bounds were one source. Laws and regulations emerged
during the nineteenth century to enable such bodies to be legally obtained by
medical schools, doctors, and other appropriate individuals. Public revulsion
at the infamous Burke and Hare murders (who murdered people to sell the
corpses to the anatomist Robert Knox, in Edinburgh, in 1828) led eventually to
the Anatomy Act of 1832. Similar legislation was passed in other jurisdictions.

One of the first jurisdictions established in the United States was in the
state of Pennsylvania, which created an "Anatomy Board" in 1883 to oversee

the process of bodies being sent to medical schools. It would distribute and deliver dead human bodies of people who had died in public houses, public hospitals, poor houses, convalescent homes and the like, to universities and medical colleges, who would receive a set number of remains each month. However, the payment exchanged was never for the *bodies*, but for the *processing costs* (Stroud 2018: 16.2–16.3). And another source were of course graveyards themselves; mortsafes (iron cages) and other devices emerged in response to the work of "resurrection men" (who could sometimes be medical students themselves).

The British Empire, and the whole world-system that Britain's colonial extraction was part of, naturally included human remains. When domestic supplies of cadavers could not meet the demand created by the growth in medical schools over the nineteenth century, supply companies found sources abroad, particularly in India. How India came to become a major supplier of human remains is a complicated knot of intersecting cultural practices and traditions, and globalizing politics and economics, and would need another whole book to untangle. Suffice to say, for nearly two hundred years, skeletons prepared for medical schools came from the cemeteries and graves of Kolkatta. The caste who traditionally performed cremations became the people who would process bones. In the 1850s, the Calcutta Medical College was one of the main organizations for processing and supplying human remains (Carney 2007, 2011; see also Hefner et al. 2016—they describe the Indian sources of human remains for anatomical study and tested eighty-five human remains from osteological laboratories across the United States to see if actual collections support this story. They found a high degree of homogeneity, suggesting that these study remains thought to be from India were indeed from India). To be clear, *exporting* human remains was permitted, but obtaining them was another matter. In 1985, the official, sanctioned export industry came to a halt when a dealer was caught selling over 1,500 skeletons of children with no very good explanation of how he came to have them (Hugo 2016a; Hefner et al. 2016: 1440–43). Suppliers of skeletons for medical study turned to China (which banned the trade in the run-up to the 2008 Beijing Olympics; Hefner et al. 2016: 1442), but over the years illicit suppliers have resumed activity in India (Carney 2007), with periodic arrests of bone traders making the international news (e.g., Suri 2017). Thousands of bodies go unclaimed and unidentified each year in India, and after a period of time if no one claims the remains they are supposed to go to domestic medical colleges to be used in medical training (Shelar 2017). Nevertheless, an active smuggling of human remains for other markets continues (Ray 2018), even domestically. We have been shown screenshots of Facebook groups where medical students in India (and Bangladesh) buy, sell, and swap human remains in order to meet the requirements of their studies. (The actual public dissection of a human body is not commonplace anymore and we direct the reader to Brenna 2022 for more on that history, but we know of one recent occurrence—the case of decorated WWII and Korean War veteran David Saunders who died at ninety-eight from Covid-19 [Yang 2021]. His will requested that his remains be donated to science at Louisiana State University. However, his donation was rejected due to the Covid diagnosis. After being turned down by LSU, his widow reached out to private company Med Ed Labs, who promised to use the body for "medical and surgical education and training." This training in fact consisted of the body being sold to Death Science, a media company that, in collaboration with the touring exhibition Oddities & Curiosities Expo, dissected his body in front of paying ticket holders in the ballroom of a Portland, Oregon, hotel!)

This is admittedly little more than a sketch of a very complicated history and process. Our point is merely to demonstrate that the people whose remains were so procured for "medical collections" were not people who were in any position of power to resist what happened to them. They were dehumanized in life and dehumanized after death. Rachel Watkins (2020) explores how various "official" study collections of human bodies become objects and contrasts the work of the Cobb Skeletal Collection at Howard University, and the New York African Burial Ground project of the 1990s, with other study collections. Montague Cobb established his teaching collection from the 1930s to the 1950s; under the laws at the time, unclaimed bodies could be distributed to medical schools for dissection. Why would a body be unclaimed? Sometimes, it could be because the person was simply unknown, a person who had fallen through the cracks. Sometimes, it could be that the family had no way of paying for burial. A person might be working in the city, their whereabouts or fate unknown to their family. The point is, no one volunteered to be a cadaver. That they ended up on the dissection table was a function of structural patterns of violence that had everything to do with laws about regulating spaces of Black and non-Black experience (R. Watkins 2020: 23; Zimmer 2018: 50). Adam N. Zimmer has treated the records of cadaver origin for the Huntington collection, mapping the remains back to places of abode in New York; they find,

New York City's policy of cadaver collection, once purported to opportunistically and indiscriminately take bodies of New York's most marginalized whenever available . . . actually targeted predominantly black, segregated neighborhoods regardless of social class . . . the "objective" nature of cadaver acquisition seems to have had different criteria for acquiring white versus black and brown bodies. Such differing criteria suggest that cadaver acquisition, dissection, and subsequent curation were all used as tools of social control during a period of increasing fears by New York City's affluent white community about a growing and increasingly mobile black populace. (Zimmer 2018: 50)

Montague Cobb—a Black scholar—believed that the personal stories, the demographic information, and the identities were critical elements for students to study alongside the cadavers (and skeletons) to understand the broader social context for the patterns and pathologies and so on that the students identified. Having these data meant that the remains retained their humanity, part of a strategy for countering arguments based on race "types" (R. Watkins 2020: 23). He did not teach his students to identify "race" from the skeletal remains; rather, he taught them to evaluate remains alongside all the other points of information to establish biological and social profiles. In this, he was largely unique among anthropologists at the time. In the 1980s, the collection came under the auspices of Michael Blakey and was made available for wider study (Blakey 1988, 1995; R. Watkins 2020: 24). Blakey established a policy for repatriation "based on an understanding that the circumstances under which individuals in the collection were not claimed at the time of death reflected social and economic circumstances . . . . It is significant that remains from an anatomical collection were positioned as research subjects in a way that did not relegate them to that existence indefinitely" (R. Watkins 2020: 24). This remains a relatively unique policy.

Medical and anatomical collections were pulled together rapidly at the end of the nineteenth century and the early twentieth century. Much of the research on these collections has focused on the collectors and their motivations (e.g., Redman 2016). Much less has focused on the individuals being turned into research subjects, the ways they came to be, and the stories of their lives as human beings. When the African Burial Ground project was underway, those enslaved individuals' remains shared space with the Cobb collection for a time. The excavation and study of those individuals was done in consultation with descendant communities in ways that were influenced by the principles built into the Cobb collection, and all those individuals were honored with care and recognition and reburial. This rarely happens. As of this writing however, students at the University of Pennsylvania have successfully lobbied the University to remove and bury the skulls of enslaved people currently kept in its collection of human remains. This collection, we note, was created by Samuel George Morton in the hopes of proving the "racial superiority" of Europeans (Bishara 2020).

In the human remains trade on social media today, "from a former medical collection" is often all we know about the individual. To cite a "former medical collection" is an attempt to absolve the current holder of a skull from blame. If anything, it should be seen as an even deeper mark of shame:

> It was no accident that several prominent medical schools were located in the antebellum South, where the bodies of slaves were commodified for their labor while alive, as well as for purposes of medical instruction in sickness and after death. (J. Davidson 2007, citing Savitt 1982)

Few schools of anatomy at the end of the nineteenth century and into the twentieth century exhibited as much ethical care as that under the control of Cobb. At many institutions, bodies were procured from recent graves, and from unethical undertakers—Davidson discusses the memoirs of Dr. Charles Rosser, published in the 1940s, that casually recount an episode where some medical students covered the cost of tuition by obtaining bodies for dissection. With reference to historical maps of the time, it is apparent from which funeral parlor the bodies were probably originally taken (J. Davidson 2007: 205). In Dallas, the stealing of Black bodies shows up archaeologically—in the excavations of the Freeman's cemetery in Dallas (a Black cemetery that was on land slated for an expansion of US Highway 75), the excavators were able to see, in the phasing of the burials, the direct impact of the establishment of medical schools in that city. For instance:

> The placement of two adults into one tight-fitting coffin was bad enough, but their specific positions appear to flout propriety; placing one man's body on his back in the superior position, and then positioning the other's body prone on his stomach, where his head (if present) would have been face down in the groin of the other dead man. The head was missing, presumably taken as a trophy, objectified and commodified. (J. Davidson 2007: 206)

The phrase "from a medical collection" covers not just the theft of mostly Black or Brown bodies and the casual dehumanization of poor or other subaltern bodies, but also their dissection, their casual deposition, and the taking of "trophies."

Davidson goes on to make an estimate of how many bodies might have been used in the teaching of anatomy up to the passage of a state law in 1907 which made it legal to use the bodies of "indigents" for dissection. In the anatomy classroom, six students were assigned to a body, according to memoirs of former students. There were five practicing medical schools in Dallas between 1900 and 1907. 1,947 students were taught over those seven years: thus 324 individuals. Now, do the math. Elaborate that ratio against all the medical schools that opened and taught in the nineteenth and early twentieth centuries across North America. Black bodies for dissection were even traded outside of the United States. In his memoirs of his days as a student at McGill University in Montreal, Dr. Griffith Evans in 1862 remarked that "plenty" of Black bodies were smuggled out of the US, "packed in casks, and passed over the border as provisions, or flour" (quoted in D. Francis 2001: 4).

A common rite-of-passage for medical students, the dissection of human bodies also served to desensitize future doctors: and it is not insignificant that the bodies that future doctors learned to treat as things were Black bodies:

> The racist views of the American medical profession in the nineteenth and early twentieth centuries, once held as normative, have been decentered but modern

health care maintains a legacy of structures that still conspire to slight African-Americans and other minority groups. In 2002, the Institute of Medicine released a report to Congress that documented a pervasive and widespread disparity within the country's health care system, resulting in a measurably lower quality of health-care for racial minorities compared to Euroamericans. This was found to persist even with parity in income and insurance levels. (J. Davidson 2007: 215, citing P. Clark 2003)

The human remains trade—the trading in human materials stripped of their humanity—is like buying and selling the evidence from the broader crimes of structural racism. Authentic (i.e., not resin replicas) human remains on the market today are sourced from archaeological sites, from recently opened graves, from crypts, ossuaries or repositories still important to descendant communities, and from deaccessioned museum or university collections that themselves might have many unknowns in regards to how they were collected. In a more general sense, today's human remains trade represents a highly tangible material consequence of laws designed to control the bodies of others, too-often Black and Brown bodies, especially in the United States and Europe.

It is within this milieu that today's private collection and online trafficking of human remains rests. Practically every hour of every day, public comments and private messages between buyers and sellers flow, money is exchanged, and human remains are shipped near and far. This includes alleged historic and archaeological collections, deaccessioned "teaching collections," alleged former "medical specimens," and much more. As will be explored in much more detail in later chapters, the justifications given by collectors often include a motivation to collect out of a "love of death" or otherwise stated respect for the dead elevated to a passion to bring them into one's home, live with them, or "study them." Thus, boundaries between perspectives on the dead can blur.

Two Vignettes of Contemporary Grave Robbing

Russia (observed by Shawn on Instagram)

The first thing to understand about our work, is that it doesn't take much time, once you start looking, to find human remains for sale on Instagram or many other platforms. In two minutes, I had a page of results—skulls, clavicles, vertebrae, finger and foot bones, long bones. Many in their own display cases, some turned into "art." But one photo stopped me cold. There, on an old tablecloth in someone's kitchen, a skull with green and brown patina. "Looks like they just got that one," I thought.

Peering closer, I realized that the post was one of those Instagram posts composed with more than one photograph. I clicked the "next" button. Same skull, different view, but the skull was dirtier. "Next." The same skull, but with lots of dirt on it. "Next." A clod of earth, with green grass and moss on it, and within the dirt, the ridge of the eye socket. I swore out loud. The skull had been just dug out of the ground, and the pictures uploaded in reverse order.

"Human skull for sale. DM me for info." All the subsequent comments were in a mix of English and Russian. Sometimes people leave geolocation on their phone when they take photos, and these locations are included in the metadata of the post. I checked; no data. I looked through all of his other photographs; one hit—for a city in Southeast Asia. "Gotcha!" was my initial thought. However, when I looked at the photo with the location ID attached to it, it sure did not look like what I imagined that particular Southeast Asian city to look like. Indeed, Google street view for that location brought up a very different picture. Maybe location IDs can be spoofed?

Paging through the rest of the man's photographs, I saw other human remains displayed for sale, but it seemed like this wasn't his main focus. Most of the pics were from bodybuilding competitions. The banners in the background had Cyrillic writing, so perhaps Russia? Then, one photograph of the man and a woman (who appears in many other photos) was tagged with the woman's Instagram account. I clicked through to her account; lots of photos of domestic life with the man who was selling the human skull. And all of her photographs are tagged with location IDs for a city in western Russia and its environs.

Looting of war graves along the Eastern Front of World War II is rampant, in Russia and its former satellites. This looting is often considered within the purview of "dark heritage"—an area of research seeking to understand everything from the online collecting of war memorabilia to public engagement at memorials or places of past atrocity (e.g., Thomas, Seitsonen, and Herva 2016; Herva et al. 2016; Bull and De Angeli 2021; Westmont 2022; Rohrlich 2022). The clod of earth on the skull in the photo showed that the burial was very shallow, hence recent. My bet: World War II war dead. There are plenty of online fora in Russia for buying and selling war memorabilia, and I suspect that if anything else of value was found (dog tags, medals, buttons, weapons) they would've been sold there. But human remains? Those are for Instagram. Instagram's filters and Western gaze means that human remains make great photographs. This particular account owner is not really interested in selling human remains that much. Given the context of the rest of the photographs, it looks like this was an opportunistic find. But nevertheless, without Instagram and the market that it provides, perhaps this burial would not have been disturbed.

(In a grim turn of events, in the context of the current war between Russia and Ukraine, informants have sent us videos and photographs of Russian soldiers using human remains probably disinterred in Ukraine, and probably from recently deceased people—to judge from the photos—as props in rallies to build morale. We cannot vouch for the truth of these videos, but we are told by archaeologists who monitor Russian social forums connected with the metal detecting trade that there has been an explosion of activity in Ukraine by Russian soldiers, so it does seem likely that graves or the dead will have been disturbed like this).

Cameroon (as shared with Damien Huffer by a representative of the EAGLE Network; https://www.eagle-enforcement.org/)

A colleague made the introduction for us—first by email then WhatsApp. In this day and age, those of us who try to monitor trafficking of all kinds need to become adept at following leads wherever and whenever they come our way. "We had 3 more arrest operations . . . in Cameroon that included human remains." This is definitely a sentence that can pique one's interest. I needed to find out more.

"Any publicly available information about those arrests; how many individuals, how many remains were being smuggled, evidence of the arrested also being the looters, etc.?" I asked. When an as-yet-unknown informant reaches out with potentially useful information, it is important to try to establish a baseline first. Do they really have useful information? Are they actually able to share anything useful? With so many examples of human remains trafficking online, chasing wild geese doesn't help civilian researchers like us, let alone provide useful "intel" for law enforcement. As discussion moved to WhatsApp, what was revealed turned out to be quite shocking.

In a small village somewhere near the Cameroon-Gabon border, my new contact and his team made arrests of several individuals seeking to sell the complete mummified corpse of a woman—a woman who had been dead for six months and was allegedly known to one of the smugglers. The photos I have seen are, understandably, disturbing. The arrested were apparently not known to authorities before, but they admitted under interrogation to have succeeded with previous sales. This group of five promised their intended buyer twelve more such corpses.

When I asked how on earth they were obtaining these bodies—were they from historic or modern cemetery looting, for example—the answer came back, no. Are we looking therefore at an instance in which a specific mortuary custom was carried out whereby the deceased are left to dry out (in the open air or hidden from view)? However, instead of being kept with the family or community, smugglers attempted to sell the now mummified remains. And to what end? To sell again overseas? For other purposes? We might never know. Glimpses of the "beginning" of a process that often ends with remains for sale online are hard to come by, but are all the more valuable due to the often-accidental nature of their discovery online or through informants on the ground.

How We Locate the Commodified Dead Online:
An Introductory Primer

Our work began in 2017, looking at Instagram, since that seemed to be the most active locus for the trade among English-speaking internet users. On Instagram, we begin with the search box, having logged in with an account created specifically for the purpose of learning what the trade looks like on Instagram. Using a "dummy" account is important because as we search, Instagram learns what we are interested in, and begins to make connections for us. What keywords might be relevant? Sometimes, it is as easy as typing in "humanskullforsale." From the results, we quickly develop a list of terms to look for. A lot of folks are participating in this trade from their smartphones. They use the same lists of hashtags on all their posts which are probably triggered by a shortcut or autocomplete text, given their consistency. We then start scraping Instagram for results, making our computers act like a human, paging through each result, one at a time, and copying down all the publicly exposed metadata or descriptive information that hides behind each post (see Appendix A).

Scraping is the collection of data from public online sources using automated tools. Ethically, this can be complex since many users have an expectation that what they post is for their community (however defined), not academic researchers. It is the difference between chatting with a friend in a crowded square and chatting with a friend while someone hovers nearby listening in (we go into the ethics of all this in more detail in the next section). However, if someone is posting online in the hopes of making a sale, they have become rather like the hawker in a marketplace, whose voice is meant to be noticeable. Those are the interactions that our scraping observes (Richardson 2018 explores these tensions in detail). The result is folders filled with thousands of images and videos, and a text file filled with all of the metadata. At this point, we can start to filter for interesting posts. One way we filter is by constructing search patterns. Normal searching looks for the explicit thing you specify—$324.55 will *only* find that exact string of digits. A search pattern looks like this: \$[0-9]{3}\.[0-9]{2} and will find *any* combination of three digits with a dollar sign and cents. We have *lots* of search patterns, because vendors are aware that Facebook and Instagram automatically look for signals that something is for sale to monetize it for themselves (or, more rarely, to enforce the commerce guidelines on the site). Sometimes, vendors will get creative: 3S4.99 using the letter S as a 5 and so on. Sometimes, vendors will overlay text onto the image itself in an effort to defeat text-based search.

Now that we have a smaller collection of posts to examine in more depth, we begin to look at the images. After a while, you become inured to seeing pictures of skulls and bones. We ourselves run the risk of forgetting the humanity of the individuals whose remains we see. Every day, we see wet specimens (human flesh, or portions thereof, kept in jars of formaldehyde) or skulls that have been modified by "artists" into disturbing pastiches of pop versions of what the sellers imagine Voudon or Santería (Regla de Ocha) altars contain, vampires or Klingons, jewelry or furniture. What we are trying to identify are taphonomic markers. What evidence of the physical postmortem contexts of this skull can we see? We're looking for traces of dirt, different colored stains, scratches, holes, or cultural modifications (made during life or shortly after death). If we had the skull physically in front of us, there would be a lot that we could tell from it concerning this person's life. The evidence that we can see in Instagram photos is still rich—it can tell us a lot about the circumstances of this person's remains after death, and the circumstances of how they were turned into a "thing" to be traded. We can see clues suggesting a skull was recently taken out of the earth (or had at least been buried at one point), and the kind of environment it was initially interred in (which might indicate grave robbing). We can see evidence for modifications that might be called "culturally authentic," and modifications that are clearly meant to appeal to a Westernized audience.

Our research also continues to try to understand the cumulative impact of so many photographs of human remains for a given user/collector, and indeed, the wider "community" of collectors. What kind of "sensibility" does this particular image participate in? What kind of "look" are they going for? We can use automatic scene and object description for this, using neural networks that have been trained by Google and Microsoft and others for visual search (and other uses, including facial recognition) to automatically describe *all* of the images that we have collected. We understand that a scene built up of dark wooden cabinets, red velvet, and dribbly candles has a different "sensibility" than a scene composed of lab benches, glass shelving, and crisp labels.

Then there are scenes where someone has bought an Ikea bookshelf, one with a lot of glass shelves and window-paneled doors, put it in their living room, and stocked it with human skulls. Based on the co-occurence of individual elements automatically detected by the computer, we build up a sensibility similarity network based on these scene descriptions. There are certain kinds of scenes that occur over and over again, and some scenes (based on their network positioning) exert more influence than others. There are DIY implementations of pop-culture stereotypes of "the museum" (especially, a rendering that looks much like the nineteenth-century ethnographic museums of Western colonialism). There are *Wunderkammers* and cabinets of curiosity. There are scenes of the colonial adventurer/Indiana Jones trope. There are scenes that bring to mind gothic pawn shops. There are scenes of heroic outdoorsy-ness. There are more Ikea cabinets filled with the dead than you'd imagine. We discuss this in more detail in Chapter 3.

We have been using convolutional neural networks, a technology that mimics the way the eye and the brain makes sense of an image (the critical paper of Krizhevsky, Sutskever, and Hinton 2012 launched the current boom in neural network approaches to images; see also Schmidhuber 2015; Witten et al. 2017). CNN (convolutional neural networks) is currently the state-of-the-art for image recognition. The algorithm converts the information in the image, that is the color values of the pixels, into a series of present/absent evaluations. It pans across the image performing a series of these evaluations (called convolution) where each calculation is sensitive to a different kind of arrangement of pixels. These values are passed up (or not) to the next layer such that each successive layer responds to more complicated patterns or shapes (see Chapter 3 for more examples).

By analogy with the brain, each layer is imagined as a series of connected neurons. Each neuron responds to a different aspect of an image and all of these layers activate in different weightings of connections. The combination of those weightings allows for the identification of what's going on in the image. The result is a mathematical representation for every single image. In automatic image captioning, the final layer of neurons is used to assign the labels. We're not interested in the labels that come with the model so we look at the second to last layer, which is the mathematical (a vector) representation of the image, and use t-SNE (t-Distributed Stochastic Neighbor Embedding) or other kinds of clustering algorithms to spot patterns of similarity within the images (van der Maaten 2014; van der Maaten and Hinton 2008). This gives us a macroscopic view of all the (machine-visible) patterns inherent in the tens of thousands of images collected (see Huffer and Graham 2018 for a detailed discussion of the approach as applied in our research). See Appendix B to learn how to do this for yourself.

Another approach that can be used to determine what the machine is actually seeing is to set two neural networks in opposition to one another—so-called generative adversarial networks. In this approach, one network plays the role of the detective, and the other network plays the role of the forger. The detective network is our standard neural network for identifying images, while the "forger" network feeds images that it creates itself to the detective. The detective network is fed several thousand images, against which it compares the forger's image. When the detective determines that the forger's image does not match in particular ways, that information feeds back to the forger which makes subtle alterations. In this back and forth, the forger network eventually begins to produce images that the detective accepts as authentic images. If we then study those generated images, we can learn something of how the original network looks at images (an approach suggested to us by the work of Melvin Wevers, who has used this approach to study the evolution of automobile advertising in newspapers, Wevers, Smits, and Impett 2018).

As an example, we trained an adversarial network on 1,500 images downloaded from Instagram under the tag `skullsforsale` (see Huffer and Graham 2018). We used Gene Kogan's version of Taehoon Kim's code for a TensorFlow implementation of deep convolutional generative adversarial networks, which has been modified slightly to enable it to run on the paperspace. com cloud machine learning platform. The result resembles a gallery of paintings of memento mori (Figure 1.2). While striking, it is important to reiterate that these are *not* human remains but the machine's *understanding* of what skulls look like. In this first attempt, this gallery with its numerous near-duplicates shows us that the network has not been trained on a large enough corpus. But it has identified a series of nearly similar images from the same Instagram user as being most representative of the sample and so generates many

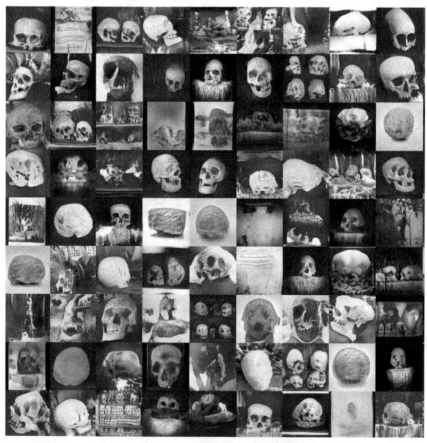

Figure 1.2. Imaginary skulls generated by Deep Convolutional Generative Adversarial Networks, trained on 1,500 images collected from Instagram. Originally published in Huffer, Wood, and Graham 2019, figure 3, CC-BY 3.0.

slight variations of that picture. On a larger dataset of 6,700 images tagged with `skullforsale`, the resulting image produces nightmarish concoctions of what seems to be manipulations of nasal bones, orbital sockets, and calvaria (cranial vaults) (Figure 1.3). The reader will also note strange areas of pink and purple in many of the images. By re-viewing the original data, we believe that what the machine is seeing in this case (and thus, generating as a key signal to defeat the detective network) are texts that have been overlaid on the original image, "for sale!" and phrases in that vein (Figure 1.4). Note that the post's associated metadata and comments do not indicate anything for sale. Putting the text into the image would seem to be an attempt to avoid scrapers and crawlers, and it happens enough that a neural network can pick that up as an important signal that something worth investigating further is going on.

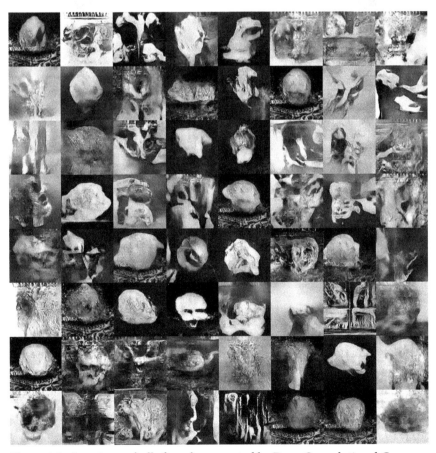

Figure 1.3. Imaginary skulls for sale, generated by Deep Convolutional Generative Adversarial Networks trained on 6,700 images collected from Instagram. Originally published in Huffer, Wood, and Graham 2019, figure 4, CC-BY 3.0.

Available , Dm w/ inquiries

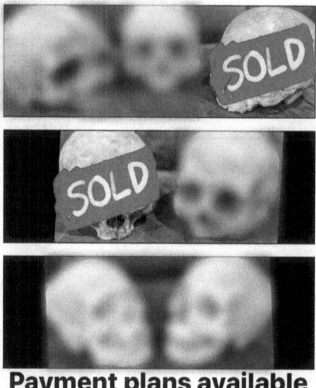

Payment plans available

Figure 1.4. A detail from one Instagram photo where there is no mention of price in the text of the associated post. Instead, the word "sold" is digitally overlaid on certain skulls, and the heading inviting the viewer to send a direct message is added to the image itself; embedded text like this cannot normally be scraped or detected. Source: Instagram.

Between our investigation of the overarching structure of today's human remains trade using digital methods to view it at scale and the more confronting and personal ways that readers of this book might inadvertently encounter the trade as they go about their lives, lies the important challenge of understanding the (living) human aspect of *how and why* today's trade exists. The remainder of this book addresses this broad space between the qualitative and the quantitative, investigating how this collecting community obtains remains, the rhetorical and visual dimensions of the discourses collectors use, and ways we might counter, explore, or understand this trade using computational tools.

Many of these tools are drawn from methods used in the digital humanities, from text analysis, topic models, and image similarity. Using these, we can say an awful lot from a macroscopic perspective about how the human remains trade operates. Sometimes, we can say something very specific about individual skulls or bones that we see in these online marketplaces (see Chapter 4). But there are some serious ethical dimensions that we need to foreground as well.

The Ethics of This Research

The ethics of research are all about harm reduction. We begin with the living, the collectors themselves, which makes the first ethical dilemma presented by our research that of anonymization. We are scraping tens of thousands of posts from Instagram and other social media platforms, but just because somebody has put material online in what could be construed as a public forum doesn't necessarily mean that they are agreeing to have their material, their online identities, and their posts, studied and pulled together into a dataset. Just because one can scrape this material doesn't necessarily mean that it's appropriate to be sharing usernames, for instance. Although the Instagram Terms of Service specifies that users "own" the content they upload, the act of uploading grants a worldwide right to Instagram that makes it inevitable that material will spread and be collected into third-party databases. That said, an ability to "eavesdrop" or gain access to "big" datasets doesn't necessarily translate to informed consent to use information obtained (Richardson 2018; Kirkegaard and Bjerrekaer 2016).

It is important to acknowledge here that many archaeologists cultivate personal social media presences across multiple platforms for purposes of educational outreach. Many of these archaeologists freely give their time and labor to provide ethically informed content, but *their* work *also* gets collected when we survey social media related to the human remains trade.

As archaeologists, we have a "shared responsibility to push the discipline of archaeology forward into a more equitable, ethical practice," especially in the area of digital archaeology (Richardson 2018). The aspirational ethical codes and prescriptive mandated ethical frameworks that govern professional archaeological practice have been outpaced by digital technologies and their usages (Dennis 2020); Dennis reminds us that digital tools and methodologies "should be subject to the same level of ethical scrutiny as any standard or traditional piece of [archaeological] kit or methodological approach" (Dennis 2020: 213).

The emergence of automated data collection techniques and their use on digital media platforms can offer a useful look into social networks present on the platforms and the way that users react to emergent media, giving us a sense of how lay people understand the issues around human remains, or other kinds of materials that might be considered "portable antiquities" (and of course, our colleagues' interactions in these spaces as well). However, this emergence necessitates "urgent and deeper critical thinking around what such data reveals or conceals, and what we, as archaeologists, expect from our social research" (Richardson 2018). Research around data gathered from digital media platforms are frequently presented "without the inclusion of any ethical statements on how the data was gathered or what permissions were gained to use this material" (Richardson 2018). As boyd and Crawford demonstrate, "it is problematic for researchers to justify their actions as ethical simply because the data are accessible . . . . The process of evaluating the research ethics cannot be ignored simply because the data are seemingly public" (boyd and Crawford 2012: 672).

The collection of observational data such as tags, comments, and interactions raises important ethical questions about privacy, especially as it pertains to protection from abuse and harassment. Human remains exist in a legal gray area in many jurisdictions (see Chapter 4), while in others the ownership or transportation of human remains are covered by a panoply of laws, statutes, and regulations that are not necessarily enforced (unless the attention of authorities is drawn to a particular instance). As researchers, "we have an ethical obligation to ensure that participation in our digital projects does not provide an avenue for personal harassment," especially in "contexts where non-mainstream opinions are elicited, politically relevant archaeological sites are discussed, or controversial subjects are presented for public consumption" (Richardson 2018). Because we cannot know the legal situation for every user whose materials might get collected through automated techniques, we cannot therefore put individuals at risk since we cannot know what all the risks might be for an individual.

We have conducted our research with these ethical issues firmly in mind. Our general research project complies with Social Sciences and Humanities Research Council of Canada (SSHRC) ethics guidelines (2018) regarding collecting and working with social media materials, having been evaluated by the Carleton University Research Ethics Board. Following these guidelines was crucial for each study in our project, guiding our approach to data collection. We were also anxious to make our research and research tools open for others to reuse, repurpose, or indeed challenge (since that is how better research eventually emerges). However, we have modified our approach with regard to "openness" with time. In short, we no longer share datasets of social media posts. Our early research did, after a process of anonymization (removing usernames), but we now recognize that it is impossible to fully anonymize such materials. While the original source material is posted openly online with the expectation of others' reading and acting upon it—making a sale, convincing someone that it is "fun" and legal to collect human remains, convincing someone of the opposite—that is not the same thing as expecting such materials to be collected for study.

The question becomes one of whether a person has a reasonable expectation of privacy while posting publicly. If they are posting, for instance, things for sale or are inviting others to admire whatever is depicted, then it seems reasonable to conclude that they have waived that right to privacy. It follows then that all other materials collected as a by-product of the search *do* retain a right to privacy and should be eliminated from the dataset. Of course, "posted for others to admire" is the entire *raison d'être* for Instagram, and for others to admire or purchase in regard to commerce-orientated Facebook groups and Facebook Marketplace. As the Cambridge Analytica scandal so graphically reminds us (Kozlowska 2018) there might be substantial amounts of data related to an individual collector's activity patterns on Facebook now inadvertently stored by Cambridge Analytica as well. (Even the so-called Dark Web and transactions completed using supposedly untraceable crypto-currencies like Bitcoin do indeed leave sufficient digital traces for traders to be unmasked, see Paul 2018.)

Nevertheless, that does not mean that we have the right to *re-post* or identify individuals, or to facilitate ways in which those identities could become known. In any event, it seems impossible to provide true anonymization anymore. A *New York Times* investigation found that the advertising ecology and its attendant arms-race track our every movement, and that they could purchase data from data-brokers (whose tracking codes are built into myriad smartphone apps) which they could de-anonymize with ease. Movements could be tracked with a time resolution of every twenty-one minutes, on average (Valentino-DeVries et al. 2018). In our earlier study (Huffer and Graham 2017), we noted that despite trying to anonymize our data, elements of the posts *can* provide a unique fingerprint and a lever into tracking an individual across platforms—especially hashtags (see Chapter 2). Despite attempts to anonymize data, there might be other signals that could be used to de-anonymize. For the researcher interested in topics at the intersection of archaeology, criminology, trafficking, and social media, one way to move research forward ethically might be only to discuss and reflect on *aggregate* patterns where the original data are posted with an expectation of *being* public, and not to share the raw data collected in the course of the study.

This raises another ethical point: given the morally gray and dubious legality of this trade, should we be publishing in open access venues where bone traders might see our work? Traditional academic publishing (which keeps the research safely locked in professional journals to which most people do not have access) would certainly be one way of keeping our findings out of the hands of people who engage with this trade, thus avoiding unintended complications from open access publishing (e.g., Chesler 2004; Tennant et al. 2016). While we want to avoid the danger in which the publication of new research drives the trade further underground or into corners of the internet not yet being actively investigated (Argyropoulos et al. 2011), or further muddies the water between what is and is not licit, we want ordinary people (not involved in the trade) to realize what is going on. This is why ultimately nearly everything we have published regarding this research has been in open access venues. We will return to this discussion in Chapter 5.

There is a deeper, potentially more harmful, ethical problem posed by our research. Our project is also trying to use computer vision to understand the visual tropes present "behind" the online trade. It is often quite clear that what's going on in the image is not what is being officially stated in the comments. How do we assess these data at a scale that enables us to understand what's going on? If we get it *wrong* we run the risk of creating a system that could be used to *authenticate* remains as belonging to a particular people or group, thus enhancing the saleability of the remains. We will go into more detail later in this volume on the ethics of machine vision (in Chapter 4). Research in neural network approaches to data analysis is unfolding at breakneck speed, and researchers investigating many categories of trafficking or e-crime need to be having these conversations now. To reiterate, the issues we see in using neural networks, machine learning, and computer vision technologies in our particular research area begin with:

- The reasonable right to privacy even if social media materials are posted openly online.
- The potential to identify individuals from their patterns of posting.
- The potential for machine learning to be responding to extraneous other signals in the data rather than the ostensible subject matter.
- The potential for our own unexamined biases to be "baked-in" to the training data we select.
- The potential for any classifier we make to be used to "authenticate" or otherwise heighten the commercial value of the materials depicted.
- The potential for the technology to replicate the sins of the past when it comes to the ethical and just treatment of the dead.

You will notice that we rarely provide any illustrations of skulls or human remains from the trade. In this, we are following the guidance and best practices suggested by the British Association for Biological Anthropology and Osteoarchaeology (BABAO www.babao.org.uk). They recognize that photos of human remains are used for archaeological outreach and for research, and so provide guidelines that ask us to consider: "Who are the living people who may be affected by this picture?" "How is the picture contextualized?" and finally, "does this photo respect the individual's dignity?" As you will see in this volume, the answer to the first question is very complex. Most of these photos are presented in a context that is demeaning, and finally, in every case, these photos do *not* respect individual dignity. For these reasons, when it is necessary to illustrate a point with a screenshot from the trade, we have blurred out the human remains. (BABAOs ethical guidelines are available on their website; most bioanthropology or bioarchaeological organizations have similar guidelines. An excellent summary of BABAO's position is captured in an infographic by Kate Faillace available at https://www.babao.org.uk/assets/Uploads/Photographing-Human-Remains-FINAL.pdf). As an aside, BABAO also maintains a "Trading and Sale of Human Remains" subgroup, of which one of us, DH, is a cofounder. Members of the UK or global public who encounter human remains for sale on or offline allegedly from the UK, or from UK-based vendors, can screen-grab (take a copy of their computer's screen; hit cmd+4 on a Mac, or use a screen capture application on a Windows machine) and report one's findings to the group's email address.

Conclusion

On 13 May 1985, Frank Powell of the Philadelphia Police Department stood on the skids of a helicopter as it flew over a predominately African American neighborhood in the city's west and dropped a bag with two C-4 bombs onto the roof of one particular residence. The resulting explosion created a raging inferno that destroyed most of the neighborhood and killed eleven people and five children sheltering in the house (see Pilkington 2020). This was a deliberate targeting of a residence known to be a meeting place of members of MOVE, also known as The Movement (originally the Christian Movement for Life), a Black liberation group. In the aftermath of the bombing, the remains of two of the victims, Tree Africa and Delisha Africa, both children, were found. They were not returned to their families. Instead, their remains eventually became used as "teaching specimens" in instructional videos for a forensic anthropology class at the University of Pennsylvania Museum. At one point their remains were kept in a former professor's home (Pilkington 2021). It is a blessing, we suppose, that the remains of Tree and Delisha Africa were not sold once they were removed from the institution. It would have been all too easy for the remains to have been sold off, each bone labeled "medical antique, teaching specimen." At present, the brother of the victims has sued the city of Philadelphia and the University of Pennsylvania Museum for mishandling his family member's remains (Watson and Musa 2022).

Efforts to understand where the remains of Tree and Delisha Africa ended up, and how and why their existence and use was withheld from the family's knowledge until exposed by the media, speak to the larger ongoing battles surrounding the use of the dead by the living. How forensic anthropologists came to have these remains in the teaching collection is prompting societal, cultural, and scientific reckoning with the events in question (Rooney 2020). By July 2021, the two victim's remains were returned to their family (Conde 2021). The remains were reinterred as per the family's wishes and the letter of apology currently hosted on the University of Pennsylvania Museum website (Penn Museum 2021) concludes as follows: "We must constantly bear in mind the fact that human remains were once living people, and we must always strive to treat them with the dignity and respect that they deserve."

These were people once. We must never forget that.

Remains from "former medical collections" are clearly ethically dubious, as for the most part they were collected via a variety of crimes and structural forces that turned non-White, non-wealthy bodies into things to be dissected, dismembered, and then discarded.

In the case of the skull that the body builder was trying to sell (in the Russian vignette above), we see not only the desecration of a (likely) war grave, a serious crime in itself, but also an illustration of the destruction of archaeological context. Human remains recovered in archaeological contexts are understood and are meaningful to archaeologists based on the contextual associations or relationships of the body with other kinds of archaeological evidence. When these associations are broken—as by pulling bones from the earth to take back home or sell to the highest bidder—then the potential knowledge we might be able to deduce about the individual is lost. In the following chapters, we provide numerous examples to illustrate that not only is the resultant lack of context known to collectors, but it can often be a real selling point. As Yates (2022) discusses in the context of how Pasifika material culture is sold, the narratives of "violence," "savagery," or "White Saviors" frequently used also conjures up notions of the macabre or exotic. This rhetoric is also at the heart of how many categories of human remains change hands.

It is true that in the discipline's early days, archaeologists and physical anthropologists (the precursors to today's biological anthropologists, bio/osteoarchaeologists, and to some extent, forensic anthropologists) did not always treat the dead or their living descendants with respect. Sometimes, as the sad case of the MOVE bombings show, this continues. With the passing of the Native American Graves Protection and Repatriation Act in 1990 (see Chapter 4), there are now careful protocols and ethical guidelines for working with Ancestors in the United States, and for reburial or other respectful treatment, that ethical archaeologists observe, and unethical ones ignore at their peril (Márquez-Grant and Fibiger 2011; Angeleti 2022). Various institutions are starting to make known the extent of human remains in their collections, prompted by the scandal of what happened at the University of Pennsylvania (with recent statements in

2022 from the University of North Dakota and the University of Kansas). In 2021 alone, over 200,000 instances of human remains in institutions subject to NAGPRA have come to light, according to a public data dashboard developed to keep track (https://public.tableau.com/app/profile/nationalnagpra/viz/2021NativeAmericanGravesProtectionandRepatriationAct/1_Reported).

In the case of the bodies in Cameroon, we are perhaps witnessing a replay of the grave robbing that supplied the West's medical schools in an earlier age. It is just as likely that we are witnessing the first step in a supply chain that ends with a post on social media or an e-commerce platform or store website. In the summer of 2019, in the run up to the Canadian federal election, a candidate was outed for having given her partner a skull as a gift (Troian 2019a, 2019b). The candidate claimed that the skull was "European," with the tacit assumption "so that's all right, right?" When we saw photographs of the skull, as reproduced in the newspapers, we could not address anything about the cultural origins of the skull, but we could certainly see evidence of taphonomic processes (e.g., changes to the skull that result from the conditions of its burial, damage by roots, animals and so on) and what appeared to be a postmortem hole made by a pick or other tool. We think that this particular skull was only recently recovered from the earth. But that is all we could say, because as with most of the human beings whose remains are bought and sold online, a single photograph is the only evidence we have.

A single photograph; a single human life.

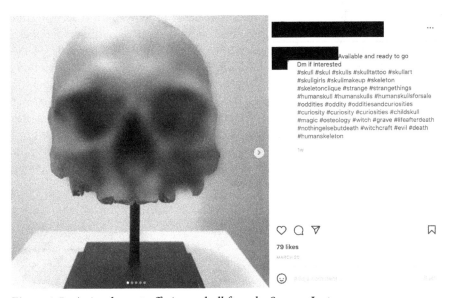

Figure 1.5. A simple post offering a skull for sale. Source: Instagram.

2

The Dead for Sale

How are human remains discussed on social media? How do dif-
ferent social media platforms' affordances affect the discussion? In
this chapter, we contextualize what we find on social media in the
broader history of the trade in human remains.

Introduction

There is a long history of buying and selling human remains that predates
the emergence of social media, of course, and the emergence of the need for
cadavers for anatomical study. To begin this chapter, we examine the history
of the private collection, sale, and use of the dead through two specific lenses:
Victorian-era mummy collection and use, and the collection and forgery of
the alleged reliquaries of saints. Once, there was demand for human remains
to place into reliquaries. Once, there was demand for mummies as things to
show, exhibit, or grind up for dust. This is not a complete examination of these
topics, as we confine our summary to the Victorian era and onwards (in the
case of mummies) and the Late Middle Ages and onwards (in the case of reliquaries). While the opening of both ancient and contemporary pharaonic
tombs, ossuaries, and catacombs has occurred in many locations from at least
the Middle Ages onwards (e.g., Klevnäs 2013; Wise 2005; Braun 2020), the
collection of human remains en masse, or their forgery to deceive gullible buyers or the faithful, is generally considered to have begun during the Victorian
Period, as colonialism and developments in Western medicine opened up new
frontiers, often at the expense of the poor, vulnerable, or colonized.

Mummies

The obsession with mummies, sarcophagi, and ancient Egypt in general across
the Victorian and then Edwardian periods, in English and non-English speaking society, in Europe, America, and beyond is well known (e.g., Stienne 2018,

2022; Dobson 2017; McCouat 2013; Wolfe and Singerman 2009; Baber 2016). We do not intend to rehash the (often shocking!) stories of how mummies were obtained for museums, found use in early medical science, were turned into medicine or pigments for art, and the like. Rather, we want to briefly explore how and why mummies began to be privately collected as *curios* in themselves that one could own (with the right connections and plenty of money), as it is this history that is the most directly relevant to today's continued desire and ability of collectors to obtain mummy fragments or accoutrements both on and offline. Whether or not the mummies purchased were recently looted (Weisberger 2019; Lewis 2021) or removed in the early twentieth century or before and only recently recovered (Daley 2018), when we discuss the "consumption" of bodies facilitated by the human remains trade, almost no other category of bodies fits the definition of this idea, literally and figuratively, as Egyptian mummies do.

In the Victorian era, the ability of medical doctors or other persons of high status and renown to acquire complete mummies and host "unwrapping parties" was seen as another way to increase one's social standing even further among one's peers. It was a visceral display of connections, wealth, bravery, and prowess, sometimes disguised as motivated purely by scientific curiosity (e.g., Riggs 2014; Sheppard 2012; Piombino-Mascali and Gill-Frerking 2019). These events straddled the line between "spectacle and science" (Sheppard 2012) and such events continue to constitute a means by which the curious public interact with (or witness the consumption of or become inspired to purchase) the dead. ("Body Worlds," the traveling exhibition by Gunther von Hagens of corpses "plastinated" into various poses, operates in a similar vein.) What does the private "consumption" and sale of mummies today specifically look like, and how is it intertwined with the myriad other reasons that dealers and institutions in the West gave for obtaining mummies from the 1800s onwards, including the subsequent mythologization of Egypt, Egyptians, and the pharaonic past itself?

Allow this vignette to serve as an example: on 12 September 2016, and 16 October 2017, two "important Egyptian mummy heads" were sold over the online auction house Live Auctioneers (Live Auctioneers 2016, 2017). Both heads were sold by Pawtucket, Rhode Island, based auctioneer "Ancient Objects," although a possibly separate company called Circa Auction Gallery is listed under the "policy for shipping" statement. Estimated sale prices were set between US$20,000 and US$120,000, but what the realized prices were is unknowable without subscription to various listservs. These remains were advertised alongside "similar listings" including wooden mummy masks, sarcophagus fragments, alleged mummy head rests, and many items besides, undoubtedly, a mix of modern forgeries and authentic antiquities. The heads were sold separately, but can allegedly be considered a "pair," one male, one female, from different Dynasties. Rough chronological age estimates are given (ca. 1,000 BCE and ca. late 2nd millennium BCE), but nothing is provided or mentioned as available to confirm any of this when one views the auction listings. Perhaps when these auctions were "live," or if one was an active bidder, more information would have been provided. To an observer after the fact, much is missing.

As we stress consistently throughout this book, it is the story that sells the skeleton. Here is the entirety of what was publicly provided by way of provenance information on the website for these two listings:

> Given by the Egyptian Government in 1877 to Dr. Christian Fenger . . . Remaining in the Fenger family until 2013. Copy of notarized affidavit attesting to provenance, signed by Dr. Fenger's grandson, is available.

> Christian Fenger (1840–1902) was a Danish-born surgeon, pathologist, and instructor who became one of the most highly regarded surgeons in the United States. For his distinguished accomplishments he was knighted by the King of Denmark in 1901. From 1875 to 1877, Fenger worked in Egypt, treating eye diseases. When he left, he was offered this mummy head, by an Egyptian official, in gratitude for his services. (FERIARTE 2019)

Digging further into these particular transactions, it is noted that the website listings make sure to emphasize the "superb preservation" condition of the remains. The 2017 listing makes the special note that "this is the companion piece to the (female) head we sold last year, and they are by far the finest examples to come on the market in decades, and easily compare (*sic*) to the best examples in the world's great museums." The general details of the Denmark-born Christian Fenger's time in Egypt as a doctor in the mid-1800s are verifiable (Rosen 1974), but other sources point to the unnamed Egyptian official who "gave" Fenger two mummies as "gifts," actually provided the entire body, but Fenger decided to take only the heads for ease of transport (FERIARTE 2019). What happened to these remains after the auction? We have some information about one of them at least.

The Spanish art and antiquities fair FERIARTE featured the allegedly female mummy head (the 2016 sale) in a write-up, showcasing the mummy's splendor as part of its 2019 trade fair, where it was displayed in the booth owned by Ifergan Gallery, in Malaga (FERIARTE 2019). From this, we learned that this person was "acquired in New York after a tough bidding session" for €550,000 (US$871,926), and that the two heads had allegedly been passed down from the elder Christian Fenger to his son Frederich and then to grandson Christian, who had put them up for auction in 2013. The female mummy head is still listed as a potentially available item on the Ifergan Gallery website (Ifergan Gallery 2021), with an export licence number from the Spanish Ministry of

Culture, a "certificate of authenticity," and some exhibition and publication history. No shipping information, fixed or flexible price, nor any discussion of legality or ethics is provided, however.

Regardless of how the sale or resale of these heads are accomplished, and whether or not everything advertised to be included is actually legitimate, what really speaks to us about the ethos that still surrounds today's trafficking in mummies is the statement below:

> After acquiring this piece, its current owner, the collector Vicente Jiménez Ifergan, travelled to Luxor (Egypt) to meet experts and scholars of the Book of the Dead, and to undergo a ritual of protection, respect and conciliation, for protection against the mummy's curse, a mysterious myth that has surrounded the Egyptian funerary world since Howard Carter discovered the tomb of Tutankhamun in 1922. (FERIARTE 2019)

Therein lies the inherent juxtaposition that must be going on in many human remains collector's minds, especially of very rare items with potentially "gruesome" or "troubling" back stories: the need to balance a desire to own, to consume, with one's own personal superstitions about what might happen if one acquires these remains. The trope of the mummy's curse plays up against the "fetishization" of the exotic dead. But there are other desires at play as well.

Reliquary Collection

There is a substantial body of interdisciplinary work on reliquaries, both incorporating human remains and not—their sourcing, their religious function and use, and their forgery (e.g., Dahan 2018; Gillingham 2010; Walsham 2010; Geary [1978] 1990; Malm 2017). We might view aspects of the trade in human remains as a continuation of earlier patterns in the culture of Western Christianity that sought out, and venerated, pieces of the bodies of saints. There are certainly interesting parallels. Relics—"leftovers," whether bone or other material—interceded between the everyday world and the world of the sacred, and the reliquaries built to both hide the relic and show off its existence, made them extremely portable. In early Medieval Christianity, the portability was part of the point (Smith 2012). Instead of going on a pilgrimage, where important points on the journey reinforced various elements of Christian learning, one could partake of some of that same learning by interacting with the relics. It was a kind of habit that helped establish a common identity: "In transforming Christianity into portable fragments devoid of coherent form or self-evident identity, relics translated it into something tangible that could be grasped as part of everyday life" (Smith 2012: 167). The networks of communication in Western Europe facilitated the exchange, tying places of veneration together. New churches, new monasteries needed new relics, and so demand created a market for relics (Smith 2012: 161–62; see Geary [1978] 1990 for a wider discussion of "professional" relic-thieves stealing from Roman or later graves). After the sack of Constantinople in 1204, relics from Orthodox churches flooded the market (to the point where the Pope had to intervene, Claverie 2008). What constituted deplorable versus religiously sanctioned theft or reuse of such relics, varied substantially across time periods and traditions (e.g., Trainor 1992; Harris 2014; Klein 2004). The more distinguished the relic, the more political, social, or ecclesiastical the potential benefits from holding, controlling, or gifting it (Claverie 2008; Geary 1994). To become a relic, human remains had to be those of a saint, of course; but the remains had also to be "discovered" through some sort of supernatural intercession, and then examined (Geary 1994: 200–5) so that it could indeed be declared, these are the remains of a saint! To *obtain* a relic, the most usual means were through gift, through theft, or through commerce; each route could imply different valences on the *meaning* of the relic (Geary 1994: 205–15):

> Human remains could go through a life cycle closely related to the wider production-circulation context: A human bone, given by the pope as a sacred relic, thereby became a sacred relic if the receiver were also willing to consider it as such. Likewise, a corpse once stolen (or said to have been stolen) was valuable because it had been worth stealing. Solemn recognition, by means of ritual authentication normally involving the miraculous intervention of the saint, provided assurance that the value assigned by the transfer was genuine. (Geary 1994: 215).

The story sells the body. To possess and control access to the human remains confers a kind of status on the person who owns them. This is obviously not an in-depth discussion of reliquaries and their changing roles in Western Christendom from its earliest days, nor a discussion of how the use and veneration of relics changed during the Reformation or the Enlightenment. These topics would constitute volumes in themselves. (There is increasing osteoarchaeological and forensic attention paid to devising scientifically grounded and practical means to determine how and why fragments of bodies became relics in the first place and how their use and reuse can be better understood, for instance Kjellström 2017, 2022; Immonen and Taavitsainen 2011; van Strydonck et al. 2016; Alterauge et al. 2016. These efforts are even beginning to include the use of DNA analysis, with permission from the reliquary's caretakers, for instance, as with Nilsson et al. 2010). But we can see that there are many echoes in today's modern trade in human remains with these two earlier (very complex) phenomena. And as we will see, with the eventual display of *Kunstkammern* or *Wunderkammers*, collecting the exotic has been a way to demonstrate one's social capital, one's worldliness (picking up on the tradition of the Grand Tour), not just one's wealth or piety.

Art from Bones

Reliquaries are of course often ornate and beautiful containers, whose crafts-manship serves to highlight the spiritual importance of the remains contained therein. Sometimes, those human remains are themselves treated in ways that are artistic within the context of the reliquary or its presentation, reworked into something spiritually meaningful. We think too of ossuaries where the remains are arranged to make pleasing or meaningful patterns (such as in the Capuchin crypt beneath the church of Santa Maria della Concezione dei Cappuccini near Piazza Barberini in Rome).

This impulse happens also in the decidedly secular contexts of the human remains trade online. We want to pause for a moment to consider some ways that this secular reworking of the remains carries meaning, through the "story" of a Florida musician, "Midnight Prince." Mr. Prince is a heavy metal musician, a genre well known for its "dark" aesthetic; skeletons and skull imagery are hardly shocking in that genre. But Mr. Prince's guitar is a bit different from what you might otherwise encounter at a show. It is, in fact, built from a human rib cage and spinal column. It is not uncommon to come across "art" made from human remains purchased online (see for instance the work of investigative reporter Patrick Pester on the desecration of human remains in the UK market; Pester 2022). We have seen chandeliers, clocks, and once, a skull modified to look like that of a Klingon. But this story is a bit different. We initially assumed that the story told by Midnight Prince to the reporter was true, and in good faith. It turned out to be a bit more complex. Even if the story is not true, it does, in its outline, suggest something of how we might understand secular art made from human remains as we encounter it on places like Instagram.

In an interview with CBC Radio (15 February 2021), Mr. Prince explained how he came to create this guitar, the "skelecaster." He claimed that the remains used are those of his late uncle, Filip, who died in Greece. As Mr. Prince tells it, Filip was a relatively young man when he died in a car accident. In his will, he donated his remains to a medical school. Eventually, the school had no further use for Filip's body. It fell to Mr. Prince's mother to either pay for continued storage or pay for a burial plot. To relieve his mother of the burden, Mr. Prince had the remains shipped to the United States, having completed all the legal paperwork. At this point, Mr. Prince conceived the notion that since Filip had also been a heavy metal musician, he could honor his uncle by . . . turning what remained into a guitar.

Now what are we to make of this? If we believe Mr. Prince, it is a story of a human being clearly transformed into a *thing*, and no doubt should Mr. Prince decide to sell the skelecaster he would find willing buyers. What has happened here is not dissimilar to the cults of the saints and the creation of reliquaries;

the story demonstrates something sincere, even something spiritual, for Mr. Prince, in this reworking of the remains. If the story is true, it is indeed an act to honor both Mr. Prince's relationship with his uncle, and Uncle Filip himself.

The point is, intentionality matters—not just Midnight Prince's, but also those of the purported dead man, Uncle Filip's. Filip's after-death wishes were respected. Mr. Prince honors his uncle with an action that ethically seems on a level with spreading cremains to the wind. But when we encounter human remains that have been similarly transformed for sale on Instagram, these elements are lacking. We do not know who the deceased was, nor their intentions, nor precisely *how* their remains came to be in the "artisan's" possession. The transformation into a chandelier or a candelabra is not done to honor the dead, an act that requires knowing something of who the dead person was. Rather, it would seem the art is made to partake of a morbid thrill, a transgression against "normie" culture, and for profit. And that is what appears to have happened in this case. The entire story appears to be a hoax (CBC Radio 2021). Mr. Prince will not verify his identity, nor his uncle's. He will not say which medical school or what town in Greece. He does not provide the paperwork. Indeed, the *only* thing that seems to be true about this story, is that the human remains are real. Studying the photographs posted to Instagram, we can see the markers of what we might expect of a medically prepared study skeleton. The question then remains—*whose* remains are these? The story appears to be one concocted for social media clout. It is possible, we suppose, that one could work artistically with human remains today in ways that might respect the dignity of the deceased, that take their stated wishes before dying into account. But in none of the examples of "art" we have seen has there ever been a single moment where those wishes are somehow documented. This is why we were initially interested in this story of "Uncle Filip."

Myriam Nafte studied the circulation of human remains in contemporary Western society through an anthropological lens, especially examining the reaction to human remains for research, for biomedical reasons (transplantation), in the context of Catholicism, and in the practice of a number of artists who use human remains as part of their creative oeuvre. Nafte also explored the consumption of the dead in popular culture, including the taking of war trophies and the creation of personal *memento mori*, Goth subculture, and television entertainment. She points out that far from being seen as people, once,

> within popular culture, however, human remains are seen as "things" infused with aesthetic and talismanic qualities that lend authenticity to products, exhibits, and events. The question of their legality or provenance is of no concern, as many dealers and collectors openly advertise their human inventories without any legal or social recourse. (Nafte 2014: 107)

She draws attention to how talking about the physical processes of death, in Western culture, are currently taboo while at the same time death pervades our entertainment, cinema, music, tourism, literature, and more (Nafte 2014: 110). She raises a very good point when she discusses the literature around this contradiction, and the way these representations act as a way to shield us from dealing with death-as-a-process. She asks:

> Is the concept of death further neutralized if individuals sell, collect, or display dead body parts? Is death considered innocuous when human remains are turned into material culture? When the actual corpse is in the hands of an artist, a personal collector, or on public display, is its "cultural moment" . . . represented by a narrative of death and suffering, or rather, does it assume the identity of its affiliated institution, venue, or owner as in for example "the Mütter Collection," "the Hunterian specimens," or "von Hagens's plastinates"? (Nafte 2014: 116)

Nafte makes a distinction here between the "disposed dead" and the "undisposed dead." The former are people that we actually knew in life, or were known in life: there is an association between the remains and a named individual, and the remains were treated in a culturally appropriate way; while the "undisposed dead" are those dead whose remains we find unnamed, unloved, unidentified, whether through purchase at an antique shop, sourced from a medical supply company, or laying in a museum storage cabinet:

> The absent, disposed dead are the reminders of mortality, inevitable grief and loss, while the undisposed dead among us have become the material objects of identity, the souvenirs of power, status, and victory. They no longer represent a person, or a family member but have become mediators infused with a new role expressed by the narrative of their owners. . . . [H]uman remains in the hands of the living become emblematic when they are transformed into trophies of prestige, membership and knowledge that seem to have very little to do with the contemplation of death. (Nafte 2014: 116–17)

In her interviews with artists, it becomes apparent that the artists (who are all sincere in how and why they are using the human remains) are all trying to say something meaningful about the human condition. These artists explain that their work is about celebrating life, appreciating life, and to stimulate our senses (similar phrases are used by the people who buy and sell human remains on social media) (Nafte 2014: 209). The artwork assumes part of the biography and identity of the artist, becoming neither relic nor specimen but something in-between. The power of the art lies in the way the art "resurrects" the dead to teach us something new—and in the way exhibiting such art in museums or other sites of prestige is a way to generate power (Nafte 2014: 204). Validation in galleries and museums, buying and selling, defuses the shock one might feel at the use of human remains:

The undisposed dead no longer represent a person, a family member, an ancestral line, or the parts of someone's body with memory and identity intact, but are deployed to allow us to experience a wide range of human events and emotions, that are not necessarily related to dying, nor reflect our fears of death. (Nafte 2014: 209)

But there is never any consideration of how this distinction between "disposed" and "undisposed" dead emerged in the first place, for these artists. Human remains that have been "disposed of" properly (including being transformed into relics) cannot be owned and continue to have their personhood respected, in this view. The undisposed dead body "become[s] limitless in the hands of artists . . . charged with political, social and cross-cultural meaning . . . like relics and medical specimens, these artworks are trophies of achievement and objects of veneration" (Nafte 2014: 208). These human remains no longer represent a human being, but their transformation as/into art makes them used as things to gesture to a wider variety of human experience (Nafte 2014: 209).

Buying and Selling Antiquities before the Web

The artists discussed above obtained the human remains they used in their art from medical supply companies, while Mr. Prince presumably bought the remains he used from an antique shop or from an online venue. Nafte's work points to the way human remains, when transformed as art, can also assume value through their association with powerful individuals or institutions (2014: 136–200). Before the emergence of social media, human remains that were understood to be "objets d'art" and partaking of those kinds of associations can be understood (in how they were bought and sold) as being part of the larger antiquities trade. The birth of the internet and all its means of buying, selling, advertising, and networking has transformed every category of illicit trafficking into forms unrecognizable to the pre-internet era of auction houses, museum cabinets, or antique shops.

Before the internet era (or more accurately, the emergence of the web in the early 1990s), and certainly to some extent today, the high-end world of auction houses drove the sale of antiquities to moneyed and elite institutions and individuals alike, as discussed in Chapter 1 and Yates (2022). The biggest names, such as Sotheby's, Christie's, Bonhams, Spink and Son, and others span the wholesale-retail divide and, with their reach, clout, and glossy catalogs, have driven "taste formation" among antiquities collectors for centuries (e.g., Brodie 2002, 2011, 2014, 2015, 2019; Davis 2011; Tremain 2017). As compared to material culture or archaeological artifacts sold at auction, much less attention has been given to human remains moved through brick-and-mortar auction houses in the pre-internet era. It is clear, however, that auction houses played an important role in the networks of colonial-era collecting that brought human remains to market, and into the collections of museums, universities, other institutions, and private individuals with wealth and connections (e.g., Knapman and Fforde 2020; Aranui et al. 2020; Carter, Vilches, and Santoro 2017; Roque 2010).

Although to the best of our knowledge, the amount of human remains of any kind that have passed through auction houses is unknown and ultimately unknowable, it is certainly greater than "none." Nor is it a thing of the past, and nor did the movement of human remains via the auction houses vanish with the rise of the internet. Numerous examples from around the world (e.g., Begley 2019; Rachwani 2021; Parke 2021; Campsie 2021; Valentine 2016; McCorristine 2015) continue to demonstrate that vigilance is required by descendant communities, conscientious curators, auction house employees, local law enforcement, and the public. Most importantly, these examples indicate that good public relations can result when auction houses take the complaints of concerned citizens seriously, even before law enforcement has to get involved. As we have shown throughout this book, this is a perpetual work-in-progress.

The Rise and Fall of eBay

As introduced in Chapter 1, eBay has arguably served as the first e-commerce platform to move the human remains trade from the shadows into broader public view. In this section, we discuss in more detail how and why eBay has risen to prominence as an early (and ongoing) site of availability of human remains and other categories of antiquities. Although the human remains trade has largely moved to other platforms, in many ways eBay set the stage, so it is worth looking at the history of the trade on this platform as a "preview" of how it now operates on other e-commerce platforms. Given that "platforms rose up out of the exquisite chaos of the web" (Gillespie 2017), their potential for continued misuse should not be surprising.

Most research investigating any category of antiquities trafficking on eBay, including human remains, was conducted before eBay banned most listings offering human remains (excluding hair and teeth) in 2016 (Vergano 2016). Yet, as will be discussed below, listings containing the allegedly banned categories of human remains continue to appear on eBay from time to time. What is more, it has become exploitable as a platform on which those selling within private Facebook groups or via private accounts on, for example, Instagram, can announce upcoming sales or events on much less regulated platforms. In addition, numerous other e-commerce platforms have supplanted eBay, operating in English and several other languages to serve specific markets. These platforms, such as Marktplaats.nl, Catawiki, Milanuncios, WeChat, Taobao, Zelo, and others, have substantially expanded the audience sellers can reach, and are easy to migrate between, in response to regulation or media attention.

The "Our History" page of eBay, Inc.'s official website provides a generally comprehensive timeline of how eBay grew from AuctionWeb, founded by Pierre Omidyar in his garage in 1995, to the multibillion dollar giant it is today (eBay n.d.). The timeline takes care to highlight the numerous social, economic, and environmental initiatives eBay has launched around the US and globally, the various smaller country or language-specific platforms it has acquired or partnered with to grow, the acquisition of PayPal (then their amicable separation, in 2015), and the rapid expansion of their Silicon Valley campus. What is not mentioned, however, is just how vulnerable the platform has been to exploitation by bad actors, traffickers, counterfeiters, and fraud, and how difficult it has proven to enforce bans for goods and services that law enforcement, civilians, and eBay itself agree should not be available.

A wide variety of research over the past couple of decades has illustrated time and again that eBay, like many e-commerce platforms, has continued difficulty in detecting illicit commerce on the platform, and enforcing its own rules around what may be sold. The breadth of what is known to be actively trafficked on eBay is vast. It includes human remains trafficking of all types (e.g., Huxley and Finnegan 2004; Seidemann, Stojanowski, and Rich 2009; Halling and Seidemann 2016); there is even an identified market for photographs depicting deceased children and infants from funeral homes (Dery 2010). Antiquities trafficking of many forms has also found a home on eBay (e.g., Purbrick 2013; Altaweel 2019; Dundler 2019; Fay 2011, 2013; Scott 2013; Stanish 2009), especially where smaller, much harder to trace items like coins, papyrus fragments, and the like are concerned.

Perhaps less surprising to readers, eBay has often been called out for allowing or poorly enforcing wildlife trafficking of numerous endangered species and their parts, including plants (e.g., Perdue 2021; Cox and Collins 2020; Whitehead et al. 2021; Venturini and Roberts 2020). Even when something is formally banned or seriously regulated offline, such substances or products (including tobacco and narcotics) continue to be offered on the platform (Laestadius and Wang 2018). On top of other ongoing concerns or questions pertaining to consumer or corporate fraud (e.g., Peckham 2005; Bogenschneider and Mironko 2021; Friedan and Roche 2007), the most relevant lingering issue for our purposes is the extent to which bans can be enforced on this and other e-commerce and social media platforms (Vergano 2016; M. Schwartz 2001; Mashburg 2020).

Section 230 and the Rise of Social Media

By this point, if not well before now, you might be asking yourself: How is all this allowed to happen? How have these platforms never had to legally answer for hosting the wide variety of illicit or socially harmful content that they do every day? Aside from voluntary attempts at banning specific categories of trafficked or extremist material (and ongoing difficulties in enforcing those bans, as discussed above), for all US-based platforms or webpages, the answer more or less comes down to one section of one law. At the heart of the matter, we can point to Title 47 U.S.C. § 230 of the Communications Decency Act. It has been called "the 26 words that created the internet" (Kosseff 2019, 2022). It reads:

> No provider or user of an interactive computer service shall be treated as the publisher or speaker of any information provided by another information content provider. (47 U.S.C. § 230)

The idea was to promote the growth of the web by shielding providers from the content that people created, in the same way that the telephone company could not be held liable for the things people said while chatting. Section 230 was enacted in 1996, which was a very different world. Comparatively few people had access to the internet, and in those days, web services were imagined more like pipes through which information flowed. It did not make sense to think of a computer service as a publisher, if the metaphor was "pipes" or "information superhighway" or even just "a better kind of telephone." The provider was clearly a piece of infrastructure with a very minor effect on how information moved over, through, on, or in. However, as the web evolved and became ever more like broadcast television (that is, certain content only available at certain sites), the pipes metaphor no longer worked.

A better metaphor we think is "publisher," which is explicitly what Section 230 argues against. But as these platforms have evolved over the years, they have assumed more and more the functions of de-facto publishers. In particular, it is in the ways these platforms change not just the content itself but also its discoverability. In how these platforms' algorithms operate on the user-provided content to highlight it, promote it, recombine it with advertisements, or otherwise modify it, there is in our view a way that reasonable onlookers might consider that this kind of machine-generated editorial oversight constitutes a form of publishing. This is an argument aligned with one put forward by Catherine Tremble in 2017 who sees algorithmic intervention in posts as a kind of "development" of the material (Tremble 2017). A decade earlier there were some court cases where the findings seem to imply that even minor modifications of content could deprive the defendant of a Section 230 defense (Horowitz 2007).

Nevertheless, as various legal cases surrounding slurs, libel, obscenity, and so on went before the courts over the years after the passage of the Communications Decency Act, courts tended to find Section 230 a shield against all responsibility to moderate or do anything about the content their platforms carried, shaped, or encouraged (Goldman 2017); one could not blame the delivery service for the content and the courts did not regard these sites as "publishers." Nevertheless, this perception of Section 230 as a blanket shield is not entirely accurate. For instance, from July 2015 until June 2016 in approximately half of cases litigated, full immunity was not fully granted (Kosseff 2016; the arguments in these cases are quite specific to the circumstances, and for the most part the argument about "changing" the content was not germane). An earlier study published in 2010 found that in a third of cases examined at that time, a Section 230 defense argument did not survive (Ardia 2010). By 2018, legal scholars could argue that the rationales put forward in the early 1990s did not envision a world where the majority of communications were handled by a handful of private companies (Caplan and Napoli 2018) and so the policy no longer was aligned with its original goals. In recent years, politicians on the right-wing of the United States' culture wars have targeted Section 230 for reform via "messaging bills" which are intended to remove what guardrails there are for content these politicians regard as helpful for their particular viewpoint (Sinnreich, Aufderheide, and Perry 2021). There is currently momentum for reform of Section 230 or indeed the full revocation of the section, but of course the debate is highly partisan, which we may caricature broadly as: while those on the left focused on the harms caused by unfettered dissemination of content, those on the right worry about the censorship of their views (Goldman 2020; Cusumano 2021).

The web has been with us now for over thirty years. Regardless of one's position on the harms, goods, or necessary modifications of Section 230, or whether these platforms should be viewed as "publishers," it is very clear that what we see on the platforms can affect our behavior there. As early as 2001, Häubl and Murray (2001) found through user experiments that the structure of recommendation algorithms could modify buying behavior (infamously, Facebook conducted and published an unethical experiment in 2014 on actual users where they manipulated the display of posts in users' feeds according to how positive or negative the posts were, to see if social networks could propagate emotions; Kramer, Guillory, and Hancock 2014). When a platform combines advertising algorithms with a user's demonstrated interest in human remains, the process begins to create a positive feedback loop. It is almost a bit like the concept of "induced demand." A demonstrated interest in human remains will cause the algorithms used by a platform to feed that user more content. As we progress through this book, we will unpick how this happens. Let's turn to the kinds of signals we might find in social media that indicate "here, here are human remains to purchase!"

Signals in the Noise

Once we started looking for human remains online, we found them in a variety of places including e-commerce platforms, personal pages, business websites, and public and private groups on social media. Sometimes people send us screenshots of things they have encountered. We have seen, amongst other things:

- The heads, hands, feet, skin, wrappings, sarcophagi, and other accoutrements of mummies from both Egypt and the Nazca and Paracas cultures of Peru.
- Modified "tribal" skulls from a variety of locations and cultures, especially Southeast Asian and Pasifika peoples.
- Videos of human remains being actively looted, and deliberately sold uncleaned.
- Skulls and skeletal remains of newborns.
- Examples of remains with clear labels attesting to former residence in a museum.
- Human "wet specimens" of all kinds, including organs, skin, preserved tattoos, blood, and fetuses.
- Jewelry, home decor, and *objets d'art* incorporating human bone, teeth, hair, fat, and ashes; most recently a skull whose teeth were removed by the "artist" and replaced with nineteenth-century hand-forged nails.
- A wide range of former "medical specimens," with or without hardware (springs on the mandibles) or company labels from former osteological supply companies.

In this section, we want to consider what the bone collectors, the bone traders themselves, say about the human remains they collect, as these are the signals that then propagate through the platform and help develop a "taste" for collecting human remains. We'll start with an infamous video on TikTok that displays one bone trader's collection:

Post: "Hey everyone nice to meet you! Feel free to ask any questions you might have any comments I'll take the time to answer it!"

[00.00 shot 1. Facing the camera, five ranks of shelves behind, with approximately twenty-six skulls displayed, two of which, based their size and the undeveloped nature of the bones, are clearly infants; speech bubble overlays the video with the comment: why do you have so many bones . . . HOW DO YOU HAVE SO MANY BONES?!??]

Hello, my name is [x]

[00.02 shot 2. Cat on the floor in front of display cases with several skulls; one skull has what appears to be a historical handwritten label written across the forehead; speech bubble remains.]

This is my cat.

[00.04 shot 3. Facing the camera, new location; open shelves above display cabinets in the background, several crania displayed; speech bubble remains,]

I study osteology primarily specializing in the medical bone trade.

[00.07 shot 4. The camera pans from three articulated skeletons in a corner, over a skull display, to three more articulated skeletons that hang in the opposite corner on a clothes rack; speech bubble remains.]

and this is how and why I work with osteology for a living.

[00.11 shot 5. New scene; appears to be a small room/closet; the camera pans right to left around the room showing two rows of articulated human spines (approximately 100 displayed) hanging from hooks; speech bubble remains.]

My pride and joy is my human spine collection.

[00.15 shot 6. In the same location and stance as shot 3; the camera is steady; the individual addresses the camera with emphatic hand movements.]

And in the US, there is no federal regulation against the ownership, sale, or possession of human osteology so it's completely legal [broad smile]

[00.20 shot 7. Shot depicts cat from the same angle and location as shot 2; now petting the cat; speech bubble remains.]

I'm making this video to help answer any of the questions you might have.

Meanwhile, on Instagram, the text of some posts accompanying photographs:

> Bone Planchette jewelry. Last minute Christmas shopping? How about a piece of jewelry made with human skull fragments? All rings are sterling silver size 8. Each has a hand carved piece of skull in the shape of a Ouija planchette.

Another post:

> This human skull comes from an old European museum collection. It still retains its original museum ID tag which reads "C-C9." This specimen is in great condition overall ... We have several other pieces from the same collection which are currently available on our website.

As it happens, the vendor quoted in this particular post styles the website referenced as a "museum." The museum sells memberships and sponsorships for skulls in its collection, which is a novel spin enabling the vendor to retain control while still bringing in cash. This museum also has a very polished webstore selling human remains if a membership is not enough. We will return to the significance of the museum framing in Chapter 3.

Another post:

> Jar of human teeth. US$320.

In an article about the trade in human remains that appeared in *Wired* magazine in 2019 (O. Schwartz 2019), one collector stated, "It's not about the money . . . . We just sell skulls so we can buy more skulls. I think for the real collectors it's always that way." The article featured our work and included interviews with some collectors. The collectors indicated that what matters to them is the "aesthetic," the look and feel of the bone—"get your hands on one and live with it for a while. Because you will soon realize quite how empty it is, but also how beautiful." According to one collector, the stigma of owning human remains is "shrouded in fear and secrecy, an unwillingness to stare [death] in the face." Certainly, Western attitudes towards death have changed over the years. Many collectors, in many posts, frame what they are doing in terms of education, preservation, rescue (often in contrast to archaeologists who would keep these pieces hidden from the world out of perceived academic elitism). Collectors are performing a *service*, if we take them at their word.

In these framings, they are adopting "personas" similar to what Lauren Dundler has found with regard to antiquities dealers more generally (2021). Antiquities dealers adopt (or mix-and-match) from four general persona categories:

- A persona where there is a performance of trust and authenticity.
- A persona where there is the performance of expertise.
- A persona where the performance of a tie to the past through autobiography and story is key.
- A persona where there is the performance of ethics through knowledge of the legal context. (Dundler 2021: 51)

We can see the performance of expertise and ethics in the few posts and comments we have already shared. It is a common persona among bone traders. But in this chapter, we are going to dive more deeply into the signals and noise surrounding human remains on social media, using the tools of text analysis, network analysis, and some computer vision/image similarity tools. We use this information to develop a picture about why buyers buy and why sellers sell.

Why Instagram?

Why Instagram? The short answer is, when we started, that is where the action was. It is also where a sizable portion remains, even as it ebbs, flows, and proliferates across other platforms. Archaeologists and criminologists first stumbled across human remains being sold on eBay twenty years ago (Huxley and Finnegan 2004), followed by Etsy in 2010. The World Archaeological Congress

(WAC) was alerted to some human remains being sold and sent a request to Etsy to remove them (WAC 2010), but the post is *still* online. The seller now directs patrons to her Facebook page to discuss any human remains purchases. Etsy added human remains as a prohibited category of materials in 2012, but that prohibition is occasionally breached. eBay's policy in 2012 was "humans, the human body, or any human body parts" are prohibited, but "clean, articulated (jointed), non-Native American skulls and skeletons used for medical research" were allowed (Marsh 2012).

In 2016, eBay changed its policy to be concise and clear: "human body parts or items containing body parts are not allowed." It seems this policy shift had a real impact. We were able to find specialist human remains auction aggregator websites preserved in the Internet Archive, and from these, scrape sales figures going back to 2010 straddling the change of policy in 2016. Obviously, we are not recording every sale. But if we look at the relative pattern of sales from 2010 to 2020 in aggregator data we have, and the way human remains were described on the auction site, there are three clear phases. First, there is a period of rising sales and clear descriptions of what is being sold that runs from 2010 to 2012. In 2012, the policy on human remains allowed for "non-Native American" remains to be sold. From 2012 to 2016 there is a drop in the sales trend, a significant decline compared to the years previous, and the language gets similarly cagey about what (and who) precisely is being sold. In the third phase, from 2016, the sales seem to stop almost completely. Insofar as the incomplete data we were able to find in the Internet Archive tells it, eBay's ban seems to have been immediately successful. However, the platform remains used by sellers to increase attention to items on display or for sale on other platforms.

Where did the vendors migrate to? They went to Instagram and Facebook, and a variety of other, perhaps country or language-specific, e-commerce platforms. We started looking at the trade separately at about this time, though we had yet to combine our forces. This migration is why in this chapter we will be discussing how the trade looks from the perspective of Instagram for the most part.

Sales Figures

The investigative journalist Kristin Hugo (2016) gives us a sense of what human remains trading looked like on Facebook during 2015–16. She was able to generate a breakdown of price and quantity for several categories of human remains (e.g., bones, teeth, and organs) with the highest prices requested for mummified crania from Peru. Prices ranged from US$36 for a bottle with human eyelashes, to US$8,000 for a mummified fetus. Huffer and Chappell

(2014) and Huffer, Chappell et al. (2019) provide more detail about the diversity of human remains offered on Instagram and via brick-and-mortar stores with an online presence for the period 2013–16. At that time, the same general price pattern prevailed.

Table 2.1. Summary of sales figures in Huffer and Graham 2017; collected from Instagram.

Year	Number of Posts	Total US$
2013	3	5,200
2014	25	9,900
2015	61	30,000
2016	77	57,000

In those studies, the researchers clicked through search results, following hashtag links to manually collect the information. We set out to automate that process. We started collecting posts and the associated metadata on Instagram in 2016; we automated paging through search results (using the same scraping technique as discussed above) to get a sense of the scale of activity. We wanted to know about not just individual prices but overall sales volume. The trawl surfaced posts that went back to 2013. Now, not every post named a price, but in that initial trawl we found that volumes and dollar amounts jumped precipitously as eBay's market declined (Table 2.1).

In the years since we published those initial results (Huffer and Graham 2017), we have revisited Instagram to collect more data, publishing an update in late 2020, and another update from another trawl of Instagram conducted in early 2022 that we recount below. Each time, we have attempted to use the same general methodologies, although this is quite difficult, since the underlying "application programming interface" (API) for Instagram (that is, a way to programmatically query Instagram to get data back, rather that manually reloading the browser to look at materials) has changed several times since then. In 2021 we also looked at a prominent Dutch-language online marketplace, and we began exploring TikTok. Early on we also noticed the existence of private Facebook groups which do a lot of business in the bone trade as well. While there is a moral argument to be made to covertly move in those groups (see for instance MacBeath 2022 in the context of online animal trafficking), we have not formally investigated the content of those private groups. Sometimes members of the public send us screenshots of conversations in these private groups, so we are aware of the kinds of things discussed in private by people who trade in human remains. We have restricted ourselves to analyze only the posts made on the open web, that do not have an expectation of privacy (see the discussion of our ethical approach above).

In our 2020 revisit, we searched through the scraped posts for clear indications of sale, using what is called a "regular expression" or search pattern to find strings of numbers with the $ or £ or € symbols. We found 193 unique accounts that stated a price openly, across 833 unique posts compared to our first investigation where there were 22 unique accounts across 1,400 unique posts.

In the first three quarters of 2020, the value of sales expressed in USD was over US$164,000 (Table 2.2). That figure is not the true figure; it necessarily is an under-representation of the true value, since our figures only come from posts we found where the vendor was bold enough to state a price up front. Over the years, the number of bone traders willing to *openly* state a price has declined. Many sales take place after private negotiation in direct messages or other private venues, so the actual potential sales volume, if traders get the price they want, is likely much larger.

Notice that this second set of figures from 2014–16 do not match up precisely with those recovered from our first investigation. Both sets of data point to an uptick in sales in 2016. The posts the most recent study found that overlap in time with our earliest study are largely *not* the same posts as we studied then. That is, while we might find many posts from a given year, they might not be the same posts we found before. The difference is that when we did our original scrape, we were much closer in time to when the posts were first put up, but as we get further away in time, the greater the likelihood that posts get taken down, accounts get made private, or posts or accounts get deleted. In January of 2022 as we wrote this chapter, we did another final, but partial, data trawl to get a sense of the most up-to-date figures. This time, we searched only for a single tag: "humanskullforsale." The scrape pulled down 2,725 posts. Of these, only thirty-four posts openly named a price, from eight unique vendors. These eight vendors posted human skulls with a combined asked-for value of US$85,258.

A slightly different trend is visible on other platforms. Given the frequent descriptions of allegedly Dayak or Asmat culturally modified human crania seen in Instagram posts, and since Indonesian Kalimantan, Malaysian Sarawak and Sabah, and West Papua—the homelands of the Dayak and Asmat peoples—were once controlled by the Dutch (among others), we have also conducted a preliminary analysis of the Dutch e-commerce platform, Marktplaats.nl (Huffer, Simons et al. 2022). Marktplaats functions similarly to eBay, as an auction website. We found 263 posts offering human remains for sale on Marktplaats, from 151 sellers. Up until the onset of the Covid-19 pandemic, the value of sales was growing markedly. We cannot speculate on why sales on Instagram should continue to grow while on this platform they start to decline in 2020, but future monitoring of both sites

Table 2.2. Summary of sales figures in Graham and Huffer 2020; collected from Instagram.

Year	Total US$
2014	US$ 8,329
2015	US$ 6,927
2016	US$ 9,593
2017	US$ 48,750
2018	US$ 10,983
2019	US$ 71,200
2020	US$ 164,247

might show this to be a Covid-related blip, or perhaps a shifting from one platform to another (Table 2.3).

Before online auctions, human remains were also handled by the traditional art-market auction houses such as Sotheby's or Christie's. Auction catalogs from the pre-social media era might be one way of seeing the longer evolution of this trade in human remains. Our colleague Donna Yates, an archaeologist and criminologist, tracks these catalogs. She shared some data she has encoun-

Table 2.3. Summary of sales figures initially presented in Huffer, Simons et al. 2022; collected from Instagram.

Year	Total Euros
2017	19,067
2018	35,566
2019	42,897
2020	8,235
2021	912

tered on human remains from Near and Remote Oceania that have passed through the Christie's and Sotheby's auction houses since 1971. In this data, whose representativeness it is not possible to ascertain, the US dollar denominated value of the human remains traded is extremely low—both in aggregate, and for individual human remains auctioned off. The majority of sales in this data occurred in the 1980s. The auctioned remains themselves were mostly of "overmodelled skulls." These skull modification traditions of overmodeling involve adding clay and other adornments including human hair to a skull. Overmodelled skulls of this kind were usually from the Malakula cultures of Vanuatu or the Iatmul of the Sepik River region, Papua New Guinea. When provenances are provided, they indicate remains collected by colonial adventurers and administrators. The catalog descriptions are restrained, almost scholarly, and tend to circle around the "artistic" merits of the remains. Sometimes a description will nod towards the role these human remains played in the communities from which they were taken, which contrasts with how human remains are usually described on social media. One gets the sense of something slightly distasteful yet nevertheless worthy of the attention of customers who can appreciate and love the macabre, savage, or strange. The theme of exoticness we will see is also present in both the comments on social media posts, and in the composition of the accompanying photographs.

Scraping Instagram

In 2016, we began to query Instagram for posts related to the buying and selling of human remains. We initially employed a variation of a snowball sampling strategy, beginning with known collectors on Instagram to see what common hashtags were employed. From this we developed an initial list of hashtags to guide our search (Table 2.4).

Table 2.4. Hashtags with which we initiated our search.

#humanbones
#humanskulls
#oddities
#curiosities
#realbone
#trophyskulls

We collected several thousand photographs using a tool written in the R statistical programming language (Barbera 2015). This package allowed us to search Instagram by hashtag, and then to download both the images and associated metadata. Unfortunately, Instagram changed the way their public API worked in June 2016 such that only those seeking to commercialise users' data could access it in this way. A second package, this one written in the PHP language (Kapishev 2016–22) enabled us to continue exploring these posts, although with less rich metadata. Each time we went to update our data and do another sweep of the human remains space on Instagram, whatever tool we had used previously would no longer work. We have spent a lot of time looking for ways of recovering the metadata that Instagram *does* provide. Our current approach is detailed in Appendix A. Instagram's own help pages suggest that their search function will return all posts with a particular hashtag, so while it is ultimately impossible to tell, we feel our samples are representative of the last several years' worth of posts connected with this trade.

In that first year it took us to collect data, Instagram grew from 400 to 600 million users (Chaykowski 2016). We initially collected some 20,000 posts and rows of data. While the snowball approach enabled us to collect a rich corpus of materials to analyze, cursory paging through the images showed that we were collecting materials far removed from our target. There is, for instance, a thriving community for buying and selling taxidermy on Instagram. Through some common tags, the taxidermy trade overlaps with antiques and "oddities" more generally, which points to vendors of all kinds of materials trying to leverage related areas of interest to drive traffic to their own area. Human remains are to be found this way, but not efficiently. We needed to sharpen the focus, to map out the human remains trade, so we changed our question. We started by asking, what are some common tags that vendors use? We changed our perspective, and asked: If we assume that a person new to the community wanting to buy or sell human remains will *explicitly* use the "#humanskulls" or "#humanbones" hashtag, what will they find on Instagram? What does Instagram look like from that perspective?

This route provided us with a much clearer way to map the trade. We collated the "humanskulls" and "humanbones" posts for a total of 13,410 individual posts. we retrieved 77,293 posts. As with the original scrape, our 2020 update included only accounts set to public. In the interval, accounts that might have been public earlier could have been deleted, abandoned, or marked private.

Some posts got captured more than once since we only scrape for one hashtag at a time and people use multiple hashtags on a given post. After removing duplicates, we had 71,646 unique posts. Remember that not every post is something-for-sale! The visuality of Instagram posts can be imagined as a kind of "digital sensorium" that draws out certain kinds of emotional responses. Some people have no intention of buying human remains, but just like to look at them. There is a culture of visual consumption of human remains that does not require ownership of the remains but rather participation in the network of followers of those who do (discussed below; see also Graham, Huffer, and Blackadar 2020).

Digital Humanities Meet the Human Remains Trade

The digital humanities are a broad area of research that can encompass a wide variety of approaches. As a series of methods, it takes a braided approach to the objects of traditional humanistic study. In the first strand, it uses the tools and techniques of data science and other digital technologies to ask new questions that could not be asked before about literature, historical documents, or the archaeological past; very often, these questions emerge as a function of *scale*. In our case, instead of studying a handful of posts or small case studies, we are able to look at thousands upon thousands of posts and consider *aggregate* patterns of word use in those posts describing the trade. We can consider aggregate patterns in photographs. The other strand of digital humanities involves taking our traditional humanistic approaches, where we read closely and contextualize nuance, and applying this approach to digital media, culture, and platforms. In this next section, we will do both.

Reading Social Media at a Distance

There are a variety of approaches for seeing interesting patterns in a large collection of unannotated or unstructured texts (by "unstructured" we mean, "hasn't been categorized"). As a function of our desire to respect privacy in the posts, (and reduce our own exposure to the cumulative impact of viewing thousands of posts of human remains often treated without respect) we opted for a "distant" reading approach that relies on various computational techniques. To read thousands of posts at once really means to step back and see what patterns in language use emerge from a distance. At its simplest, we are merely counting and categorizing words. When things get more complex, we are looking at word uses vis-à-vis all the other words in all the other posts and comparing these distributions, which requires some more complex statistical modeling.

The typical bones-for-sale post, aside from the image(s), contains a certain amount of text mixed together with a long tail of hashtags. We can count the words and tags within the posts, and compare these against the normal distribution of words in the English language (as evidenced by the Trillion Word Corpus compiled by Brants and Franz 2006 and further processed by Norvig 2008). We filter out the common day-to-day words (also known as stop-words, e.g., "the," "and," "of") and end up with the most common words in this corpus of Instagram posts that are otherwise uncommon in day-to-day English. Thus, we get a sense of what this community speaks about most often: skulls, oddities, macabre, curiosities, taxidermy, goth, handpainted, crafty, curiosity. We can see that this community frames their engagement with human remains as an experience with the other—skulls and human remains are objects valued primarily for their ability to invoke the thrill of owning something taboo. The words taxidermy, goth, handpainted, and crafty point to another interesting pattern in this corpus: the reuse of human (and, clearly, animal) remains for artistic reworking, as well as other forms of art inspired by bone motifs.

We can delve deeper into the language of the posts with a more complex statistical approach called a word embedding model. In this approach, the idea is to ask, "what if we could model all relationships between words as spatial ones?" (Schmidt 2015a, 2015b). Because, in English, word order conveys meaning, the proximity of every word in every post can be explored at once, in a multidimensional space. Directions in this space are called vectors. We can explore the vectors through this space (say, from masculine pronouns to feminine pronouns), and see what the space looks like from that perspective. An advantage of this approach is that it can then be used for a kind of algebra of meaning, where if the vector for words like "king" looks like *this*, and the vector for words like "man" looks like *that*, then we can subtract the vector for "man" from the vector for "king" and end up with a new vector—one that happens to be very similar to the vector for "queen." This approach then lets us work out, at scale, how concepts like "this item is for sale" might be expressed through a variety of words. Ben Schmidt, a history professor at New York University has done this with professor ratings from RateMyProf.com, and finds a clear gender binary in students' language, where words like "genius" are closest to male pronouns while words like "nice" are closest to female pronouns (Bartlett 2015; Schmidt 2015c).

Let us just consider the basic proximities for two phrases we often encountered: "notforsale" and "forsale" (these were hashtags, and hence, no spaces between the words). Knowing which hashtags turn up in closest proximity to each other will tell us more about the contexts in which these tags are used. The words or tags that end up closest to a notforsale vector include:

antiquetaxidermy, naturalbone, deadperson, realhuman, iliveinamuseum, internationalshipping, funforever, antiquesforsale, medicalspecimen

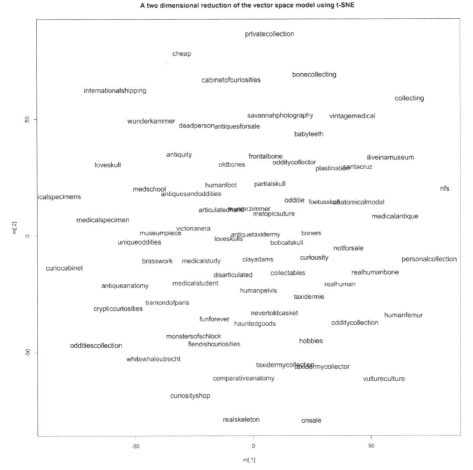

A two dimensional reduction of the vector space model using t-SNE

Figure 2.1. t-SNE graph of the word vector space "forsale-notforsale." Originally published in Huffer and Graham 2017, figure 2, CC-BY 3.0.

The fact that words are present that clearly indicate something is in fact *for sale* suggests that the #notforsale tag might not really mean what it apparently says.

Words closest to the forsale vector include: frontalbone, boneprocessing, overtheline, anatomicalmodel, collectable. When we look at the complete arrangement of words in posts arranged along the spectrum from forsale to notforsale, we find that a word like "oddity" and its variants seems to fall more or less equidistant from either end. Something like antiquebones or personalcollection are found towards the forsale end of the spectrum and might be understood as signaling the potential for a sale when they are used. We can also observe words at this end of the spectrum that seem to make bones more collectable or desirable: medicalspecimens, patina, deformity.

We can also take *two* such lines through the space of these words and cross them to create a kind of quadrant mapping of the space. We can extract from the model the spectrum from "forsale" to "notforsale," and another spectrum from "good, better, best" and "bad, worse, worst" and lay them at right angles to each other. In this way, we end up seeing which words in the forsale—notforsale space carry negative or positive connotations.

In the forsale column, many of the words in the positive row are words connected with the online store for handmade crafts, Etsy. Also prominent are words connected to moving those remains around ("ships," as in, to transport). The word "gifts" reveals one marketing tactic, as in, "makes perfect christmas gifts" [*sic*]. The Christmas 2016 marketing push seems quite prominent

	forsale			notforsale			
	blackandgray	hydrodipped	bad	*powerful*	*thehouseofmasks fully*		negative
	2000	blackngrey	forgot	*successful*	*eyed*	*often*	
9	rosa	peony	u2022	*four*	*masks*	*philippines*	
	labo	taxidermyforsale	monster	*large*	*sum*	*000*	
	skulladdict	mandala	ude48	*mostly*	*especially*	*bodies*	
6	kult	tattoocommunityboy		*french*	*although*	*two*	
	o	tatuaje	epoxy	*gates*	*correct*	*shirtless*	
	dolls	tattoosociety	finished	*punishment*	*earlier*	*willy*	
3	labookult	coveruptattoo	sorry	*form*	*position*	*remains*	
	rockabilly	acrylicpainting	flames	*became*	*cave*	*normal*	
	woodburning	catrina	tom	*sarawak*	*usually*	*were*	
0	forsale	skullandroses	udc89	*ground*	*buried*	*though*	
	homedecor	halloweenskull	81	*temple*	*wooden*	*good*	positive
	paperart	beunique	bonesforsale	*following*	*published*	*bye*	
9	creeplife	ttddhomedecor	plate	*forms*	*realhumanbone*	*sciencemuseum*	
	smallbiz	gothdecor	christmasgift	*1940s*	*poison*	*knife*	
	xmas	ttddskulis	eu	*skullcap*	*lucite*	*beeswax*	
6	disponibile	christmas	brown	*ancestors*	*1950*	*brain*	
	skullfashion	tatu	track	*nfs*	*artifacts*	*mutter*	
	etsyuk	dd4sale	ships	*physician*	*vrolik*	*phrenology*	
3	artforsale	etsygifts	skulldecor	*swedish*	*massive*	*stockholm*	
	grunge	w	fauxtaxidermy	*sleeping*	*trepanation*	*collecting*	
	gothichome	19	uk	*professor*	*arteries*	*calvarium*	
0	etsystore	shopping	circleoflife	*provenance*	*veins*	*notforsale*	
	0	1	2	3	0	1	2	3

Figure 2.2. Exploring the vector space defined by binary pairs, "good"/"bad," "for sale"/"not for sale." Hints of various dynamics at play can be viewed in contrasting, but related, terms, e.g., as with "acrylic painting" falling in negative space and "skull decor" falling in positive space. This might be a glimpse into the taste or aesthetic of those who create skull-related art, which may be important for understanding what creates the taste and demand for human remains themselves. Originally published in Huffer and Graham 2017, figure 3, CC-BY 3.0.

in this initial dataset as well. In words associated with the negative column are many words demonstrating the close affinity of this community with tattooing. It may be that the word we used to construct the negative end of the positive-negative vector, "bad," is being used among the tattooist subcommunity here as its very antonym. In the notforsale column are words signaling academic authority or jargon. Given that notforsale is a tag associated closely with antiquesforsale, is it an indication of "for sale at a price I won't name publicly but it is clearly extremely valuable"?

When we re-ran this analysis a few years later in 2020, in the vector notforsale the closest words were: oddities, skull, cabinetofcuriosities, curiosities, skulls, taxidermy, odditiesandcuriosities, humanskull, odditiesforsale, art . . . which looks to us like that winking nod remains.

When we look for words or tags closest in the model to forsale, we find these are actually several usernames connected with making art *depicting* human remains. This is dissimilar to what we found in 2017, where there were more words connected to particular kinds of bones and their desirability. If we look at "sell," we find the closest words are: skullsell, heavyskulls, cannibal, cannableskull, legal, prohibited, [username redacted], [username redacted], possess, zeldaskull.

Cannibal and cannableskull [*sic*] suggest the association with the exotic, while "legal," "prohibited," and "possess" point to a concern to ward off the inevitable potential buyer's question: is this legal? The final tag, "zeldaskull," points back to making art based on the video game franchise, *The Legend of Zelda*. Thus, between 2017 and 2020 there is an indication of more of a concern towards the legality of the trade and at the same time being more explicit that, yes, this item may be purchased.

If we explore the idea of "legal" discourses in more depth by looking at the vector of words around "legal" and "prohibited," the result almost reads like a post itself. We took the distances in the vector and expressed them as a dendrogram. The words that turn up are: requirements, prohibited, legal, law, ownership, respectful, anywhere, shippable, and then a number of dollar denominated prices (but without a $ sign). It is interesting that expressions of price also fall along this vector, and that the majority of these are denominated in Canadian, rather than American, dollars. In 2019 in Canada there was a brief moment when the human remains trade made the national spotlight, and perhaps might account for a sudden interest in the legality of the trade amongst potential Canadian buyers and sellers. During the 2019 Canadian federal election a candidate was revealed by news media (not by us) to have bought a human skull and to have given it to her partner (Troian 2019a, 2019b). In those news stories, our work was cited, and we were invited for comment, since the 2017 article was readily found by the journalists. Thus, in a roundabout way, we can see in the current discourse perhaps a hint of the impact of our earlier work.

We also explored the material we collected using a statistical technique called topic modeling. A topic model is a model of how writing works, where there are only a limited number of bags of words to draw from. Any document is an admixture in different proportions from these different bags, and these bags contain all the possible words in a corpus of documents in different proportions. If we can accept that, then the computer can look at patterns of co-occurrence of words (from the next word all the way to the beginning and end of a text) and decompose the entire body of materials into its constituent bags. Then we can look for change in these topics over time for the entire collection of posts, or see which topics are most present in a particular post (Graham, Milligan, and Weingart 2015: 133–58). One post might be mostly topic 4—for instance—with a smattering of topic 2. The computer outputs a topic as a list of words and their proportions where each word contributes different amounts to the coherence of the topic. Words can appear in multiple topics but do so in differing proportions. A word like "lead," might appear frequently in a topic about leadership ("lead," "victory," "win") but less so in a topic about heavy metals ("well," "poisoned," "lead") in the same corpus. But what precisely the topics *mean* requires the interpretation of the investigator (the technique has been used in archaeology to explore how field notes both record and form a type of archaeological knowledge e.g., Mickel 2016). A topic model doesn't provide the answer; as a model, it provides lenses for looking at our information. When we use topic models, we fit several with varying numbers of topics to see which lens, as it were, provides the best insight.

Our first attempt highlighted topics like this:

- sale real osteology bone medical oddities sold shipping worldwide specimen
- bones anatomy skeleton medical death museum medicine tattoo doctor photo
- tribal asmat bone dayak tribalart kapala tibetan trophy tin headhunter

Note the close association of topics clearly connected with buying and selling, and topics related to trophy skulls and other Indigenous ethnographic materials. While a post might not necessarily mention a trophy skull being bought and sold, the patterns of discourse are very similar. These remains are not being discussed with respect, but as commodities to sell. There are other topics connected with the mechanics of the trade—giveaways, a gift for Christmas, a Halloween raffle. When we look at individual posts where these giveaway topics are present, we also see topics around authenticity (building up that persona of a knowledgeable authority), which perhaps means that these giveaways are working as a loss-leader (a strategy to attract new customers) for a particular vendor.

The first time we built a topic model around the posts we collected, we noted that there was a clear topic related to tourism (featuring words like catacomb, Paris, travel). While many people share pictures from the catacombs of Paris (and elsewhere) it appears that they do not use the same descriptive tags as individuals interested in collecting bones. Indeed, that one topic appeared to be the dividing line—when we calculated the similarity of topics—between people who were interested in skulls and bones as a motif/inspiration for their art, and for those who wished to possess the dead.

We built some more topic models a few years later with the newer data that we had collected (Graham and Huffer 2020). What is striking in the model we built in 2020 is the relative *absence* of words connected with, for example, the Asmat or Dayak peoples, Tibetan Kapalas or the practice of headhunting among the diverse cultures who practiced it. The continued association with Halloween, Etsy, tattoo culture, and witchcraft remained strong. It is important to note that Asmat, Dayak, and Tibetan remains were, and are, still being traded and are indeed mentioned in the posts we collected. What this *model* indicates is the relative role—or not—of words like Dayak or Tibetan in forming a coherent topic visible at a macroscopic level. We can interpret this to mean that there are fewer overt mentions of this particular material compared to other kinds. While in 2017 there was a strong topic related to tourism (catacombs and so on), that topic does not seem apparent in 2020. This perhaps suggests a divergence in hashtag use where tourists to catacombs and ossuaries are no longer represented in our data. The practice of giving away human remains as a kind of loss-leader that was apparent in 2017 definitely continued in 2020.

Reading Social Media Posts Closely

An alternative approach to these distant, computationally mediated reads is to examine every post ourselves, and all of the comments for each one, and to categorize them in some way. One typology of categorization that might be useful is Sedef Uzuner's typologies of what he calls educationally valuable and less valuable talk, drawing from the literature of online education and assessment of the humble discussion forum (Uzuner 2007). At first it might not seem obvious, that a typology for a discussion forum is an appropriate tool to use here. However, these posts are multifunctional—they are advertisements, but they also try to draw the viewer into the hobby. They try to create an interest in collecting bones. They provide a means for a seller to perform what they know (or think they know) about osteology or the cultures that the remains are said to be from. In their way, they educate the viewer into the norms of this pastime. They also help to signal the persona of the bone trader as an authority to be trusted (Dundler 2021), and trust and familiarity appear to be crucial to facilitating any kind of commerce online (Gefen 2000). As an experiment, we collected roughly two hundred posts and comments from both Instagram and TikTok, and then proceeded to read through all of the comments and classify them according to Uzuner's typology.

Posts or comments with "educationally valuable talk" composed about 10 percent of what we collected. All these educationally valuable posts were of a type that Uzuner calls "exploratory," where the intent is to pose a question or clear up confusion. These comments revolved around questions concerning the origins of the bones, and sometimes comments asking if the vendor has read a particular book that might cast the act of collecting in a better light. Many of these posts were ultimately questions about price, the first step in the haggling process. With respect to posts that contained educationally less valuable talk an overwhelming majority of them presented as "affective," that is, posts that indicate an emotional response—heart emojis, or statements like "I love this!" or "So beautiful!" or encouragement to the vendor to keep up with the "good work" of collecting. Some who leave comments that we classify as "affective" explain how they have similar human remains in their own collection.

On TikTok (see also Chapter 3), the picture is a little more complex. The majority of comments attached to the vendors' videos we collected were of the "less valuable" talk, again in the "affective" category, but clearly belonging to Uzuner's subcategory "adding social presence"—in essence, the equivalent of scratching on a wall "I was here!" These comments were by people making the same few jokes over and over again, to paraphrase: "when the cops enter your house, they'll be so confused"; "my spine/leg/etc is wrecked can I have one of yours"; "oh boy those bones are in better shape than mine!" Nevertheless, in general there is far more educationally valuable talk on TikTok compared to Instagram. There were questions about pathology, questions about size of adolescents versus adults, questions about how to differentiate bones, questions about where do the remains come from.

Most of the comments, while still brief, are longer than what one tends to find on Instagram. What we certainly almost never find on Instagram, but more often find on TikTok, are comments that pass a negative judgment on what the vendor is doing. Some of these are very explicit. But most of these comments are still of a knee-jerk variety, questioning the vendor's morals or mental health.

One kind of talk that isn't captured by Uzuner's typology is of the "you-gotta-see-this" kind. On both platforms, this manifests as a comment with nothing more than someone else's @username, much like how attention is drawn to posts on Twitter and other social networks. We see the @username practice far less often in Instagram bone trade posts, which again points to fundamentally different ways of using the platforms. What seems clear from this close read is that TikTokers are more willing to push back while simultaneously engaging in "educationally valuable talk." We will return to TikTok in particular in Chapter 3.

Hashtag Stuffing

In our first exploration of data from Instagram, we wondered if there was anything meaningful that could be deduced from the long trains of hashtags on posts. That is, not just the presence or absence of hashtags but the precise sequence of tags in a given post. It turns out, there is.

We used a statistical package for the R programming language by the historian Lincoln Mullen called "textreuse." This is a package that compares every document within a corpus with every other document, based on five-word sequences of text at a time, to measure how similar the texts are (Mullen and his colleague Kellen Funk have used this package to study the evolution of American legal history in the nineteenth century and see how different jurisdictions reused civil code from other jurisdictions over time; Funk and Mullen 2018).

A score of 1 indicates a perfect match. We found several hundred posts scoring 1. This was not an error: in every case, the post is a unique post with a unique photograph yet using the exact same caption in its entirety. People selling this material or discussing this material use the same language time and time again. For example, take this post:

> Real human skull for sale, message me for more info. #skull #skulls #skullforsale #humanskull #humanskullforsale #realhumanskull #realhumanskullforsale #curio #curiosity.

There are a number of posts by this user, using the exact same caption and which the textreuse package scored at 1. A post at .9375 similarity has one extra hashtag appended to the text (and, of course, a different photo):

> Real human skull for sale, message me for more info. #skull #skulls #skullforsale #humanskull #humanskullforsale #realhumanskull #realhumanskullforsale #curio #curiosity #dead.

We continue the analysis until we are at around .5 for our score:

> Skull and arm £400 for the pair. One of the fingers on the hand is missing its tip and the whole arm needs glue removing and tidying up a bit. Real human skull for sale, message me for more info. #skull #skulls #skullforsale #humanskull #humanskullforsale #realhumanskull #realhumanskullforsale #curio #curiosity #dead.

That one phrase, "Real human skull for sale, message me for more info," and that sequence of hashtags seems to be as good an identifier for this individual as any username. Indeed, we find through general web searching of that sequence of hashtags that this particular individual is cross-posting to Facebook as well and thus proves a salutary reminder that what is facilitated on one social network likely propagates across multiple ones.

Placing so many hashtags into a post is also a kind of search-engine optimization technique known as "hashtag stuffing." To type so many tags over and over again on a phone or tablet is difficult, and so we are probably also looking at text shortcuts and text expansion macros to make the process easier and more consistent. Hashtag stuffing is the social media equivalent of "keyword stuffing," or the practice of loading the metadata of a web page with keywords in an effort to distort the search results for that page, making it appear higher on the page.

Social Networks

Collecting all this Instagram data also gives us the usernames of the people posting, the people leaving comments, and information about who follows whom. The animating idea of social media is to create networks between users after all, so we turned to formal network analysis using these usernames to see these connections. What kind of audience do the most popular accounts that are openly selling human remains have? What does this network look like, and what does that tell us about the trade? The topic modeling we discussed earlier seemed to imply a roughly tripartite division in the interests motivating the use of the humanskull and humanbone tags on Instagram, so we wondered if and how that would emerge in the networks themselves.

Ideally, one would systematically obtain the list of followers for each and every user account that our scrape collected. Then, we would obtain the list of followers of followers, and then the list of followers of followers of followers ... until we had the networked shape of the entirety of Instagram. When armed only with laptops from our local tech store, that simply is not feasible. As an initial experiment, we instead took the twenty-two accounts that named a price in our first scrape (Huffer and Graham 2017) then scraped the lists of followers for those twenty-two accounts. This gave us a network with 138,014 individuals connected by 172,208 links. These individuals are not necessarily implicated in the human remains trade. Rather they provide a proxy here to indicate influence and impact of the individuals whose materials we did collect.

We converted this network so that we had a network of twenty-two accounts connected by the followers they had in common (Figure 2.3). This makes for a network (also sometimes called a graph) where the size of the connection reflects the number of communal followers. We can then look at some of the structural properties of this graph. We were interested in community detection, a statistic which identifies clusters of individuals who have broadly the same pattern of connections, and centrality, a way of identifying the relative importance of an individual in a network. We found that there were three distinct subgroups (Huffer and Graham 2017). The first group, when we looked at them in more depth, all appeared to be what we might call specialists, or accounts explicitly selling mostly human remains. The second group who seem to have a much wider variety of materials than just bone we referred to as the generalists. Finally, we could identify a group that, once we examined their accounts, were users who for the most part enjoy looking at pictures of human remains but who sometimes sell parts of their collection.

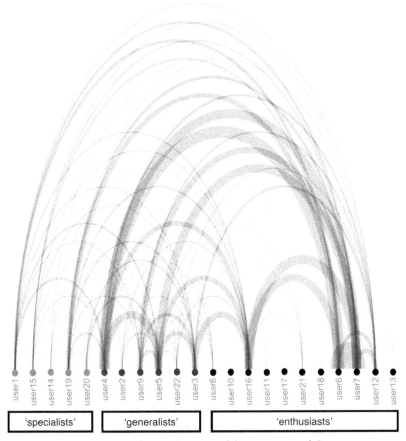

Figure 2.3. An initial network visualization of the structure of these communities. Originally published in Huffer and Graham 2017, figure 6, CC-BY 3.0.

This first attempt at network analysis did not go very far, and in 2020, we tried again. We were able to retrieve the followers for seventy accounts, which covered all the 2020 posts that discussed dollar figures above. That is to say, the network we could stitch together appears to be representative of the state of play for 2020 (Figure 2.4). The result is a network of 235,593 accounts con-

Figure 2.4. Social network visualization of the filtered network of seventy accounts that named a price in posts made in 2020. The unfiltered network consists of 235,593 accounts connected by 257,676 "follower" relationships at one step. Color is assigned through community detection (nodes that have similar patterns of relationships are assigned to the same cluster and colored accordingly). There is a central "core" group of vendors who are connected together, while there is a large penumbra of "one off" accounts that from this perspective have nothing to do with each other. Originally published in Graham and Huffer 2020, figure 1, CC-BY 3.0.

nected by 257,676 follower-following relationships (relationships are also called edges in social network analysis). The fact that we only have a network from the seventy accounts that posted in 2020 naming a price is because Instagram's automated blocking algorithms kicked in and stopped us, prohibiting any more connections from our IP addresses. (When you study the machine, the machine studies you back!)

The pattern that we had observed before, in 2017, of a roughly tripartite division between specialists, generalists, and enthusiasts seemed to hold. We can change focus slightly, and ask, what does this network look like if we try to see things from the point of view of the followers rather than the initial accounts we scraped? That is, rather than the direct follower/following relationships among these vendors, what if we looked at how the vendors are connected to each other by virtue of having followers in common? Thirteen of the vendors do not have followers in common, and so drop out of the network (Figure 2.5). Of those that remain, we can then see that there are still three broad communities (two large, one very small), but this time the nature of the communities is slightly different. One group deals almost exclusively in bones. The second group tends to deal in a wider assortment of antiques. The final group, interestingly, contains the accounts of tattoo parlors.

We might wonder about how pairs of nodes end up with high numbers of followers in common. Instagram's own algorithm for suggesting other accounts to follow might be one culprit. Another factor might be geography, as some of the pairs seem to be within the same general region, for instance. Indeed, there looks as if there might be a broad trans-Atlantic divide between the two major groups, but the evidence from Instagram seems weak.

When we did one more scrape in January 2022, we tried a different approach in terms of looking at followers and following. We took the accounts that together were offering over US$ 85,000 in human skulls, and just looked at the accounts that these eight themselves followed. This obviously does not give a complete view of the trade, but by looking for the accounts these eight vendors followed in common—the individuals whose Instagram accounts connect these vendors together—some other interesting patterns emerge. In fact, we can think of these weak links between the vendors as accounts that perhaps set tastes, or perhaps are vectors of supply, for the eight we are interested in.

In the visualization, we expect to see a kind of dandelion radiating around each vendor—accounts that they follow which the other vendors do not—and perhaps a few bridges or links tying them together. One vendor's account does not in fact follow anyone which is interesting in and of itself, for it suggests that this vendor's account is purely a broadcast account. The most central account, the one that joins up most of the vendors, belongs to one individual who has

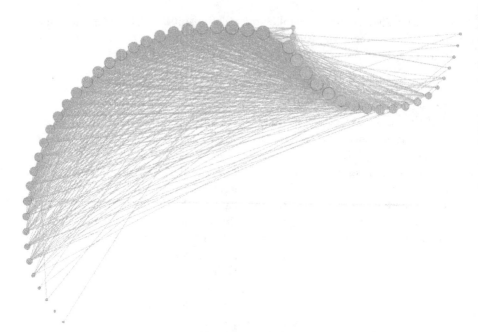

Figure 2.5. Social network visualization of the same data (235,593 accounts connected by 257,676 edges) recast so that the seventy vendors are connected to each other by virtue of having followers in common. (A person who follows vendor A and also follows vendor B is turned into an edge or tie between A and B. Each edge thus has a "weight" that represents the number of followers in common.) A vendor might not follow another but be connected by having followers in common: thus, for those followers the two vendors' posts help create a culture of consumption around images of human remains (which may or may not lead to purchases). Community detection is run again, taking edge weight into account. The result is three distinct groups. Originally published in Graham and Huffer 2020, figure 2, CC-BY 3.0.

only fifteen posts. These fifteen posts are all carefully composed photographs of human skulls. Why would these dealers all follow this one individual? The account offers nothing for sale. Just . . . well done photos of skulls. We might speculate that this account is a buyer. Or perhaps a photographer whose visuals appeal? (In Chapter 3, we tackle the possibility of mapping networks of visual influence using computer vision.)

In the next rank of central accounts that our eight vendors follow in common are a well-known UK dealer, and two lifestyle-type accounts. The dealer is probably by our estimation the UK's biggest dealer. Perhaps these eight vendors obtain their supplies through the man in the UK? And alongside that

Figure 2.6. A social network generated by focusing on the followed accounts in common for eight bone trading accounts. Accounts that only one vendor follows arrange like a dandelion head, while accounts that are followed by more than one vendor act as bridges between the clusters. The network is colored by community detection. Created by Huffer and Graham, CC-BY 4.0.

account, playing structurally an identical role, is an artist and self-described curator who maintains an extensive series of web properties capitalizing on oddities and morbid materials, and a web magazine with an online oddities store.

We will not go through every rank characterizing the accounts, but in the next rank (where rank is based on the way these bridging accounts interconnect the vendors we are interested in) are several well-known (to us, at least) accounts that shift high volumes of human remains (but again, no longer openly mention prices). The further into these accounts we wade, the less tightly focused on human remains they become, and the more all sorts of oddities or curiosities become prominent (there are a tremendous number of taxidermists on Instagram, it seems). This graph gives us a window into seeing how taste formation and sales intermingle.

One of the initial eight accounts that this scrape surfaced is interesting for the structural role it holds in this network (which, remember, is composed from stitching together when they follow the same account). Call it Account 1. Account 1 not only follows a lot of accounts, but it is also an account that most of the other seven vendors also follow. Account 1 follows about 1,600 accounts but is in turn followed by more than 15,000 accounts. Account 1 has an Etsy store (proudly sporting a banner showing over 2,000 sales), where they appear to be selling only wet specimens. Each wet specimen listing uses an image of a human skull with the word "censored" overlaid. If you click through the image of the skull for a given item, there are indeed pictures of the wet specimen for sale. The use of a human skull here we believe is a signal to people who encounter the vendor via Etsy that other kinds of human materials may also be available. Accounts like this, and the way they function as lynch pins on the networks on Instagram, become nodal points of access to other venues for buying and selling human remains.

An Evolving Picture

This then is what the trade in human remains looked like to us, as it has evolved on Instagram over the last several years. The dollar values listed for human remains are increasing each year, indicating perhaps a greater boldness or lack of concern with ethical and legal issues or perhaps the normalization of buying and selling human remains. This community primarily consists of small traders ("makes a great Christmas gift!") rather than the rarefied worlds of the antiquities trade with which archaeologists are typically most familiar. Human remains are almost always framed as the exoticized other. What makes human remains attractive for consumption is the degree to which they signal the other: the more deformed, the more ancient, the more "tribal," the better (we discuss this more in Chapter 3).

To make human remains safe for consumption (i.e., display and sale) on Instagram (the controlling gaze), there is also a concern to use the language of antiquing, to render the buying and selling of the dead like that of an every-day commodity. Advertisements for skeletal elements being offered as prizes in informal auctions is a prime example of this phenomenon. Language can be creatively contorted to often mean the exact opposite of what is literally being said, especially when signaling that something is for sale (in particular, in those posts that do not name a monetary value). Specimens traded or showcased on Instagram are being bought and sold across multiple social media platforms, including Etsy, the network for artisans (loosely understanding "social media platform" to be one that enables "followers"). In the case of Etsy, the sale of human remains has allegedly been banned for several years (Guzzardi 2012) yet our dataset demonstrates that it continues.

Instagram users employ combinations of hashtags to boost the visibility of their posts in ways that can be readily applied to identify users themselves. At a macroscopic level, the social network of individuals interested in human remains on Instagram (whether known only from usernames or via more personal identifying information) seems to split into specialists, generalists, and enthusiasts.

Real human remains are sometimes the raw materials for artwork and self-expression (and so there is an implied lack of humanity or dignity to the person whose remains have been so-appropriated). While replica resin skulls are also sometimes used for this purpose, these are rarely sought by collectors, even if occasionally high-quality casts are sold as real bone to inexperienced enthusiasts. Sometimes, the subsequent blow-up upon discovery that a resin replica has been bought under false pretences can be quite vitriolic. This is a community that does not take kindly to "scammers." (But see Chapter 4 on the veracity of claims).

Tourist photos of catacombs or other dark heritage sites featuring human remains do not, by and large, appear in our corpus of material, even though our initial search terms, "humanskulls" and "humanbones" in themselves imply no necessary connection with either tourism or trading in remains. What does appear from time to time, however, are posts presenting remains available for trade or sale that are implied to have come from such sites. This is often followed by vigorous discussion of the morality and ethicality of possessing or selling remains obtained this way, with comments often split between those for whom the robbery of crypts and catacombs is a bridge too far, and those who are interested purchasers.

Conclusion

It is easy to find human remains online. Once you know the tags and who some of the players are, the system will find more for you and draw you in deeper. There are patterns of discourse which seem to persist broadly over time. We find that the amount of money and the amount of human remains being bought and sold seems to be accelerating, and the numbers of people participating in this trade seem to be increasing. The language of posts has changed in subtle ways that we might see as a response to the increased media attention the trade has received in recent years. The overall structure of kinds of accounts and their interconnections seems to be holding.

Of course, Instagram does not make it easy to scrutinize what is going on, and its parent company Facebook (now Meta) continues to tinker with monetizing various parts of its various platforms. When eBay banned human remains on its site in 2016 the dollar value of sales crashed on that platform; the figures presented here show a large jump in stated values given on Instagram posts around that same period which perhaps can be interpreted as a shift by vendors to the newer platform. Meta (both Facebook's and Instagram's umbrella company) seems to want to encourage transactions in private groups using Facebook's own financial exchange mechanisms, though this process has not been completely realized yet, and might never be. When/if it does, we might expect to see a drop in posts naming a price for human remains as Facebook's newer systems come online and vendors shift platforms again and platforms continue to battle for users, viewer attention, and influence (Solsman 2022; Stokel-Walker 2022). Regarding TikTok, the next big development scheduled to arrive is the allowing of videos up to ten minutes long, likely as a direct challenge to YouTube (D. Goodwin 2022). This, combined with the addition of creator monetization methods (Perez 2021), has the potential to add TikTok to the long list of platforms on which money can be exchanged for goods and services. Another platform on which "influencers" can make money regardless of the content they are putting out into the world. Another commercial vector for the human remains trade.

3

Looking at Bodies

Are there any large-scale patterns in how photos of human remains are composed? And if so, what can we deduce from these patterns? Are there visual tropes that distinguish "bone trade" photos from other kinds of photography? Can we say anything about what photographs so-composed do for the people who buy and sell human remains?

The key thing about the trade in online goods is that the buyer is not able to handle the goods prior to purchase. Whether we are looking at purchasing books, cooking ware, gadgets for our homes and offices or indeed, human remains, we must rely on what we can see in photographs, coupled with what we can deduce from the accompanying text. How is authenticity signaled?

Osteologically Real, but Culturally Fake

Sometimes, when human remains are recovered, and osteologists can examine the remains in detail, the modifications to the remains we find point to another worrying trend. Sometimes, the materials are indeed osteologically real (i.e., actual bone, not resin or plastic replicas), but *culturally* fake. In October of 2015, agents of the Royal Malaysian Customs Department stopped a shipment of human remains, among which were sixteen crania. These remains were shipped from an area of the Malaysian state of Sarawak on the island of Borneo, an area in which some Dayak cultural groups (but not all) took trophy skulls from their enemies. Such trophies would be ornamented in various ways and using various tools, according to the cultural traditions of the various groups, and put on display. The patterns carved into the skulls, the locations of perforations, the additions of other materials, all of these held significance. But in the nineteenth and early twentieth centuries the area was forcibly incorporated into the wider global economy; colonial administrators, settlers, and tourists began acquiring these trophies as souvenirs. With traditional ways of life disrupted, some individuals would take or reuse skulls to create versions of the traditional trophy skulls explicitly meant to feed the curio trade, and thus obtain cash.

When the Sarawak Museum Department curators permitted Huffer and Guerreiro to examine the seized remains, it was clear that the modifications, that is the carvings, made to the majority of the skulls were created using modern electric tools (see Huffer, Guerreiro, and Graham 2021). The condition of the crania and coloration of the patina or other staining, suggested these crania were probably stolen from modern graveyards (either Muslim or Christian). After drilling, dyes and pigments were added to make the carvings look old; perforations through the skulls were clearly done by electric chisel and then stained with dye. Forgers will go to some lengths to make human remains appear to be culturally similar to materials already having some market cachet.

We have thousands of photographs of human remains. How many of them depict similar osteologically real but culturally fake remains, sold under pretenses of owning physical manifestations of exotic or "savage" customs long gone? The forgers clearly are aware of one dimension of the "tastes" that motivate the buying and selling of human remains. Notice also that this particular taste seems to be the same one behind the Christie's and Sotheby's sales we mention in Chapter 2. Federica Villa, who considers the tension between the "authentically exotic" and the "authentically beautiful" in the context of Peruvian antiquities found in Christie's listings and on eBay, points out that authentic does not have to be understood in archaeological (or osteological) terms. The reality of the object being sold is not based solely on age or provenance. Instead, the taste for the authentic can also be framed in terms of appealing to buyer's notions of *beauty* (and/or the macabre). It looks like our expectations of the real thing, and it is ancient too, so of course this item is "authentic." Villa concludes that how something is framed as "genuine" depends partly on the venue where it is being sold (Villa 2021: 135, 152).

In this case the culturally fake but osteologically real might also be, in this way, authentically beautiful and confirm people's beliefs about how human remains are supposed to look. We might expect that we can work out something of these beliefs by seeing how photographs of human remains are composed (the anthropologist Douglas Harper uses peoples' reactions to photos as part of his ethnographic research, and he argues that photos evoke a deeper response since the way the brain processes visual information is different than the way it processes text; Harper 2002: 13). What were the visual tropes used to compose these photos? In archaeological photography, sometimes, if the photos are orthorectified it is possible to measure useful metric data from photographs that have been carefully staged. They don't necessarily look like good photos to the eye, but despite the seeming distortions, the proportions and angles are all correct and true, so one can read measurements off the photos for further research. The photographs thus become archaeological evidence. We wondered, can we do something similar with the photos from Instagram, despite all the noise and randomness (as it were) introduced by so many different people taking pictures? Could machine learning cope with that, and learn to pull out useful data? And if it could, would that tell us something about how people signal materials for sale in photos? Or would it tell us something different?

Taste Formation

No one is their true self on a social media platform. We choose which items to share, which photos to post, which accounts to follow and which to ignore. We perform differently, given the emergent culture of different platforms, and we "curate" the materials that go there (Liu 2007), and these are also a function of the user's aesthetic tastes. These tastes are also formed through our intersecting experiences of class and gender in the real world. One way we signal belonging through these tastes and aesthetics is through conspicuous consumption, especially of so-called Veblen goods (Veblen and Banta [1899] 2009) or goods for which demand increases as the price increases, rather like status symbols, which achieve their status through their high price. This also neatly describes the economics of human remains trading, where we might think of human remains as the ultimate Veblen good.

We can differentiate groups in society via participation in these different taste groups. This extends to the people who view and like a given post. By participating in liking, commenting, and following particular accounts, taste groups are expanded and ideas about how to be in these spaces emerge and coalesce (K. Davidson, Graham, and Huffer 2021, drawing on Bourdieu 1984; Liu 2007; and Gans 1999). If this is true, then one way vendors/collectors/enthusiasts might signal "belonging" in the community of human remains traders might be in the way the photographs are composed. What we needed was a way of measuring the visual similarity of the thousands of photographs that we had collected.

Looking with Machines and Neural Networks

In recent years, a whole suite of approaches to machine learning have developed around the idea of re-creating digitally the way neurons in the brain interconnect and learn. The idea is, if you show enough images of a dog to the machine and tell the computer that all of these images are a "dog" then the machine learns to generalize from all of these specific instances of dogs to a kind of "dog model" represented by particular patterns of interconnections. A bit more technically: each image is composed of pixels; the image classification program is composed of mathematical functions called "neurons" that are interconnected. Each neuron "responds" to the values produced by the functions it is connected to in the previous layer and makes a decision about whether or not to pass an output value to the neurons in the *next* layer to which it is connected.

The first neurons look at the image, sweeping past all of the individual pixels that compose it. The neurons might respond to the presence or absence of light or dark shades. They might respond to the presence or absence of shapes. The strength of the connections (the weight) is, at least initially, entirely random. Some neurons might fire, but the value that they compute does not get passed to other neurons because their connection is not strong enough. But—and this is where computer vision and other machine learning techniques do the "learning" part—this neural network can *change* the pattern of its connections, changing the weights and so on through back propagation, to get better results. The network is shown pictures of dogs. At the output layer of the network, the result can be compared against a "known" picture of a dog. The difference can be worked out, and the network can use that degree of difference to reset its weights to get a better result. Over time—and this is hugely computationally expensive—the network assumes a shape that lights up correctly when it sees a dog.

Then the researcher does this again for another kind of image. And another. And another. Eventually, once the network is trained, it can be used to classify images: "What is the probability that this picture is that of a dog?" The machine might respond: "Labrador retriever: 80 percent. Chihuahua 10

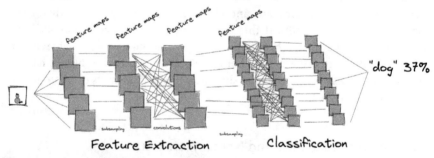

Figure 3.1. A greatly simplified representation of a convolutional neural network. The network is exposed to an image; a convolution acts as a filter or "kernel" passing over the image to identify features; these are passed progressively to the next layers according to the weights of the connections, to identify more and more complex features. The final layers assign the classification. Created by Huffer and Graham, CC-BY 4.0.

percent. Cat 6 percent. Guinea Pig 4 percent." The training data for these kinds of classifiers comes from pictures scraped from the web from all sorts of places, by companies like Google with enormous computational resources and expertise. For most of us without the resources of Google, this simply is not feasible.

There can be shortcuts though. These trained models are made available freely, and with a bit of coding, one can throw out the last layer, the existing labels (knowledge), and add one's own data instead. The final layer is retrained on the new data—a few thousand images of crop diseases, say—and the resulting model *can identify crop diseases accurately* (see for instance Kang et al. 2021). It is this ability for trained models to be retrained that has led to the incredible increase of machine learning in both industry and academia in the last ten years. Nevertheless, one problem with this approach is that it requires extremely large training datasets. It also requires that the training dataset have example images of what one is trying to classify. Knowing whether something is a member of a class requires multiple examples so that the model can learn the extent of the variability.

But . . . if we forget about labeling or classifying images, we can do something else. The output of a neural network, when we show it an image, is a vector or list of numbers, where each number corresponds to a feature of the model that has been lit up for us. A vector is also a kind of direction in a multidimensional space, and so we can measure the *degree of similarity* of two vectors. Identical images will have a similarity of 1. Images that are completely different in all respects will have a similarity of 0.

Taste in Two Dimensions

That is the key for this next experiment. We took the corpus of materials that we had scraped from Instagram, looking at the images for which we had previously studied the discourses of the text. Using code from and following the example of Douglas Duhaime (2017; a developer with Yale's Digital Humanities Lab), we fed the images into a neural network, obtaining their vectorized representation. We then compared each image against every other image, measuring their similarity (the underlying code for this procedure is now bundled together as the PixPlot package for the Python language; see Appendix B). These scores allowed us to project each image into a two-dimensional representation of that similarity using a technique called "t-distributed stochastic neighbor embedding" (Figure 3.2). Finally, we identified clusters of similarity within that distribution using a technique called "affinity propagation" (Figure 3.3; see Huffer and Graham 2018 for a more detailed discussion of the statistical techniques used).

Figure 3.2. t-SNE projection of image vectors of data collected for Huffer and Graham 2017. Originally published in Huffer and Graham 2018, figure 1, CC-BY 4.0.

Then the hard part began. What unified these clusters? *Why* had the machine gathered them up this way? What was it responding to? In general, the plot of images had four main divisions. We could see that pencil-sketches and other "artistic" interpretations of human bones were for the most part located in the bottom right quadrant, while photos of people showing off bones were in the top left. Taxidermy and animal skeletons seem to be in the lower left, while human bones on their own were in the upper right.

In the very center of the complete projection—in a sense, the most central image, too—is an image of a skull upon a shelf, with a price tag. This example is from a cluster where the images are of bones/skulls that are positioned on things—often, but not always, a shelf. The image is composed so that the foreground is in sharp focus and the other items on the shelf are blurred. Images in this cluster are reminiscent of mid-twentieth century museology, of items ranged in ordered rows, heightening the sense of "other," reducing their humanity (see Redman 2016). If we consider the photos of human remains according to their original associated text, another two clusters attract our immediate interest. They are adjacent in the t-SNE plot, and quite distinct from the location of the central cluster discussed above.

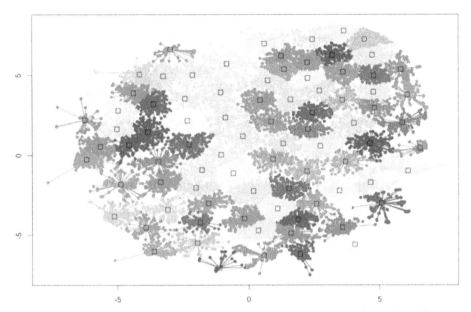

Figure 3.3. t-SNE projection of image vectors of data collected where the eighty-four clusters determined by affinity propagation are indicated by shading. Squares indicate the location of the exemplar datapoint for a given cluster. Originally published in Huffer and Graham 2018, figure 2, CC-BY 4.0.

The first cluster of interest depicts skulls that often have been photographed straight on, and largely fill the frame, while the second cluster is composed of images of skulls that are turned slightly to the left or right or upside down. In the associated posts for the images in these clusters, the language used is of the "look what just arrived in my collection" or "look what I just gave away" discourse. Some photos are indicated as having been taken in a museum, and there is at least one photograph from a well-known business in this trade where the associated post advertises that the store is seeking skulls to buy. Items marked for sale are discussed obliquely, e.g., as one post put it "new skull arrived . . . come pay your respects at [the] most amazing curiosity shop."

In the associated posts for the images in the first cluster are many explicit notices of materials for sale. A number of active businesses (predominantly in Canada, but also in the UK) account for several of the posts and clearly state the item is for sale, often naming a price. As was reported in Huffer and Chappell (2014), active businesses (with brick-and-mortar storefronts and/or online websites with catalogs, PayPal account details and contact information) are also known to exist in the US, the Netherlands, Belgium, Australia, and elsewhere.

The machine directs our attention to the framing of photographs, and the relationship of the human remains to other elements within the photograph. Exhibition design—rows of objects in cases on display—are recreated here. The interplay of foreground and background also seems to be important. Photos composed to show off a collection might also be subtly signaling that the item could also be for sale.

It would seem then that machine learning can detect visual signals in Instagram photographs that indicate the human remains are for sale: the positioning of a skull, for instance, relative to the plane of the camera, as well as the arrangement of materials on shelving (or other objects), mimicking a museum display case, with foregrounds in sharp detail with backgrounds blurred. These all seem to be invitations to the viewer to consider the availability of an object for purchase or trade. But we can do more with this data.

A Network of Tastes

Taylor Arnold and Lauren Tilton have been working with neural networks in this fashion for some time to understand print and televisual culture; they call this "distant viewing." In one of their experiments, they took the corpus of photographs produced by the US Farm Security Administration's Office of War Information during the 1930s and 1940s and vectorized the images in the same way that we did. But instead of visualizing the similarities between images as a kind of plot, looking for clusters, they took the similarities as indicating nearest neighbors, and then expressed these relationships as a network. Imagine that the nearest neighbor for Image A was Image C; and for Image C, the nearest neighbor was Image F. In their 2019 study they found that these chains of visually similar photographs, also implied a *chronological* linkage. Image A was older than C was older than F. The key to understanding this was to consider who created the photos—the photographers were often students and mentors for each other, in turn. What Arnold and Tilton found was that visual similarity, as measured by the computer, was finding chains where a photographer's earlier work was influenced by their instructor or mentor, and in time, their work influenced that of *their* students (Arnold and Tilton 2019).

As an experiment, we rescraped Instagram using the tag #humanskullforsale one day in 2020 and fed the resulting images (about 1,300 unique images) into the neural network. We calculated the visual similarity for every pair of images and took the top five most similar photos for each image, which we then expressed as a network where each image is connected to its most similar neighbors. The details of this experiment are explained in K. Davidson et al. (2021). As a network, the result looked a bit like a hairball, but we could explore it using various network measurements that considered each image's links and the strength (degree of similarity) of those links. The first thing we looked for were clusters, using "modularity" or community detection routines. In network analysis, a module is a cluster of nodes (in our case, images) that have broadly similar patterns of interconnections (in our case, visual similarity). This was useful because it quickly identified for us a series of images that really had nothing to do with human remains—crystal skulls, amulets, artworks, taxidermied animals—but that did use the #humanskullforsale hashtag as a bit of lateral marketing. Other isolated communities tended to be images that turned out to be multiple views of exceptionally different human remains (compared to the majority of pictures collected): skulls that had been heavily modified or transformed into "art" or ornaments.

We did find communities with chains of connected images where the most central image also had the oldest creation date, with each subsequent image in the chain being a bit younger (see Figure 3.4). One such chain turned out to be posts from a single vendor over four years. In the earliest photos, the skull is square to the camera on a plain shelf. With time, the shelving/cabinet becomes more ornate, more gothic. Props start to enter the frame. Simple candles give way to more elaborate (and more dribbly) groups of candles. Plain lighting gives way to a dark atmosphere characterized by deep reds and blues/blacks. It is, rather, cliché. This particular vendor has over forty thousand followers and we can see their style evolve over time as they become more prominent, and more successful in the collecting community. In the graph, other chains featuring images by other vendors and collectors connect into this vendor's visual aesthetic, as they learn and develop their own related style.

We found other communities with chains of images where the thing that unified the chain was not so much influence over time, but variations on a theme. And again, a bit of a cliché: individuals playing at being Hamlet performing the speech over Yorick's skull. Often, the image is from the point of view of the speaker. Sometimes, it is apparent that one image is created as a response to the other; sometimes it appears as if this set-up has occurred to the photographer spontaneously.

While not as neat and self-contained as Arnold and Tilton's experiment (where the photographers in their dataset all worked for the same agency and often knew each other), that we can see and trace patterns of visual influence in the much wilder space of Instagram does demonstrate how single individuals can set the taste for a much wider population. The wider public consciousness of "how to act" with human skulls is also apparent. Even if a person has no intention of buying or selling, if they indicate to the social media platform that they like these images, then they will be presented with more of them. Similarly, the people who compose such photos will learn to compose more similar images. In this way the commodification of the dead becomes realized in the photos.

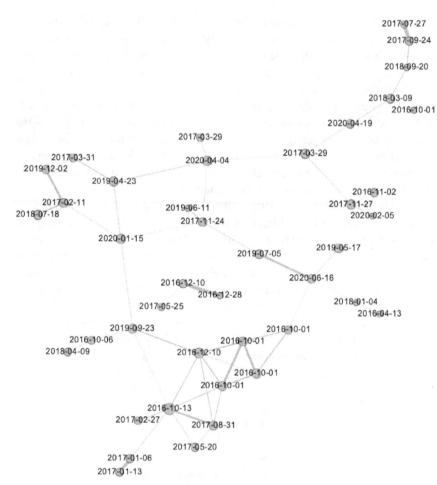

Figure 3.4. The largest "community" or module from a network of visual similarity, filtered to only show strongest similarities (> 85 percent). Darker lines denote closer visual similarity. Individual nodes are labeled with the date on which they were posted. Figure regenerated from the same data discussed in Davidson, Graham, and Huffer 2021, figure 2. Created by Huffer and Graham CC-BY 4.0.

Taste Formation via Interacting with Bioarchaeologists?

In the midst of beginning to examine taste formation among dealers and collectors, we also wondered if formal academic scholarship mediated through activity on Instagram intersected with the human remains trade. One of us (DH) examined how professional bioarchaeologists interacted with the wider public on Instagram via a hashtag analysis and a close reading of the posts the self-identifying members of this community made (that is, they said they were bioarchaeologists in their profiles; Huffer 2018). A sample of "professional" hashtags like #bioarchaeology, #paleopathology, and #osteoarchaeology were queried. These were terms that almost never crop up in our other analyses of how human remains dealers, collectors, or enthusiasts use the platform. The absolute numbers of posts was approximately three thousand, and these posts received comparatively few comments. Only a handful received more than five hundred likes. Huffer identified four common themes in the ways that this community used the tags.

There was a strong, recurring theme around balancing the ethics of doing osteological research with the pressures of study or public outreach. There was a theme around the lighter side of being an academic or student in this field. These never displayed human remains in the posts. Another theme showed a trans-Atlantic divide in the conception of what "bioarchaeology," as a term, is meant to cover. In North American posts, almost always only human remains are discussed, while elsewhere both human and faunal remains were covered by the term. Another theme spoke to the developing networks of professionalization (conferences, laboratory settings, and works being read). One instance was identified where a small-time dealer in human remains left comments looking for authentication advice. No one responded. For the most part then, it was found that the community of scholars who use these tags were talking largely to themselves, with little interaction in the wider Instagram world. (However, it is also apparent from posts shared with us from other social media channels that there are instances of individuals allegedly both practicing or studying forensic anthropology, dental anthropology, and other similar topics, participating in comment threads related to the bone trade and occasionally answering collector questions as to the possible age, sex, or "ethnicity" of crania for sale. As you might imagine, we find this quite concerning.)

Taste Formation through Other Media

The human remains trade can sometimes be found on television and while we have no evidence of people being motivated to buy human remains online because of watching a television program, it is worth considering how a TV program might *teach* a person about the trade, and so provide the terms for entry on other kinds of media. A couple of *Pawn Stars* episodes highlight many of the dimensions of the online trade that we have been discussing. Airing since 2009 on the History Channel, *Pawn Stars* follows the often-colorful adventures of the Harrison family (patriarch Richard, brothers Rich and Corey, and Corey's childhood friend Austin "Chumlee" Russel) as they run the Gold & Silver Pawn Shop in Las Vegas, Nevada (History.com n.d.). The draw of the show centers around the dynamics of the owners as they interact with each other and customers and navigate running their business, and around the wide range of items brought to them for evaluation and potential purchase by a diverse spectrum of clientele.

In Season 17, two separate episodes aired in which a collector and dealer of human remains (identified in the show only as "Stuart"), came into the store to sell some skulls. In Episode 1 ("Shooting Pawns"), "Stuart" brought in an alleged Asmat *ndambirkus* (decorated ancestral skull), and in Episode 17 ("Crossbows, Coins, and Conspiracies"), he tried to sell a purported decorated and carved Tibetan *kapāla* skull (Pawn Stars Fan 2021a, 2021b) There could be other episodes of *Pawn Stars* featuring human remains, but we found no episode synopses for any edition of *Pawn Stars* that mentions human remains for sale.

In the first video, "Stuart" admits to being "a collector and dealer of human skulls and other odd things" when asked how he came by this item. The store employee serving him admits this "is kinda creepy" (met by laughter). "Stuart" asks for $2,100 at the outset, saying that the piece is rare and in good condition; on the screen flash a few generic (but not necessarily accurate) "facts" about the Asmat and the "crazy rituals" of the "thousands" of tribes in the area. The store employee tells some stories about cannibals and head-hunting. Close-up, panning shots over the skull in a face-on view clearly indicate that this is in fact real human bone, with noticeable signs of age, staining, polishing, and minor breakage not unexpected for frequently handled human remains that were initially stored in an open-air tropical environment. Indeed, both employee and potential customer admit it's "real bone," even if it might be a "tourist piece." (We also note that the way the skull is handled, by grabbing its face, can damage it and is enormously disrespectful.)

When he counters the initial offer of $2,100, the store employee casually mentions that a collector such as the client would know that one could "buy a skull, online, right now, for $800." "Stuart" emphasizes that a skull selling for $800 "might be a little damaged, wouldn't have the cool headdress on it, wouldn't have the tribal background, but . . . ." The employee goes on to say, "Who knows what it really symbolizes." A counteroffer of $600 is given for this "fun story, and a fun idea" but a verdict that "it's basically an arts and crafts project on a skull." A bit more back and forth is offered before a final price of $800 is accepted. "Stuart" grouses that the price is "a bit low," but that's ok. He will "just put that money towards more skulls."

The clip illustrates how two individuals, who clearly have dealt with the skull trade before, approach the remains. The story is the key element. The cultural knowledge is haphazard and appeals to a vague "tribal" mythology. The interaction and haggling are entirely blasé (skulls, vintage radios, it's all the same, one feels). We encountered this clip on YouTube. In the comments under the clip, some individuals immediately question the framing of the entire arrangement and the complete lack, in the clip, of any discussion of legality or ethics of selling a human skull. The commenters all seem to be long-time fans of the show, and in their discussion, they offer a kind of push-back against this effort at packaging the human remains trade as entertainment. They feel that the store employee seemingly has *too much* information, while "Stuart" has too little (and his persona as a dealer fails in that he makes no performance related to the legal context). But this is a frequent narrative arc of the show, that the people who bring things in do not really know how much their items are worth, until the Pawn Stars set them straight.

"Stuart" returns in Episode 17 with the alleged Tibetan *kapāla*, speaking with the same employee and asking $4,800. What is most interesting about this exchange is both an admission from "Stuart" that he has been in the business for a long time, followed by a later revelation by the "expert" called in to independently assess the piece that, in fact, the bone might be real, but everything else about it is too new or of the wrong material. They're looking at a tourist "trinket" from the 1990s—another example of the osteologically real but culturally fake phenomenon. The seller is optimistic that the expert "might be able to shed some light I wasn't aware of." Who is called? Robert (Bob) Dodge, one of the founders of Artemis Gallery in Louisville, Colorado (Artemis Gallery n.d.). Complete with its own thermoluminescence "testing laboratory" (and an alleged PhD holder willing to work for them), they are notorious for no-questions-asked selling (e.g., Yates 2014a; Barford 2010). Although Bob is "definitely seeing dead people here" and indicates the skull is "definitely human," it appears "over decorated" and all wrong. A date of 1980–90 would likely put the collection and export of the skull right up against India's 1985 export ban.

An evaluation of $1,000 is suggested, a counteroffer of $400, a counter again of $3,500, and then no deal. "Stuart" leaves by mentioning he will "hold on to it to see if he can sell it elsewhere." Does that mean social media? Most likely. The comment section on YouTube once again contains discussion of the strange disposition and possible personal habits of the seller, his not being able to tell it was a "tourist piece" (suggesting that he is a rip-off artist now after a more gullible buyer), discussions of whether or not such items are "cursed," and the like. "Stuart" does not seem to be very good at the trade. But clearly, the producers of the show felt that human remains would make for good entertainment, that the exotic and macabre stories would make for a good clip. The clips we are discussing were not put online by the History Channel; a fan uploaded them to YouTube. In the comments, we see an interested public pushing back again, but on themes of authenticity. "Stuart" tries to adapt the antiquities dealer's persona of performing expertise (Dundler 2021: 51) but fails, and this is what draws the commenters' ire. Would these two clips prompt someone to start collecting human remains? We suppose that is possible but in the discussion of what sells, of how prices are set, of how the appearance of authority can be won or lost, and how the various categories of personas that signal authority are created, the clips are instructive and teach how-*not*-to-be-a-skull-dealer. Don't be a Stuart; be one of the Pawn Stars, it would seem.

The relationship between television watching and its social impacts (including of course consumer behavior, since understanding what keeps people watching television is what keeps ad revenues coming in) has a voluminous literature. We want to jump into some of these discussions as they pertain to the reality television format, for it seems that reality TV does indeed have an influence on people's purchasing behavior and beliefs. For instance, Crockett, Pruzinsky, and Persing (2007) surveyed forty-two first-time visitors to a cosmetic surgery office about their viewing habits with regard to the "plastic surgery makeover" genre of reality TV. They divided the viewers up according to how much of these kinds of shows they consumed. The high intensity viewers reported a higher degree of confidence in their own knowledge of cosmetic surgery and felt that the shows corresponded well to real life than the low intensity viewers. Thirty-four of the viewers reported that the TV shows influenced their decision to go to the office in the first place, with fourteen of them reporting that they were strongly influenced by the TV shows to go to the office. In this study at least, an inclination towards the subject gets reinforced by the television program(s) and prompts the individual towards action. A larger study of 2,148 individuals asked an allied question, "does reality television influence the public's perception of plastic surgeons as experts" and found that it negatively influences that perception—the understanding of the scope and role of plastic surgery beyond aesthetic enhancement is not understood (Denadai et al. 2015).

Another aspect of reality TV that has been shown to have an impact on the behavior of consumers is the star power of the celebrities shown, whether these are stars from other forms of media (movies, dramas, sports, and so on) or whether these stars have emerged from the reality TV format themselves (like the hosts of *Pawn Stars*). Lueck (2012) found that viewers who admire these stars seek to emulate their lifestyles. They develop a kind of parasocial relationship with the hosts of these shows (a phenomenon that has been documented for at least as long as television has been part of the media landscape; see the summary in Tran and Strutton 2014). Studies of how viewers feel connected to these hosts or stars (along various dimensions) have been mapped to explore viewers/consumers' purchasing behavior for products endorsed by the star. Tran and Strutton found evidence that implies "viewers generally may see themselves, or want to see themselves, expressed in what they do (or buy) that makes them feel more 'connected-with' the celebrity endorser [or host]" (Tran and Strutton 2014: 303). A study of college students found a similar parasocial effect (Jahng 2019).

Collectively, these reality TV shows that intersect with the human remains trade may be more effective than we thought in creating a taste for human remains. For those already inclined to collect or enjoy collections of human remains, they reinforce that inclination; the shows reinforce beliefs about the domain that do not match with the reality of it, and through promoting para-social bonds, buying/consuming human remains or photographs/collections of human remains gives a venue to express an identity that helps foster a sense of broader community. It also implies, we would argue, that certain bone-traders, through the dominance of their presence on various platforms, become a kind of celebrity with whom users can form similar kinds of attachments. This is especially true if the users comment or like posts or otherwise engage with the bone-trader, adopt the use of their hashtags or terminology, or exhibit other forms of digital appreciation and mimicry. But unlike reality television, the kinds of celebrities who emerge on the social media of the bone trade do not always get it their own way.

Taste Formation and Resistance on TikTok

Short form video platforms, such as YouTube and TikTok, are also an avenue for creating taste. In the summer of 2021, a video on TikTok was heavily re-posted across several social media platforms, attracting conventional media attention too. Unusually (for TikTok), it was about the trade in human re-mains. Thus, we were presented with the opportunity to watch how knowledge of the trade exploded into broader public consciousness on a comparatively newer platform. This video was discussed in Chapter 2, with our transcription.

TikTok is known for fun or goofy uses both imitative and adaptive, like lip-syncing to popular music, copying, sharing, or subverting dance styles, and mixing videos together into new forms. What makes those videos possible are the many unique creator features of TikTok such as the ability to post videos with pre-selected or self-made soundtracks and backgrounds, tag other users, and importantly for purposes of extending one's reach, the ability to "stitch" with other user's content. A "stitched" video reuses a certain amount of some-one else's video allowing the second creator to respond to, or expand upon, the first person's video. Such videos carry the #stitch hashtag and name the user whose materials have been reused. "Duetting" is another means by which media is shared, with the newest means of sharing being to "repost" from one's FYP or "for you page," a page that TikTok puts together automatically to show-case videos the TikTok recommendation algorithm calculates will draw your attention.

The means by which content is created and shared allows for videos and users to more easily "go viral." Going viral is one of those terms without any precise definition, though we all know it when we see it. Some scholars and marketers say something has gone viral when a piece of media has received more than the arbitrary threshold of 100,000 views, while others maintain all that matters is the rate at which the media is viewed and engaged with over a short period of time (Wadbring and Ödmark 2016; Nahon and Hemsley 2013). Regardless of how we define virality, the more important feature is the long tail of all videos, since there will likely be something of interest to the user in there somewhere, once the algorithm deduces your interests. The longer a viewer spends watching a video, the more that TikTok learns that this video is interesting and so the more likely the video will be served up automatically to other users with similar attention profiles. The precise mechanics of Tik-Tok's attention algorithms are of course a secret, but massive experiments conducted by the *Wall Street Journal* (2021) using hundreds of fake accounts seems to support this understanding of how the algorithm works.

While many users have attracted well-deserved attention due to the creative, humorous, or socially conscientious nature of their content, the platform has also attracted numerous studies and media exposés detailing how illicit or exploitative content has found a home as well (e.g., Feddema, Harrigan, and Wang 2021; Hu et al. 2021; Petersen et al. 2021; WSJ Staff 2021; Weimann and Masri 2020). There is not a built-in payment option included with account creation, as with for instance Facebook and Instagram, but payment for goods and services can be negotiated in messaging or via movement to PayPal, TransferWise, and related international payment services (however, TikTok announced on 28 September 2021 that it was rolling out "TikTok Shopping," an e-commerce feature that will allow "business" accounts to commercialize their videos; Perez 2021).

It should come as no surprise that prominent members of at least some trafficking communities have taken to the platform to reach new audiences or indicate that sales can be arranged via their account on other platforms, such as Instagram. The account we discuss here, which we will call "Individual 1," was created in February 2020 and first rose to prominence *outside* TikTok on 10 August 2021, when Individual 1 posted a video displaying over one hundred articulated vertebral columns adorning his apartment's closet clothing racks. Using off-kilter camera angles, cuts, and pans in the video, he creates a kind of frantic energy as he shows off the collection, calling it his "pride and joy." The video was reposted across social networks as other people encountered it. Conventional news outlets then picked up the "story." We first encountered the video via our own personal Twitter accounts. Before August 2021, we do not know how many followers Individual 1 had on TikTok. They have posted prolifically since 2019, with the earliest posts documenting daily day-in-the-life of a student while shifting slowly towards mostly bone-related content as they started up their business.

A Network Lens

We used Andrew Nord's TikTok-scraper (https://github.com/drawrowfly/tik-tok-scraper) to download videos and associated metadata from TikTok according to two hashtags: #bonetok and #**********.

The first is a general tag used by TikTokers interested in both human and vertebrate faunal osteology, while the second is a hashtag that replicates the user-name of Individual 1 whose videos garnered general attention in August 2021. The first tag functions almost like a library call-number, a way of finding videos that surround a general interest. The transformation of Individual 1's username into a hashtag is an interesting development. Bonilla and Rosa (2015) talk about the way a hashtag is not just a kind of finding aid, but also a kind of *place*, a field-site, where ad-hoc publics come together (2015: 6). They were developing this idea in the context of the #Ferguson hashtag on Twitter, which references the shooting of Michael Brown, a Black teenager, by police in Ferguson, Missouri in 2014. They argue that if we look at hashtags as places, we must recover the context of the "utterances" made there, and so have to focus on the individual "experiences, practices, and socialities" in that place (Bonilla and Rosa 2015: 6). For the second tag then we will try to consider it as a place, via an experiment of looking for visual similarities in the composition of the videos.

Once we obtain the videos and metadata, we represent this data by recasting it as a network of videos to hashtags, so that hashtags are connected to other hashtags by virtue of appearing on the same video. The resulting network can be thought of as surfacing the connected concepts that users employ to conceptualize the communities they are engaging with. It is a network map of "ideas" that surround the initial post. This map can then be queried for structural patterns. We look for groupings or clusterings of the videos (formally, "modularity," or the idea that nodes that have similar patterns of inter-connectivity amongst themselves form a community) or high connectivity between them (formally, "betweenness centrality," or the idea that a node is important because it sits on the highest number of shortest paths between all pairs of nodes).

Hashtags that belong to the same clusters suggest a general topic or "idea," while hashtags with a high betweenness centrality could be understood as ideas that broker pathways to other discourses, "gateways" as it were. It is important to understand that what we are generating, by looking at patterns of hashtags, is not how users *find* videos on TikTok, or a divination of how the algorithm uses hashtags for its recommendations. When users give a hashtag to their video, it is a way of signaling how they understand its broader content or perhaps conversations in which the video takes part. Thus, if we build a network from this data, we are obtaining an emergent, higher-level view of these conversations.

We scraped TikTok for videos on 23 August 2021. We will summarize what we found; the interested reader should go to our original paper (Graham, Huffer, and Simons 2022) for the full details. But in essence, the network of connected ideas that we found bears some resemblance to what we observe on Instagram but has crucial differences. It is a messy network with six major subsections (Figure 3.5). Unsurprisingly, the tag sitting at the center of it is "bones." Other central tags included variations on "for you page" (FYP, FY, for you), which are all attempts to get one's video onto the coveted first page on TikTok that a user sees. This may be done deliberately to drive more traffic

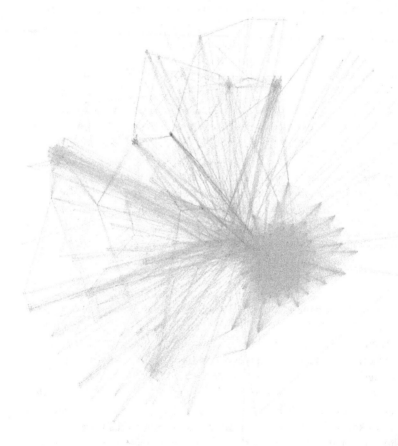

Figure 3.5. A visualization of the network of hashtags connected to other hashtags by virtue of appearing in the same post in our TikTok scrape, colored by modularity (communities of similar interlinkages). The visualization is not particularly useful, other than to demonstrate that clusters of hashtags do differentiate structurally in their use. Originally published in Graham, Huffer, and Simons 2022, figure 2, CC-BY 4.0.

to their own content, or, tangentially due to content creators wishing to share something they find important or amusing, whether or not new viewers of the particular video go on to follow their account. "#Vultureculture" is a hashtag that we encounter on other social media platforms and covers not just human remains but also taxidermy and various subcultures devoted to animals. "Witchtok" is interesting in that it gives us an intersection into another very active TikTok subculture that is also known to acquire, use, and debate the use of bones within their community of practice. Some hashtags with a lesser degree of centrality, like "stitch" or "greenscreen" are related to the affordances of TikTok and how the particular video was made. "Bonetokhelpme" is interesting in that it points to perhaps some of the earlier uses of the bonetok tag, for identifying animal bones encountered while walking in a park or down the street.

The six major subgroups that constitute the overwhelming majority of the nodes were determined by looking at their patterns of interconnections, where the tags are more strongly linked among themselves than with the rest of this

Table 3.1. The six major subgroups within the TikTok network.

module 3—constitutes 44 percent of the entire network. Top tags: bones, fyp, vultureculture, witchtok, skull, foryou, foryoupage, oddities, stitch, skeleton, bonetokhelpme, nature, bonejewelry, oddity, collection, crystaltok, witchtok, teeth, humanskull, boneart, skullart, pagan,witchyvibes, crafttok, bonetiktok, goblincore

module 2—constitutes 18 percent of the entire network. Top tags: skulls, bone, viral, taxidermy, art, witch, flowers, witchcraft, artist, pheasant, dogsoftiktok, deer, halloween, commission, pink, feathers, haunted, bonesinabucket, cleanup

module 12—constitutes 10 percent of the entire network. Top tags: creepytok, skulltok, witchy, spiritual, spiritualtiktok, creepygirl, crystals, deerskull, creepy, witchythings, etsyshop, smallbusiness, creepycool, deadtok, artistsoftiktok, specimen, crystal

module 0—constitutes 6 percent of the entire network. Top tags: osteology, anatomy, skulltiktok, bigone, horrortok, deathpositive, biology (but also includes: skullcollector, wunderkammer, skullcollection, oditiktok, skullcleaning, tattoo, cazaska, osteologist, cemetery)

module 14—constitutes 4 percent of the entire network. Top tags: bonecollector, storytime, anthropology, humanremains, duet, respect, anthropologytiktok, archaeology

module 19—constitutes 4 percent of the entire network. Top tags: greenscreen, spooky, museum, voiceeffects, goth (but also includes truecrime, ghosts, neworleans, deadbody, truecrimetiktok, cemeteriesoftiktok) network (the network analysis routine found that it could determine twenty-eight separate groups in total).

Modules 3 and 2, which together account for almost two-thirds of the network, seem to be a kind of meta-level of tag use where the user is trying to game the system to achieve virality, with modules 2 and 12 also having a more promotional feel supporting artists or business that might not necessarily be involved in the *human* remains trade. That module 12 points to "etsyshop" as a tag demonstrates that one platform might serve as an introduction to another. Module 0 veers more into the display of human remains, while module 14 seems to circle around pushback and discourse over the morality/ethics of collecting. Module 19 gets into the "showy" aspect of human remains as a kind of decoration. The stitch tag points to a TikTok feature enabling one to remix someone else's video with your own. Seeing it as a tag is both an encouragement to remix and a signal that a piece has been remixed. Such posts are also signaled in the original metadata in a field called "mentions." Note that mentions are a distinct piece of metadata, and that these mention networks are a subset of the total number of unique users whose material we scraped.

We can query the network from our #bonetok scrape to show us only the nodes that explicitly mention other nodes—these are call outs, shout outs, direct challenges or responses meant to be seen. When we look through this lens, we find a subgroup of creators who are all professional archaeologists or archaeology students responding to Individual 1 directly (and sometimes, to each other). We note that Individual 1 does not respond back. In fact, the only times Individual 1 can be connected with another user more than once was the result of Individual 1 making his stitch videos featuring an otherwise unrelated video where the person depicted asks, "What is the rarest thing in your collection?," inviting responses from across TikTok. Individual 1 then shows off many parts of his collection, including his infamous spine wall, over several videos, with the same clip from the source video as introduction each time. Other responses he makes are to demonstrate his alleged knowledge of human anatomy, responding to videos that ask questions like, "What is this thing?" (In this case, pointing to the philtrum, the area of skin underneath the nose on the upper lip.) In this network of mentions, there are no posts *supporting* Individual 1; rather, they separate out into subclusters by the presence/absence of secondary conversations over the morality and ethics of bone collecting, and occasionally highlight inaccuracies in the osteological information provided. These responses too will feed the algorithm, teaching TikTok about the human remains trade.

Individual 1's account became its own tag. On 20 September 2021, TikTok reported that the tag had had 4.6 million views. What does it look like or mean when an individual user becomes a meme or new hashtag in their own right on TikTok? And what does this imply for the archaeological consciousness of TikTok? We cannot speculate as to what this might mean for Individual 1's actual business, though he posted another video in January 2022 thanking everyone for their support bringing "public awareness to osteology" as he held up a print edition of a major newspaper that had done a story on him.

We scraped the #********** tag (the frequency of posts, and again extracted from the metadata of the hashtags-to-hashtags network (to get a sense of the overall discourses), and the user mentions. Again, we find the same general patterns. Individual 1 doesn't reply to any of the users explicitly mentioning him except for one, and it is to answer a question posed in the comments (rather than in a new TikTok) about why teaching with a real skeleton is better than using a replica. He presents a facade of being interested in human remains for their educational usage. As many of his earlier videos especially demonstrate, he is quite content to be entirely cavalier with the human remains he controls (allowing and encouraging his cat to play in and with them in earlier videos, for instance).

Composition of the #********** Tag Videos

What about the composition of these videos?

We extracted keyframes from each video we collected under the #********** hashtag, using the open-source software ffmpeg. A keyframe is, roughly, a point in the video where the content has largely changed from what came previously. Then, we sought to explore the image similarity of all of these keyframes. Some videos had only very few keyframes; some had many. A video with many keyframes indicates many cuts and changes of scene or intermixing with other videos, carrying a frenetic energy. We then used a convolutional neural network as we had done before (this time, using the PixPlot python software by the Yale Digital Humanities Lab, which is based on the same code we used earlier by Douglas Duhaime). The result is an interactive visualization allowing the user to zoom in and explore different clusters of images by eye; Figure 3.6 is a screenshot from this interface. We should note that this approach can create clusters with keyframes from *different* videos appearing in the same cluster. Thus, the results should be understood as being about the composition of individual shots that comprise a video.

The approach found twelve visually similar clusters of keyframe images. Two clusters are of materials related to an ultimate fighting athlete who got caught up in the scrape because of hashtag overlap. It is interesting that both the network analysis of the hashtags, and the visual representation of this similarity via PixPlot separate this material out. The keyframes in these ultimate fighting videos feature a great deal of text, much of it with a kind of neon highlighting, over a closeup of a person's face. We removed these images from

Figure 3.6. The visual similarity of keyframes from the videos rendered into a webgl visualization using t-SNE to organize the images in three dimensions. Originally published in Graham, Huffer, and Simons 2022, figure 7, CC-BY 4.0.

further analysis. However, there is one keyframe from an individual engaging in bonetok that gets categorized in these two extraneous clusters. It shows a screenshot of a listing from Individual 1's commercial online storefront, for a skull of an alleged Sámi individual, the Indigenous people of northern Fenno-scandia. Over the image the user, an archaeology student, has laid the text, "If you didn't think you were doing something wrong, you wouldn't have taken it down . . . right?"

Cluster 1 is composed of keyframes of a woman, addressing the camera directly, against a wall with a completely neutral background. There are no other images in this cluster.

Cluster 2 features several images that are visually very busy—complex scenes with domestic furniture, sometimes bookshelves or workbenches. There is usually a person in the scene.

Cluster 3 features keyframes that depict an individual facing the camera, often from the torso up, in a room where there is something going on in the background (window, wall hanging, mirror, and so on).

Cluster 4 depicts the TikTok user where they have employed a greenscreen effect to place themselves, from the chest upwards, on top of the comments thread for a given post.

Cluster 5 is very similar to Cluster 4, but the focus is cropped to the TikTok user's face.

Cluster 6 again shows images of the user employing a greenscreen effect to place themselves, mostly from the torso upwards, over the top of specific posts by the #********** account; these "background" posts are drawn from other social media platforms in addition to TikTok.

Cluster 7 images are characterized by extremely dark lighting or indeed a kind of credit roll aesthetic depicting overlying text. One in particular reads, "This situation with ********** proves yt [*sic*; slang, "white"] people shouldn't be trusted." This speaks to a theme picked up in the comments on the initial video, where several individuals left comments related to the settler-colonial/ scientific racism origins of human remains collecting, which will be discussed in the next section.

Cluster 8 are images associated with one TikTok user who also participates in witchtok communities, dressed in black gothic clothing and makeup, against a black background so that her face appears in high contrast. This visual approach is sufficiently distinctive in the larger corpus of material we scraped to make its own cluster here.

Cluster 9 is composed of keyframes where the user's face fills the frame.

Cluster 10 features users facing the camera from the waist up, against a light background (paneled walls, often) where the user's words are also displayed in the foreground.

TikTokers, or at least, the ones responding to Individual 1, use a variety of techniques to get their messages across. Notably, the use of overlaid text in the images further complicates the videos and would not normally be caught in the trawl of metadata retrieved through scraping, which points to the need to develop methods that address the full range of multimedia that social media encompasses.

Individuals who indicate in their profiles or in their videos that they are professional in some capacity (including students) here at least are creating visually simple videos—facing the camera, perhaps using greenscreen effect to illustrate the content they are speaking to, or placing text over top of their own image to emphasize their words, in marked contrast to the frantic energy of Individual 1's videos. Some individuals remix (one or more of) the original #********** posts with their own (so-called hand-stitching) to underline the contradictions in the original posts. Some users will mix in screenshots of comments and frame their posts as a response. The playfulness and versatility that TikTok facilitates by making it quite easy to adapt and reuse others' content in one's own materials promotes different kinds of responses that largely seem to map against whether a user appears to be for or against collecting, with the against posts providing clear and critical responses, sometimes taking a sober approach, other times appealing to the visceral upset that many individuals feel when first realizing that there are people who buy and sell human remains today. The pro-collecting posts seem to revel in creating visuals that range from the playful to the shocking.

As one of the anonymous reviewers of the initial version of this case study pointed out, it is an act of protest to refuse to use the same techniques and props that Individual 1 uses. The very *contrast* is itself an eloquent "no" to what this person does and represents. On Instagram, we do not see this kind of engagement, this kind of refusal. Individual 1's attempts to leverage TikTok *on the face of it* are only successful if we look at likes. It seems to us that he has instead created a community of active resistance to the human remains trade. Inadvertently, he seems to be successfully teaching TikTokers why the trade in human remains is unethical. We turned to the comments left on Individual 1's original video to explore this idea more.

Topic Models

We collected all the top-level comments on Individual 1's original August 2021 video in February 2022. We also selected a large, interesting subthread of comments to collect and analyze separately that circled around the legality of what Individual 1 was doing. Altogether, that provided us with 2,028 comments to explore. To give a sense of the flavors of the subthreads within the comments, we reproduce below the comments with the most likes and replies:

- "'don't worry it's completely legal' is the kind of answer that makes me worry more": 41,600 likes but only 54 replies, and most of these are either @ symbols to attract someone else's attention, questions of "why is this legal," and patient explanations that what is legal isn't always what is moral/ethical.

- "legality and morality are not the same": 35,400 likes and 281 replies, and is discussed further below.

- "'And here is my spine collection' then it's not really 'for science' anymore but a room for your trophies": 19,800 likes, 61 replies.

- "There's absolutely no way you have this many bones ethically. And the fact that you aren't answering questions about it tells me all I need to know.": 11,200 likes, 96 replies.

- "these were people not rocks to collect. have respect": 7841 likes, 110 replies.

- "I'm an actual anthropology student who focuses on human remains and osteology and this is totally not okay": 6592 likes, 69 replies.

- "some real colonizer energy we've created here today": 4167 likes, 41 replies,

- "I have a PhD in biological anthropology and I work in clinical anatomy. While it may be legal it is certainly unethical.": 3215 likes, 33 replies.

- "the fact that your PRIDE AND JOY is human spines says enough tbh": 1612 likes, 13 replies.

There were also multiple comments, framed in a variety of ways, calling out Individual 1 for not actually replying to anyone's questions in the comments, despite his "promise" to do so.

We created several topic models and found that a model with six topics seemed to express the full range of ideas the best. The first two topics (that overlapped slightly) are composed of words expressing incredulity that people collect human remains. The main difference between the two topics is the expression of that incredulity—one topic is characterized by comments along the lines of "I have questions," while the other has comments imagining ghosts, or the surprise/shock/horror that visitors to Individual 1's home might feel. Another topic turns around the imagined interactions with, and effect on, Individual 1's cat (and, deeper within the results, questions of ethics). A fourth topic focuses on the legality of what Individual 1 is doing, and frequently contains comments that specifically reference settler colonialism, white supremacy, or scientific racism. Topic 5 is composed of words that are used like those in Topics 1 and 2, and again, focuses on the viewer's reaction, expressing desire to have or to collect bones of their own (frequently making a joke of it), while Topic 6 is similar to 3 and focuses on potential bad effects of owning bones (including legal issues). The topics are all more or less similarly sized, demonstrating a fairly equal distribution of the topics across all the top-level comments.

We ran the same analysis, but this time on the long thread where TikTokers were arguing over the morality/ethics of this trade (as a subthread, this was not considered in the previous analysis). This time, we found that seven topics clearly emerged. The largest topic captures the flavor of the debate well—the words "rape" and "consent" feature prominently, which ties back to a recurring theme in this thread comparing the lack of consent of the people whose remains Individual 1 collected to a commenter's argument, to paraphrase, that "rape is similarly about lack of consent." Topic 3 is a topic composed largely of replies to the previous discourse and its rape analogy, as is Topic 6. The difference with Topic 6 is that it uses "murder" as its analogy, as in, to paraphrase, "murderers presumably think they're in the right too." Topic 2 draws attention to the problem that the origin of these human remains is not known, and some commenters raise the historical sourcing of anatomical study skeletons from India and China. Topic 4 is a discourse about the *form* of others' arguments (the strawman fallacy is charged) and the fact that so much about the human remains trade is (paraphrasing again) fundamentally *unknowable*, while Topic 7 is again concerned with the form of argument and the shifting of goal posts. Finally, Topic 5 is similar to Topic 1, but remains distinct through a concern with "society" as well.

A number of comments and replies (in the top-level comments, and in the subthread) contain someone's username, and emoji characters signifying some sort of emotional reaction; these posts serve as a kind of topic on their own (though because of their brevity, not one formalized in the topic model), a flag to attract other users' attention. Nearly six hundred of the top-level comments contain the "@" symbol, which is prepended to a username for this purpose.

This distant read of the top-level comments, and of the one large subthread, show again that TikTokers are viewing Individual 1's post *not* within the framing that he wants but rather through their own understandings of colonialism, law, and ethics (several call him out expressly for his claim of being on TikTok to answer questions but ignoring everyone's comments). It is a kind of discussion that we do not really observe in the comments on human remains posted to Instagram, where any kind of legal topic is more of an invocation by the original user who made the post that "yes this is legal."

Peer Pedagogy

It is evident that this whole episode was the first time many users on TikTok encountered the human remains trade. It is also evident that some users were already well versed in the moral, ethical, and historical issues of the trade. In this episode, these worlds collided. The kind of learning that happens on these kinds of platforms in these collisions is messy and informal, and, as Michael Dezuanni (2021) reminds us, constant. Dezuanni, drawing on a variety of research connected to how "peer pedagogies" work in online platforms, especially video based, explains that

"Peer Pedagogies" recognizes that in digital contexts individuals often learn from other individuals, regardless of if the "teacher" in the relationship is directly known to the learner, and regardless of if "teaching" is intended or purposeful. For instance, peer pedagogies and learning are frequently central characteristics of the relationships that form between "micro-celebrities" and their fans. (Dezuanni 2021)

Dezuanni's research explores the phenomenon of #booktok. Like #bonetok, this hashtag unites a variety of people around talking about books via TikTok. Dezuanni's research identifies two kinds of videos in the #booktok world. One is reader-centered and involves a kind of conversation around books, new authors, and the worlds depicted within the covers. The other involves a kind of habitus where books are status objects to be consumed. We see a similar broad bifurcation in the videos we have scraped and analyzed here. Individual 1's videos promote "a habitus," a normalizing and a glamorization of the bone-collecting lifestyle. Other videos (without perhaps the same reach) use the same kinds of techniques visually and rhetorically to show off collections and inspire others to do the same. Within the #bonetok world though, there is also a peer pedagogy around ideas of osteology, ethical engagement with osteological research (human and other animals), and a desire to provide public knowledge about how human remains were obtained and commodified in the market in the first place, including but also apart from responses to Individual 1's content. These videos facilitate and invite conversation around the topic, while spilling over into other "universes" in TikTok. They use a restrained and careful, quiet framing to highlight and contrast with Individual 1's videos—a deliberate countering of his work.

We were struck by how TikTok, as a platform, seems to facilitate push back in a way that other platforms do not. In our research on Instagram for instance we have very rarely come across posts that call out another user, or engage with the ethical and moral issues presented by bone trading to the extent that can be regularly seen on TikTok, at least for now and in relation to Individual 1's particular account. Similarly, the interconnectivity of tags shows a wide range of discourses that frame people's engagement, with both pro- and anti- sides, in a way we have not seen on Instagram. Our research on Instagram shows how Instagram forms tastes and works as a platform for connecting buyers and sellers. Here, we see Individual #1 using TikTok like shock advertising while at the same time through the peer pedagogy that Dezuanni identifies, other users create opportunities for pushback and discussion of the moral, ethical, and legal issues around human remains. Critical engagement is being done by students and other archaeological practitioners on TikTok in this regard.

Who Pushes Back?

Given the prominence of archaeology, osteology, and history students and practicing professionals challenging and contesting the bone trade on this evidence, let us take a brief moment to explore some demographics. What are the demographic categories involved here, on TikTok as it intersects with the bone trade? Are there differences with those individuals who appear in Instagram photos? It is worth pointing out that on Instagram, in the materials we have collected, very few vendors or collectors post photographs of themselves or provide biographical details in their user profiles, while there are comparatively far more examples from TikTok where users do post photos of themselves or otherwise provide demographic information (whether they trade or collect bones or contest these practices). We have not categorized users according to demographics in our research nor have we tried to confirm the demographics of vendors and collectors (the ethical protocols that guide our research dictate observation only). *Our impression* is that the trade in general skews heavily male (although we have observed some prominent accounts on several platforms where the individual is femme-presenting).

Demographic data are ultimately what all social media platforms profit from, in the sense that knowing very fine-grained information about the user base is the key to monetizing social media. Hootsuite, a platform for managing social media from a commercial perspective, compiles statistics periodically on various marketing categories. Hootsuite reports that 43 percent of Instagram users ages sixteen to sixty-four also use TikTok, and 82 percent of TikTok users also use Instagram (Sehl 2021). On Instagram, twenty-five- to thirty-four-year-olds represent the largest group (for advertising purposes). We can narrow those age ranges down and find that Tiktok has a far larger share of Gen Z users (broadly, those born between 1997 and 2012, so ten- to twenty-five-year-olds) than Instagram, 37 to 33 million people (Cyca 2022). In the United States, 61 percent of TikTok's user base identify as female in these surveys (Cyca 2022) while for Instagram that number is 43 percent (Sehl 2021).

In the videos discussed above, crafted in reaction to Individual 1's video, the ones that push back using a neutral video aesthetic, simple backgrounds, and by addressing the camera face-on, are primarily by femme-presenting individuals. *If* the same demographic proportions held true for the user base for both platforms that engage with the human remains trade (and that is by no means certain or data that we can access), we might be able to say that part of what we are observing here in the way TikTok users engage the human remains trade is a function of Gen Z perspectives on how to "be" online. *If* there is such a thing as a suite of values that can characterize an entire generation (whose parameters are defined for marketing purposes), then a report by the McKinsey consulting group might be useful here. The report suggests that Generation Z values "truth" and "believe[s] profoundly in the efficacy of dialogue to solve conflicts and improve the world" (T. Francis and Hoefel 2018: 2). Combine this perspective with the affordances of a platform that encourages remixing and pushback and peer pedagogies (and is as yet unmonetized in the sense of effecting direct sales), and perhaps we see the emergence of a powerful avenue for contesting the trade.

The Sensory Affect of Displaying Human Remains

We have seen something of how tastes are formed for collecting human remains on two social media platforms, considering the photographs as existing within networks of influence. In this section, we wonder if we can use these photographs to imagine if there is anything we can say about what human remains *do* for the people who collect, themselves? Here, we approach this question not through a criminological or sociological lens, but via an archaeological lens. What is the *affective* impact of collecting remains: how do they make collectors feel? The key thing about archaeology is that it sees meaning in how physical materials are arranged or put into relationship with each other and their environment. Working with these assemblages are a cornerstone of archaeological method. (One of the reasons why looted and unprovenanced materials are doubly destructive is that the act of looting destroys these relationships, and the lack of provenance makes what we *can* tell from the materials doubtful because we cannot trust our deductions.)

To understand what human remains do for the people who collect them is to try, for a moment, to extend a moment of grace to the people who buy and sell human remains and to look at what their collecting creates: new assemblages that put the human remains and other materials into new contexts and relationships. The archaeological biography of these remains continues, but only for a moment: the act of photographing and creating these new assemblages is still a moment that extends the duration of the original acts that made these human lives into things in the first place, a thought to which we will return. How can we study these new assemblages, these new sites, and what might they mean for the construction of the past in the present? Are these sites of enchantment (Perry 2019) for these collectors (see Graham, Huffer, and Blackadar 2020)?

The digital places in which we find these archaeological materials require a literal digital field archaeology and survey strategy. We cannot study and contextualize every photograph we collect manually, but what if we were to treat these individual accounts as archaeological sites in a system of relationships intertwined with the physical world, and treated the posts as features within them? (We are drawing here on Hamilakis' [2017] take on assemblages of the kind promoted by Deleuze and Guattari [1980]). We could use machine learning to describe these features automatically, see how they connect across sites, and use network analysis to characterize the sensory *affect* that these interconnected digital places exhibit (see also Gibbs et al. 2014 for a more manual approach). In our experiment, we will use the Microsoft Azure Cognitive Services platform, which describes each photo with a series of tags.

Like potsherds on the surface that the archaeologist studies and maps and from which they develop an (informed) imaginative idea of what lies beneath, these tags become our sherds, evocative descriptions of scenes through which we can use our imaginations and our own experiences to approach something of the synaesthetic impact on the collector of having these human remains. In our research to date, we have asked what we can learn from the text, and from the images, as individual artifacts. However, what we are trying to do here instead is to consider their photographic practice as emerging out of relationships between the people involved, their own (real-world and virtual) places, and their things.

As Frieman and Gillings write, criticizing ways of "extracting and compartmentalizing vision" in the past:

> What is needed is an archaeology that is sensitive to the rich and complex way in which individual sensory threads are woven together, their interdependencies and the tensions that can arise between them. Put simply, having successfully extracted vision from the sensorium we need to rise to the challenge of putting it back, and in so doing explore more fully the role played by the senses in shaping and structuring understandings (both past and contemporary). (Frieman and Gillings 2007: 6)

This means that, just as in sensory archaeology (e.g., Skeates and Day 2020; Hamilakis 2013, 2014; Frieman and Gillings 2007; Tringham and Danis 2019; Tringham 1991), we also have to engage in "evocative writing," a writing that draws on our own mnemonic and autobiographical accounts (Hamilakis 2014: 11), to sense and make sense of the results of this digital remote vision, this remote sensing. Tringham and Danis (2019: 52) draw our attention to Skeates's methodological suggestions (Skeates 2010: 4) for how to do this—reflexivity, inventory, experimentation, thick description, and creative writing. What follows is offered in that spirit.

Whatever else this trade is, it is an engagement with human history and the past. We accept that there is some connection, some engagement with history, that holding or owning human remains does for people who participate in this trade, beyond the mere dollar value. If we are ever to hope to persuade them not to trade in human remains, we need to try to understand what being in this trade does for these people. Let us try some "evocative writing" from a sensory archaeology perspective. Let Shawn tell you a story about a horse skull, and let us wonder, given this example of SG's own entanglement with that horse's skull, can we understand something similar to the sensory experience implied by these photographs for these people who collect or sell?

> Our house was in the woods, about two hundred feet from the road. The bush was all tall white pine, their crowns spread out and touching one another, but otherwise long tall poles with dead branches all the way down. The air was always dry and dead in the bush, sometimes broken by the crash of falling branches when the turkey vultures took flight, their long wings smashing through the trees. Our house stood in a little clearing; our lawn was mostly green moss and lichen. We had a shed around the back, sitting deeper among the pines. If I opened the door, I could smell the warm smell of pine boards, the cold damp of the dead pine needles, oil and gas from the lawnmower and the chainsaw.
>
> On a shelf made of rough pine there was a box; in the box, the skull of a Percheron workhorse. The skull came from a farm up by town; they were digging a new foundation for a barn and came across the burial pit for this workhorse. Somebody thought I'd find it interesting and had brought it down to us. Horses were last used up there around the 1930s, so the sandy acidic soil had done its work quite quickly. The skull, as I remember it, had no smell at all, in that shed in the bush. But I now associate the contrasting smells of that space with the non-smell of the skull, if that makes any sense: cold + damp + oil + gas + rough_textured_wood + crashing branches = horse_skull. And so the photo of that skull I have evokes the smells and sounds of my father's house.

What does a photo of a human skull evoke for someone involved in this trade, or for someone who enjoys looking at the photos other people share? A social scientist might interview the people collecting bones (and archaeologists have interviewed looters and collectors before; e.g., Kersel 2008), but it is very difficult as an archaeologist to transparently arrange interviews with a collecting community actively engaged in highly suspect behavior (journalists have; see O. Schwartz 2019, for instance; Yates [2014b] discusses the ethics of concealing one's archaeological identity from informants). But we want to approach this as digital archaeologists. If we treat the assemblage of photographs created by an individual vendor or collector as a site, if we treat each photo as an archaeological context, we can use various digital methods to explore from a sensory perspective the meanings of these sites, these photographs.

Field Survey of a Digital Field

Andrew Reinhard has described one facet of archaeogaming as the use of archaeological methods in virtual environments (Reinhard 2018), where these virtual environments are understood as hyper-realistic, high-resolution 3D graphical environments, often experienced from a first-person perspective, whether through a screen or through a virtual reality headset. He argues that we can, in fact, perform archaeological surveys within these environments because the difference between the virtual and the real world is not very important as far as understanding human culture is concerned. However, these game spaces are not the only virtual environments that archaeologists encounter. We have now lived with the web (as distinct from the internet) since the early 1990s, and so we do not think of the experience mediated by a browser as being "somewhere else" anymore. With the rise of powerful smartphones and mobile computing, the web feels even less somewhere else, even less virtual, than it did before. Instead, it is just another overlay, another dimension of information that intersects our lives in ever more intertwined ways.

Digital historians such as Ian Milligan point out that the event horizon for historical scholarship—what dates and events count as history rather than current events—is now firmly within the era of the web (Milligan 2019). His research deals with web archiving and the textual exploration of websites as archives of human activity. Similarly, we argue that personal social media pages that detail engagements with material culture are within the ambit of the digital archaeologist: they are places where different kinds of informational entities (a larger concept than cyberspace in that anything that manipulates information, alive or not, online or in the real world, can be seen as being along the same spectrum; see Floridi 2002) intersect and are entangled in rich assemblages. The question is, what are the materials that we are studying? Is it the photo? The text of the post? The comments and likes that overlay it? The metadata that underpin it and reveal even more entanglements and interconnections? The things in the photo and their interrelationships, both in physical spaces and in this digital space? The interaction with other elements of the user's profile page?

Clearly, a single post on Instagram is extremely information-rich (as of November 2022, if a person appends /?__a=1&__d=1 to an Instagram URL, the full metadata for that page or post are exposed in JSON format; see also Appendix A). Everything depicted within a photograph on a post can be considered the organizing principle for creating a sensory impression of a site, emerging through the interplay of everything collated on individual profile pages or through searches. In the same way that remote sensing in archaeology does not actually sense the past or actual things (it senses variations in the Earth's magnetic field caused by the presence/absence of a wall, or the local relative moisture of the soil compared to somewhere else, and so on), our digital archaeological remote sensing of these websites operates at one step removed, patterns of pixels that have been probabilistically learned by the machine as corresponding with some thing or concept. By using an analogy to field survey, we suggest a way of looking at the tags assigned probabilistically by the machine as "sherds of meaning." Reassembled, they give us a way of assessing different fields or regions of the web from a sensory perspective; it permits us to understand the feel of the digital space the vendor is creating within which they wish to sell.

In our earlier experiments with using computer vision to understand the mass of materials we had collected (Huffer and Graham 2018; Huffer, Wood, and Graham 2019), we were pessimistic about the ability of models like Google's Inception v3 to identify what was in these images, because it was trained on a limited number of categories, and none of these categories were germane to human remains. Indeed, we found that Google Inception would often guess "jellyfish" when the picture was of a skull displayed on a dark background, as pictures of jellyfish similarly have a bright, smooth area of color contrasted against the black of the ocean deep. However, since our initial experiments, it appears that the major technology firms have made huge strides in identifying materials within photos, a process known as automatic image annotation or tagging. Microsoft offers an API for their image tagging service, via their Azure service, which when shown an image returns tags based on thousands of recognizable objects, living beings, scenery, and actions. When tags are ambiguous or not common knowledge, the API response provides hints to clarify the meaning of the tag in the context of a known setting. Tags are not organized as a taxonomy and no inheritance hierarchies exist. A collection of content tags forms the foundation for an image description displayed as human readable language formatted in complete sentences (Farley 2019).

For this experiment, we examined all the images collected from two major vendors of human remains on Instagram (Vendors A and B) and three minor vendors (Vendors C, D, and E), where "major" and "minor" were determined by number of followers (anything over 10,000 was determined to be major). Additionally, all images found by searching the Instagram tag "humanskulls-forsale" on 5 February 2020 were collected. Finally, we scraped the British Museum's Instagram page. In total, this gave us 10,432 images in a comparative perspective.

What Does the Machine See?

The output of the first step in the process, the assignment of descriptive tags for a scene, produces lists of tags and probabilities for each image. Azure hedges its bets with its statement of probability, which is a function of its original training set or a measurement of the input photograph against the "platonic" ideal for a "person" that it knows. We may make some observations on the output at this stage. Azure seems to be very good at identifying skulls, even when these are partial fragments, and it seems to mean "human skulls" for the most part. It will qualify "skull" with "mammal," "primate," or "anthropological" when the skull has had cultural modifications or additions made to it (which also hints at a latent racism in Azure's training dataset perhaps).

While there are very few actual reptiles in the photo collections, Azure frequently tags a photo with "reptile" or "dinosaur." Examining images tagged like this shows an interesting example of a kind of machinic pareidolia (i.e., seeing a pattern, object, or meaning where none exists). The vendors will display and sell partial bones, parts of the knee, or a quarter of a pelvis with a bit of femur (thigh bone), for instance, which they mount and light as they will other more complete bones. These photos, if you squint at them, can look like a long saurian neck with a head.

For one specific vendor, the photo with the strongest "museum" assignment (>90 percent) depicts in the foreground an apparently Dayak skull, on a coffee table, with a display case containing more skulls in the background. The display case contains other skulls in bell jars, arranged across four shelves. Other images with strong "museum" assignments show close-ups of adult or infant skulls, arranged on glass shelving. One shows a skeleton laid out on what looks like hessian cloth, taken from an oblique angle looking along from the feet towards the head, an angle of display that would not be out of place in a museum.

In any event, the presence of a display case, glass shelving, or a stand seems to be one of the strongest indicators for "museum" to Azure. Other images with the "museum" tag, but not as strongly assigned, seem to have dramatic lighting in common, an object sharply defined in the foreground, and a uniform background, which seems to recall museum or auction house catalog photography.

There is also a curious "doughnut" tag, which, in the larger network of tags, is part of the constellation of connections describing bones and their origins. Examining the tags for individual images that have the "doughnut" assignment, we find patterns like this: doughnut, 99.70; indoor, 96.43; museum, 61.36; stone, 37.83; wall, 98.31. This particular image depicts a skull, heavily damaged by root action and with a dark patina, displayed on a wood block against a beige wall, and with a large square hole in the left parietal bone. Azure has done a good job describing the scene, even if it has misunderstood some of the particulars. Other "doughnuts" include more skulls with similar cuts in them, but also skulls in dramatic lighting that highlight one eye socket over another.

What is an "artifact" to the machine? Looking at the images tagged thusly, we see that one vendor constructs their photos such that the background is a soft-blurred table, slightly angled to take up one-third of the field, with black matte walls/background, and the skulls (or other bones) in three-quarter profile on wooden lacquered stands. When Azure assigns the tags to these images, it also can be read as describing the scene: table, 98.42; indoor, 98.14; museum, 97.16; skull, 96.91; sitting, 95.47; art, 93.88; animal, 84.43; artifact, 75.47; bone, 74.01; wooden, 72.25; sculpture, 70.25; vase, 66.45.

In the collection of photos retrieved from a search of Instagram for "#humanskullsforsale," there is a curious tag, "arthropod." Arthropods are invertebrate creatures with exoskeletons. This is another case of machinic pareidolia. Examining these images, we actually find depictions of human remains in or on the ground, sometimes articulated and apparently in situ, sometimes disturbed and scattered. We see skeletons in the earth; the machine sees exoskeletons. The associated posts largely come from a single vendor (who was hitherto unknown to us, and who advertises that they will obtain remains to order).

So What Does It *Feel* Like?

The machine sees different elements in an image and composes rich sets of tags for each image to capture the objects it identifies, the nouns, and sometimes adjectives. It can clarify what it means by collating nouns together, e.g., painting, abstract, monochrome, outside, atmosphere. The machine sometimes experiences a kind of pareidolia. When we unpack it, it might also point

Figure 3.7. An example of the method, depicting a visualization of the major tags assigned to Vendor C's photographs. Nodes represent tags, edges represent photographs. Radial axes lay out where each spar is a subcommunity; subcommunities are also indicated by color. The size of the node indicates relative importance. *The unconnected component is not depicted.* The layout obscures some of the smaller subcommunities. Originally published in Graham, Huffer, and Blackadar 2020, figure 3, CC-BY 4.0.

to a way to automatically flag images for human inspection (the "doughnuts" or the "arthropods"). We can then treat these assignments as a kind of network and begin to pair nouns together tied by their co-assignment to photographs; the emergent clusters give us an affective sense of what this site (this vendor, the results of this search, this museum) is like, what effect or feeling is evoked when visiting the site.

To the eye, the networks look more or less the same. Sometimes network diagrams do not actually help us understand what the network is telling us. It is more useful to analyze the networks for subcommunities and then discuss what these communities or clusters tell us. The "most important tags" in these networks are identified by calculating eigenvector centrality. In this measure, a node is important or central by virtue of being connected to other important or central nodes.

At the time of this research, Vendor A had well over 30,000 followers. The tags for this vendor are fully connected: there are no isolates, indicating a singularity of purpose. Six distinct subcommunities of tags (out of 25) account for >90 percent of the unique tags. There are 408 unique machine-assigned tags describing this vendor's images.

Table 3.2. Descriptive tags assigned by the computer to photographs posted by Vendor A.

Module	Percent of Tags	Most Important Tags
11	41	indoor, person, wall, human face, floor, clothing, sitting, black and white, man, table
1	16	outdoor, ground, tree, building, sky, grass, tire, water, vehicle, land vehicle
0	13	animal, skull, mammal, bone, reptile, dog, primate, black, cat, carnivore
3	12	text, drawing, book, cartoon, painting, sketch, art, poster, screenshot, abstract
2	6	weapon, tool, handgun, rifle, sword, melee weapon, cold weapon, blade, dagger, shotgun
7	3	statue, sculpture, museum, bronze sculpture, metalware, dark, ceramic, ancient, chain, monochrome

Vendor B had over 10,000 followers. Six distinct subcommunities of tags (out of 16) account for >90 percent of the unique tags. There are 126 unique machine-assigned tags describing this vendor's images.

Table 3.3. Descriptive tags assigned by the computer to photographs posted by Vendor B.

Module	Percent of Tags	Most Important Tags
0	35	indoor, person, wall, sitting, table, floor, human face, smile, man, dog
1	26	outdoor, clothing, ground, grass, footwear, tree, cave, building, sky, seafood
4	14	animal, skull, bone, mammal, primate, reptile, skeleton, anthropology, doughnut
2	10	statue, sculpture, art, drawing, museum, bronze sculpture, sketch, painting, mask, cartoon
3	4	tire, basket, container, wheel, autopart (These are all of the tags in the module.)
5	3	shelf, different, bunch, flower (These are all of the tags in the module.)

Vendor C had just over 1,000 followers. The tags for this vendor are in two broad clumps, indicating two very distinct interests. Six distinct subcommunities of tags (out of 10) account for >90 percent of the unique tags. There are 197 unique machine-assigned tags describing this vendor's images.

Table 3.4. Descriptive tags assigned by the computer to photographs posted by Vendor C.

Module	Percent of Tags	Most Important Tags
3	24	art, statue, museum, bone, sculpture, skeleton, anthropology, artifact, fossil, mask
1	18	skull, animal, reptile, wall, person, close, hand, food, cave, turtle
0	16	indoor, cluttered, tool, tableware, glass, bottle, bowl, sewing machine, counter, engineering
2	14	wooden, table, black, vase, sitting, dark, dessert, bronze, lamp, bird
8	11	mammal, floor, wood, shelf, cabinet, household hardware, furniture, door handle, cat, carnivore
6	8	text, symbol, book, design, handwriting, menu, earthenware, pottery, screenshot, font

Vendor D had just over 1,000 followers. The tags for this vendor are fully connected. Six distinct subcommunities of tags (out of 10) account for >90 percent of the unique tags. There are 105 unique machine-assigned tags describing this vendor's images.

Table 3.5. Descriptive tags assigned by the computer to photographs posted by Vendor D.

Module	Percent of Tags	Most Important Tags
1	30	indoor, floor, black and white, wall, cat, statue, sculpture, carnivore, food, table
6	26	text, person, drawing, sketch, painting, human face, aquarium, cartoon, book, hand ("Museum" occurs in this module in 15th place.)
0	15	animal, skull, mammal, primate, bone, reptile, dinosaur, skeleton, crocodilian reptile, snake
4	9	invertebrate, insect, butterfly, arthropod, spider, moths and butterflies, oven, crab, beetle (These are all of the tags for the module.)
5	8	drink, soft drink, cocktail, cup, water, dairy, reef, bottle (These are all of the tags for the module.)
3	7	weapon, kitchen utensil, knife, gun, scissors, melee weapon, pair (These are all of the tags for the module.)

Vendor E had less than 100 followers. The tags for this vendor are fully connected. There are no isolates, indicating a singularity of purpose. Two distinct subcommunities of tags (out of 3) account for >90 percent of the unique tags. There are 23 unique machine-assigned tags describing this vendor's images.

Table 3.6. Descriptive tags assigned by the computer to photographs posted by Vendor E.

Module	Percent of Tags	Most Important Tags
0	70	indoor, wall, skull, animal, dinosaur, bone, skeleton, mammal, primate, reptile ("Museum" appears in this module but at 86 percent probability, and so has been filtered out.)
1	22	butterfly, invertebrate, moths and butterflies, text, insect (These are all the tags for the module.)

On 5 February 2020, a scrape of the Instagram hashtag "humanskullsfor-sale" retrieved 116 unique posts. There are 166 unique machine-assigned tags describing the images returned by a search for the Instagram hashtag. There were seven modules in one connected component. Six distinct subcommunities of tags (out of 7) account for >90 percent of the unique tags.

Table 3.7. Descriptive tags assigned by the computer to photographs retrieved under the #humanskullsforsale tag.

Module	Percent of Tags	Most Important Tags
1	23	art, different, colored, several, drawing, invertebrate, arthropod, plant, flower, painting
2	19	skull, bone, skeleton, fossil, anthropology, primate, extinction, museum, close, jaw
4	19	animal, mammal, outdoor, dirt, wooden, cave, reptile, trunk, deer, antler
5	19	text, person, hand, cartoon, poster, man, screenshot, book, various, human face
0	11	indoor, floor, pan, lined, cluttered, food, vegetable, table, bread, furniture
6	8	sculpture, statue, ground, dirty, old, stone, ancient, door, weapon, tool

The British Museum currently has over one million followers on Instagram. On 28 February 2020, a scrape of the Instagram user account for the British Museum downloaded 462 unique posts. There are 373 unique machine-assigned tags describing the images. There were 10 modules in one connected component. Seven distinct subcommunities of tags (out of 10) account for >90 percent of the unique tags.

The absolute number of assigned tags indicates the visual richness of the collection. The clumping (or not) into single connected components, as well as smaller diameter or shorter average path lengths, may indicate thematic unity in the vendor's presentation. The number and composition of submodules indicates internal variety within that composition. The disconnected component in Vendor C's materials accounts for 6 percent of the tags: *sky, outdoor, mountain, cloud, nature, desert, landscape, area,* and *stone,* and clearly indicates that the vendor uses their account to also post their personal interests or holiday pictures, which are sufficiently distinct that they do not interconnect with the vendor's business; this contrasts well with all of the other vendors whose tags all cycle back to their business interests. Remember, this is apparent to a hu-

Table 3.8. Descriptive tags assigned by the computer to photographs posted by the British Museum Instagram account.

Module	Percent of Tags	Most Important Tags
1	19	building, stone, outdoor, black and white, window, abstract, monochrome, sky, ceiling, roof
5	19	indoor, person, museum, statue, sculpture, clothing, different, woman, dark, wall
2	15	gold, bronze, brass, fashion accessory, coin, silver, metal, pendant, gemstone, platinum
3	13	plant, vase, ceramic ware, porcelain, painted, jar, ceramic, cup, displayed, tableware
4	13	art, text, painting, drawing, human face, sketch, cartoon, book, child art, illustration
7	12	black, animal, ground, cat, carnivore, mammal, sitting, reptile, horse, laying
0	5	water, reef, underwater, diving, swimming, aquarium, scuba, fish, ocean floor, water sport

man eye, but the machine makes this distinction as well, which is an important consideration as we scale up to the tens of thousands of photographs and posts that we have collected. This might also be useful for comparing vendors' behaviors across platforms, for we know that these vendors are active on Facebook and other social media platforms, and we might hypothesize that they compose sales images differently for different audiences or platforms.

It is worth pointing out that some of the least eigencentric tags (that is, tags that do the least work in holding the network together) might be worth looking at too, since these might be the words that Azure adds to provide context to its most likely labels, e.g., in module 2 for Vendor C, some of the least important words are *collection, display case, lots, drawer, chest of drawers, cabinetry,* and *filing cabinet,* which tells us something about the way this vendor displays their materials. Considering the least central words reminds us of discussions in the Digital Humanities regarding text analysis techniques, such as topic modeling or term frequency—inverse distribution frequency about whether to include stop-words. Stop-words are the very frequent words such as "the," "of," "and" which seemingly do not carry much weight for determining larger patterns, yet they are very telling when we do such work as author attribution or stylometry (see, for instance Laramée 2018; Froehlich 2015). Is what we are doing closer in concept to topic modeling, or closer in concept to stylometry? We do not have an answer for this yet.

The frequent tag "text" is interesting. Vendor A's module 3 and vendor C's module 6, for instance, point to the ways in which vendors embed text within the images to indicate items for sale, a practice that hides posts from the more usual practice of analyzing the text of captions for materials for sale. The permanent embedding of text into and onto the image itself seems to convince the machine that the text is an artistic embellishment, design motif, or perhaps some sort of signature.

We will conclude by asking, "What is a 'museum' to the machine?" And what is the sensory affect thus created? The result we get also tells us something of how individual sites (user pages, search pages) on Instagram portray themselves:

- Vendor A: statue, sculpture, museum, bronze sculpture, metalware, dark, ceramic, ancient, chain, monochrome.
- Vendor B: statue, sculpture, art, drawing, museum, bronze sculpture, sketch, painting, mask, cartoon.
- Vendor C: art, statue, museum, bone, sculpture, skeleton, anthropology, artifact, fossil, mask.
- Vendor D: text, person, drawing, sketch, painting, human face, aquarium, cartoon, book, hand.
- Vendor E: indoor, wall, skull, animal, dinosaur, bone, skeleton, mammal, primate, reptile.
- Instagram Search: skull, bone, skeleton, fossil, anthropology, primate, extinction, museum, close, jaw.
- British Museum: indoor, person, museum, statue, sculpture, clothing, different, woman, dark, wall.

The only actual museum in this experiment has a far more equal distribution in terms of the size of its subcommunities, representing much more varied content, but at the same time, these subcommunities are all still interconnected, suggesting an overarching ideal guiding what gets posted (e.g., the underwater pictures depict underwater archaeology). This more equal distribution is most likely an artifact of the museum's social media pages being perhaps curated by several employees, perhaps each from different departments of the museum, and each given individual rein to select representative photographs. This approach to digital outreach is common throughout the museum world. When vendor tags do not mesh into one connected whole, this seems to indicate the mixing of professional (bone trade) and personal interests in a single account. Thus, Vendor A represents a more disciplined or "professional vision" than some of the other vendors.

In terms of the sensory affect, Vendor C leaves us with a tactile impression of an artist at their craft, working with materials and showing off the process that culminates in an artwork for sale. This work takes place in busy workshops, but also sometimes in the open air. However, this affect is subsumed underneath the construction of something that the machine recognizes as a "museum." Nevertheless, Vendor C's images are disconnected, and are interspersed with images that create an image of the person, their holidays, and their other interests. Vendor A's pictures are interconnected into one whole, but that whole portrays a site that is in some ways darker and more gothic, more dangerous, and yet still signals a "museum." Vendor A has created a space full of materials somehow dangerous, exotic, communicating a forbidden thrill to own, hold, and display (contrasting human remains with pictures of weaponry, in dark velvets and dramatic lighting).

An actual museum, the British Museum, leaves a sensory affect that is more equitably distributed than in the "museum" created by the vendors, where none of the clusters dominate, and we get a sense of a rich storehouse of treasure and artworks of all kinds. A search for a particular Instagram hashtag, one devoted explicitly to selling human remains, also brings up the idea of a "museum," but to very different *affect*. We might see this as circumstantial evidence that many bone sellers going for a "museum" look seem to collectively choose the style of an old-school Victorian era museum, more akin to the *Wunderkammer*, but not seemingly *au courant* with the aesthetic of more recent museological trends for the display of human remains.

In the text alongside many of the posts, many vendors voice a love for the beauty of the remains, and sometimes suggest that they are saving the dead for study and appreciation. Perhaps by choosing the aesthetic of the dusty museum trope, they project the message that they can help new buyers begin their own "timeless" collection? Or perhaps this intersects with comments we have observed from time to time on the accounts of some of the major vendors, about who has the right to collect and study human remains and in general, disparaging archaeologists who "keep it all to themselves"; in which case, perhaps the message of the images is "if they can do it then so can I." In turn this raises an important point. There are many human remains in the possession of museums that got there through dubious ways, which offers a kind of moral cover for the collector. While the Native American Graves Protection and Repatriation Act (see Chapter 4) has prompted a re-examination of collections of Indigenous peoples in museum collections, and moved repatriation to the foreground, other peoples collected in institutions still require a reckoning— see for instance the student activism that prompted the Penn Museum at the University of Pennsylvania which has the human remains of enslaved people in their collection, to promise to repatriate and rebury these remains (Diaz 2020).

This was an experiment in trying to create an affective digital archaeology through machine vision. By focusing on the system of interrelationships in the machine-determined tags, we present not so much a rigorous scientific method, but a digital humanities heuristic, a co-creation of meaning between the human investigator and the machine viewer. By getting the machine to contextually tag thousands of images with what it sees, we get a sense of the sensory experience that these vendors are trying to create for their online store. This online sense is partly a function of how their actual physical store is arranged. However, the online traces are to the physical world of lived experience as the archaeological traces in the ground are to the physical world of lived experience of the past. In neither case is it actually feasible for us to go there. What counts is the look, feel, and experience created by the online space.

Conclusion

While many of the posts that vendors or collectors make are designed to facilitate a sale, trade, auction, or show off one's collection, the fact that these posts are being made on Instagram or TikTok points to another important dimension to the trade: the creation of a taste for collecting human remains. We have not used the language of influencers to frame this discussion, but that is what is going on. Taste is arguably carefully cultivated across platforms as dealers often cross-post sales to reach multiple audiences, and thus must adapt their posts to the particulars of each platform and actively adjust the content or aesthetic look of their posts to match what potential buyers expect or cover up what they feel is too risky to state upfront (such as mention of prices or keywords with the potential to be flagged by platform algorithms). This occurs with greater and lesser degrees of success.

Villa's concepts of the authenticity of beauty, and the authenticity of the exotic (Villa 2021), are both present in the construction of the photographs, across platforms. We can see the evolution of this construction over time on Instagram through calculating visual similarity and cross-referencing this with the metadata about the day a photograph was taken. When these same visual similarity data are cross-referenced against the language of the posts, we start to see the subtle visual cues that something may or may not be for sale. The underlying marketization of human remains is in this way normalized, making Instagram a vast catalog showing its users how to consume digitally mediated human remains. It is still an ongoing area of research for us, but it seems as if this careful construction and learned way to represent human remains does not translate well to TikTok. Through using TikTok's affordances to create breezy, informal, frantic videos, Individual 1 prompts pushback and opportunities for peer-to-peer learning that are mobilized against the bone trade. The intersection of TikTok's affordances with perhaps a different demographic is creating a different dynamic that bears watching.

Computer vision, and careful use of tools to examine the structural connections between accounts, enables us to engage in distant viewing; the elements that we see give us a strong sense of how a taste for collecting or viewing the dead can form. It is not the case that the human remains trade works the same way across all social media platforms. Some are more social, and more open to pushback, than others. In the next chapter we examine these elements more closely.

Through an experiment where we had the computer describe the scenes found in photographs collected from the trade, we can now say something about what photographs of human remains and the remains themselves do for the people involved. It is telling that the result of looking at these images of human remains is to create a sensory feel that harkens back to the ethnographic museums of the late nineteenth century and the early twentieth, the kind of museum that might have put these human remains on display in the first place. There was no necessary reason why this sensation should have been the result of looking at these thousands of images computationally. It emerged because the ethnographic museum has been argued to be a *weapon* whose main function is to make the violence of the past endure (Hicks 2020: 185). Dan Hicks, who is curator of the Pitt-Rivers Museum in Oxford, is specifically talking about the emergence of the ethnographic museum as a category of museum, not their current operation or role in repatriation debates. We maintain that human remains buyers and sellers today either consciously or unconsciously mimic the same forms of acquisition, display, and rhetorical speech about how and why they collect that were used in the first place to dehumanize the cultures from whom remains derive.

We need to unpack that thought for a moment. In his study of the so-called Benin Bronzes, Hicks outlines how the theft of the material culture of the people of Benin was a deliberate consequence of the corporate-militarist colonialism, destruction for extraction for profit, of Britain's era of small wars. These were the wars of the late nineteenth century and early twentieth century that sought to punish states, nations, and peoples who did not bow to British corporate interests. The British would manufacture an outrage, and then use the outrage to justify a vastly lop-sided military engagement. With the technological superiority granted by the use of the Maxim machine gun, rockets, mortars, and grenades, British victory was assured. The range of these weapons made them into "guns that shoot twice" (Hicks 2020: 1–17), in that there is the first retort when the trigger is pulled, and then the second blast some moments later when the shell/bullet hits its (indiscriminate) target.

By blasting a people and their material culture into fragments—and then looting and selling what remains—the British were involved in a kind of "chronopolitics" (the use of time to control a people, Hicks 2020: 113) that transformed a living culture suddenly into an archaeological site, a safely neutered past, a "lost world." The museum's role in this was to make the violence of the past endure into the present by putting the trophies of this violence on constant display: the museum shoots twice by re-enacting the violence every time someone looks at the cabinet (Hicks 2020: 149). In this framework, we can think of "archaeology [as not] the study of fragments of the past, but the science of human duration" (Hicks 2020: 36). The photographs of this enduring violence (Hicks 2020: 15) similarly shoot twice.

For Hicks, the objects on display in these museums, the photographs, constitute an ongoing crime scene. The ethnographic museum provides the ongoing justification for empire by demarcating who belongs and who is beyond. The chronopolitics are stark:

> To slaughter populations, and to destroy cultural sites, and to throw royal treasures to the market, is to turn time itself into a war zone—and here archaeology and anthropology became one of the "imperial applied sciences" that were central to Chamberlain's policy of "constructive imperialism." (Hicks 2020: 190)

When people build their own private museums that harken to the late nineteenth century and early twentieth century ideal of the ethnographic museum, stocking their shelves with the nameless and faceless dead, they are similarly participating in a chronopolitics of erasure and destruction. The violence is made to endure. And it makes these people, the collectors and vendors, complicit in an ongoing crime, adding duration to the racism that turned individuals into mere things, adding duration to the harms inflicted on communities. To collect human remains is to participate in the project of Empire.

Collectors of human remains, as we have seen, will claim an interest in the beauty of the bones, or saving them for their own scientific study, or preserving them because their source countries allegedly cannot—that is, they mimic the same arguments deployed since the 1980s of the universal museum (Hicks 2020: 200–8) used by a wide range of high-end antiquities collectors to justify their actions. But a "propaganda of archaism" suffuses what they do: it puts the violence responsible for the creation of the remains safely in the past.

The Lies behind the Bodies?

A magical phrase: "not available to residents of Louisiana, Georgia, and Tennessee." The truth is more complex. What can we say about the legal landscape?

Is it *really* legal to buy and sell human remains?

The answer is, it depends.

It should be a straightforward question to answer. Vendors will often claim, in their posts and on their store-front websites, why yes, yes it is! *If* you live anywhere but Louisiana, Georgia, and Tennessee (and this is part of what Dundler [2021] argues is a key component of one of the "personas" that antiquities dealers in general adopt—the ethical individual who knows the relevant laws). Let us take a look at the relevant legislation. In our research to date, the major vendors identified (especially those who claim willingness to ship worldwide "wherever it's legal") are largely based in the United States, Canada, and the United Kingdom, so we will limit ourselves for the most part to the states, provinces, and territories of those countries. Tanya Marsh, a legal scholar, compiled the relevant laws related to human remains as they pertain to the United States. In what follows, we are drawing on her research, supplemented by our own digging through various laws, statutes, and legal memos.

The first thing to understand is that for most selected jurisdictions, the legal traditions are building on the foundation of English common law. The question is, can human remains be considered *property*? Property is traditionally divided in two, with "real" property (rights in landholding), and personal property. Here, we follow Mimnagh (2017). When someone dies, that person's property is generally disposed of according to their wishes. Disputes over the *body* of the deceased were traditionally handled by ecclesiastical courts (this remained the case until well into the latter half of the nineteenth century).

Over time court cases did emerge over theft from graves, for instance, where it was alleged that the defendant was stealing from the bodies. In general, stealing *from the dead* could not happen because the dead could not own property (as in the Haynes case of 1614, where Haynes successfully argued that stealing grave goods did not constitute theft). In other cases, such as that brought by the parents of deceased conjoined children against a physician who had disinterred them (*Exelby v. Handyside* in 1749), the justice found that the parents did not "own" the corpses of the children, since dead bodies are not property. Yet, this rule has been modified over time (as with various Anatomy Acts) to prevent "resurrection men" from profiting from the sale of human remains.

In general, it is the act of exhuming without sanction that gets criminalized, rather than treating the body itself as something that *is* property or that *has* property rights (Mimnagh 2017). The idea that human remains are not property ultimately has its origin in legal traditions going back to the Roman jurist Ulpian at the start of the third century, who opined under Roman law that God owns the body, while its occupant (as it were) is merely the administrator or custodian of it. Marsh (2015: 14) points out this is consistent with ecclesiastical law as it later emerged: once a human body is consigned to the earth it is no longer something that can be owned. In ecclesiastical law, the idea that a human corpse is not property has been traced back to a decision by Lord Edward Coke, and Marsh points out,

> read narrowly Lord Coke . . . simply states if a member of the Church of England had been buried on consecrated ground, owned by the Church, his body had been entrusted to the Church until the Resurrection of Jesus Christ and therefore his heirs had no cause of action in secular courts if the remains were disturbed. However, these statements have consistently been read broadly to mean that no property interest may exist in a corpse from the moment of death regardless of religious affiliation or method of disposition. (Marsh 2015: 13)

Nevertheless, as the nineteenth century progressed, and the supply of corpses rose to meet the needs of medical and surgical training, and outrage among the living over the disrespect visited upon graves grew, the idea that one could say something about who owned remains and what should be done with them after death found traction. The Anatomy Act in England of 1832 did make an allowance for individuals to specify that their bodies could be used for dissection (Mimnagh 2017: 5–6). In general, when there has been a conflict between the wishes of the deceased and their executors or heirs regarding the disposition of the body, it is the wishes of the living that have prevailed. The remains remain mere things.

So much for general principles. What do the actual laws say? In the United States, a quasi-property right in a dead body prior to disposition has emerged over the twentieth century (Marsh 2015: 15), and now a great deal of the existing laws concerning human remains focus on regulating the funeral services industry, including transport of remains both within and between individual states. A certain number of states regulate human remains in terms of tissue harvesting (and transplantation). Some states make a distinction between human remains of the recently deceased that are still (for want of a better word) fleshy, versus skeletal remains. A number of states prohibit the trafficking of human remains from Indigenous peoples. A smaller number explicitly prohibit the trafficking of human skeletal remains *tout court*. A similar quasi-property right has similarly emerged in other jurisdictions (Frerking and Gill-Frerking 2017).

Summary of Pertinent Laws

We summarize below the laws as we understand them in some of the main jurisdictions where we know major bone trade vendors are active; again, please do not take this as legal advice. Our point is that there *is* quite a large body of law that seems to us applicable, that there might very well be legal avenues for dealing with the trade in human remains.

United States, Federal Law

Federally, the treatment of human remains of Native Americans is covered by the Native American Graves Protection and Repatriation Act (NAGPRA), Public Law 601, US Statutes at Large 104 (1990): 3048–58, which makes buying, selling, transporting, or using for profit the human remains of a Native American a felony. The act asserts that cultural items (which explicitly includes human remains) uncovered on or recovered from federal or tribal lands belong explicitly to the lineal descendants or closest culturally affiliated groups. The act provides for Native groups to have full consultation on excavations or other licensed research. Anyone who discovers human remains by accident on federal or tribal lands must notify the authorities. Federal agencies and museums that hold human remains were directed by the act to conduct inventories of their holdings, in consultation with tribal governments and notify the appropriate organization to arrange for repatriation.

Halcrow et al. summarize the effect of this law best when they say,

> NAGPRA is a law and set of procedures with a limited scope that seeks to affirm tribal sovereignty and to ensure that the ancestors of Native people are treated with the same level of care and protection under the law that has historically been afforded to other human remains in the United States. (Halcrow et al. 2021: 216)

The law affirms the human dignity of Indigenous peoples and the Ancestors. The passing of this legislation represented a seismic shift in how archaeologists and biological anthropologists worked with human remains and with Native peoples in the United States. Its passage was a result of the patient work of activists and a process of enacting state-level legislation. It is one step towards acknowledging and repairing the damage caused by the long history of abuse of non-White skeletons to provide physical "evidence" for the now-discredited concepts of racial superiority and racial criminality (Halcrow et al. 2021: 212). The passing of NAGPRA was a key element in putting repatriation onto the agenda of museums and governments worldwide. The importance of this law lies beyond its immediate legal effect in the US (see for instance Aranui 2020; Fforde, McKeown, and Keeler 2020; Nash and Colwell 2020).

US States

In what follows, we are highlighting material compiled from Tanya Marsh's magisterial *The Law of Human Remains* (Marsh 2015). This compendium dates to 2015, and various laws may have since been updated. Many offenses are criminal with fines and jail time associated. Marsh examined the individual statutes for each American state, from funeral home regulation to abuse of dead bodies. Here, we are quoting the relevant regulations from *select* states where there seems to be laws *directly relevant* to the buying or selling of human remains, to demonstrate something of the true scope of relevant laws. Not every state is listed. (For instance, in Pennsylvania the law is silent on buying or selling human remains, but desecrating a body is an offense, as is receiving stolen goods. These were the charges laid against Jeremy Lee Pauley in 2022; see Wallace and Lauer [2022].) The reader should consult Marsh and/or search the relevant state's website using these phrases for the full statutes. A good place to start is the "State Burial Laws Project" from the Washington College of Law at American University, https://www.wcl.american.edu/burial/. Remember, we are highlighting the panoply of laws and ways that trading in human remains is framed at the state level in the United States, not offering legal advice; things are not as legal as bone traders might imply.

Arkansas

It is against the law to knowingly "mistreat or conceal . . . a corpse in a manner offensive to a person of reasonable sensibilities." Disturbing a grave as a consequence of agricultural activity by mistake is exempted (but if done knowingly, that's another matter). Anyone who buys or sells or barters human skeletal remains or grave goods has committed an offence, as well as anyone who displays human skeletal remains for profit or as part of a commercial enterprise, which is an offence with *each day of display* being a separate offence. Arkansas Code Annotated § 13-6-406 (2015); Arkansas Code Annotated § 13-6-407 (2015).

Connecticut

"Any person who delivers or receives a corpse for the purpose of speculation or pecuniary profit shall be fined not more than one thousand dollars and imprisoned not more than one year." Human remains collected or excavated within the state cannot be sold or purchased or transported. Connecticut General Statutes § 368i-19a-288 (2013); Connecticut General Statutes § 184a-10-390 (2015).

Delaware

"A person is guilty of trading in human remains and associated funerary objects when the person knowingly sells, buys or transports for sale or profit, or offers to buy, sell or transport for sale or profit." Delaware Code § 11-5-VII-1333 (2015).

Florida

It is a crime to remove or interfere with burials and associated artifacts including skeletal remains. It is an offense to buy or sell or participate in the trafficking of the dead body of a human. Florida Code § XLVI-872.02 (2015); Florida Code § XLVI-872.01 (2015).

Georgia

It is illegal to exhibit or display the human remains of "American Indians" unless part of an accredited educational institution or with the express written permission of lineal descendants or the Council on American Indian Concerns. It is an offense to remove or receive a dead human body for the purpose of selling or purchasing. It is unlawful for anyone to buy or sell dead human bodies, or to transport dead bodies for sale in other states. It is unlawful for anyone to remove a dead human body from a grave or other burial place like a vault or tomb for the purpose of selling or dissecting it. It is also unlawful for anyone to receive or buy a dead human body that the person knows was obtained in this way. Georgia Code § 31-21-45 (2015); Georgia Code § 12-3-622 (2015); Georgia Code § 31-21-41 (2015); Georgia Code § 31-21-43 (2015).

Idaho

No one may possess any artifact or human remains taken from a cairn or from a grave or publicly display or exhibit these; no one may sell any human artifacts or human remains taken from a cairn or grave. Idaho Code § 27-502 (2015).

Illinois

It is an abuse of a corpse if a person moves or carries away without authorization, or knowingly dismembers, severs, or mutilates any part of a body. Disinterred human remains shall not be transported within the state unless accompanied by a permit for disposition of a dead human body. Anyone who destroys, damages, or desecrates human remains is guilty of a felony. Anybody who buys or sells or offers to buy/sell a human body or any part of a human body is guilty of a misdemeanor. A person cannot own any skeletal remains unless they comply with the *Human Skeletal Remains Protection Act*. Illinois Compiled Statutes § 720-5/12-20.6 (2012); Illinois Administrative Code § 77-500.50 (2013); Illinois Compiled Statutes § 720-5/12-20 (2012); Illinois Compiled Statutes c. 127 § 20-3440/6 (2015).

Indiana

If a person conducts unlicensed archaeological investigation and discovers or disturbs human remains without an approved plan, they commit a felony. A person who receives, retains, or disposes of human remains is guilty of possession of looted property, a felony. Indiana Code § 14-21-1-26 (2015); Indiana Code § 14-21-1-36 (2015).

Kansas

It is a crime to knowingly obtain or try to obtain unauthorized control of a dead body or the remains of any human being. It is an offense to sell, trade, give away, or discard skeletal remains known to have been from an unmarked burial site. Kansas Statutes § 75-2748 (2015).

Kentucky

It is an offense to intentionally excavate or disinter human remains for commercial sale. Kentucky Revised Statutes § 525.105 (2015).

Louisiana

It is an offense to interfere with a cemetery. It is unlawful to trade in human skeletal remains from an unmarked burial site. Removing remains from a cemetery with intent for sale is an offense. Purchasing or receiving human remains, knowing that the same has been removed unlawfully from a cemetery, will be punished. Louisiana Laws Revised Statutes § 8: 678 (2015); Louisiana Laws Revised Statutes § 8:653 (2015).

Maryland

"Human remains" means the body or any part in any state of decomposition. A person may not knowingly buy/sell or transport for sale or profit, or offer to buy/sell/transport unlawfully removed human remains. Maryland Code Health Occupations § 7-101 (2015); Maryland Code Criminal Law § 10-403 (2015).

Massachusetts

It is a felony to buy or sell or possess for the purpose of buying, selling, or trafficking, the dead body of a human. Massachusetts General Laws, c. 272 § 72 (2015).

Michigan

It is a felony to dig up, disinter, or move human remains from the place of burial. Selling an unclaimed human body is a felony. Michigan Compiled Laws c. XXVI § 750.160 (2015) (amended 2016); Michigan Compiled Laws § 333.2663 (2015) (amended 2016).

Mississippi

It is a felony to purchase or receive a dead body unlawfully removed from the earth. Mississippi Code § 97-29-21 (2015).

Missouri

Any person who purchases, sells, profits, or transports for sale or profit any human remains or cultural items without right of possession commits a felony. Missouri Revised Statutes § 194.410 (2015).

Montana

A person may not knowingly buy, sell, transport, barter, or display human skeletal remains or burial material. Montana Code Annotated § 22-3-808 (2015).

Nebraska

It is an offense if a person receives, conceals, purchases, sells, transports, or trades human skeletal remains if the person knows or has reason to know that the remains have been removed from burial or have not been reported in a proper death certificate. Nebraska Revised Statutes § 28-1301 (2015).

Nevada

Any person who removes the dead body or any part from a grave or other place with the intent to sell is guilty of a felony. A person who purchases or receives, except for burial/cremation, knowing that it has been removed illegally, is guilty of a felony. Anybody who makes available the remains of a fetus for any commercial purpose shall be fined. Nevada Revised Statutes § 451.010 (2015); Nevada Revised Statutes § 451.030 (2015); Nevada Revised Statutes § 451.015 (2015).

New York

A person who purchases or receives a body, or any tissue or organ or part, for any purpose other than burial, commits a misdemeanor. Obtaining human remains from a grave or place of internment, with the intent to sell, is a felony. New York Laws Public Health § 4217 (2015); New York Laws Public Health § 4216 (2015).

North Carolina

It is a felony to desecrate human remains by any means including any physical alteration or manipulation. It is illegal to acquire human skeletal remains from unmarked burials. It is illegal to exhibit or sell human skeletal remains from unmarked burials in North Carolina. North Carolina General Statutes § 14-401.22 (2015); North Carolina General Statutes § 70-37 (2015).

North Dakota

If a person receives a body for the purposes of dissection (duly authorized), but that body is used for any other purpose, including sale, that person has committed a misdemeanor. "Every person who purchases or who receives, except for the purpose of burial, any dead body of a human being, knowing that the same has been removed contrary to the provisions of this chapter, is guilty of . . . a felony." North Dakota Century Code § 23-06-18 (2015); North Dakota Century Code § 23-06-26 (2015).

Oklahoma

It is an offense to display human skeletal remains previously buried in Oklahoma for profit. Purchasing a dead body, buying, selling, or bartering for profit for human skeletal remains or associated burial furniture previously buried in Oklahoma is also an offense. Oklahoma Statutes § 21-1168.3 (2015); Oklahoma Statutes § 21-1168.1 (2015).

Oregon

It is illegal to possess, display, or sell materials related to "Indian" human remains. Oregon Revised Statutes § 97.745 (2015).

South Dakota

Grave robbing is a crime. Every person who removes all or any part of the dead body of a human being from any grave or other place where the same has been buried, or from any place where the same is deposited while awaiting burial, with intent to sell the same is prohibited; receiving the same is also prohibited. One cannot buy or sell skeletal human remains previously buried within the state. Human remains previously buried in South Dakota cannot be displayed for profit. South Dakota Codified Laws § 34-27-18 (2015); South Dakota Codified Laws § 34-27-19 (2015); South Dakota Codified Laws § 34-27-20 (2015); South Dakota Codified Laws § 34-27-22 (2015); South Dakota Codified Laws § 34-27-24 (2015).

Tennessee

The import or export of human remains is prohibited. Tennessee Code § 11-6-118 (2015).

Texas

It is an offense to sell or buy a human corpse or in any way traffic in a human corpse. Texas Statutes Penal Code § 42.08 (2015).

Utah

Trafficking in "Native American" remains is a felony. A person who removes or possesses mementos from human remains with the purpose to deprive another over control of the property is guilty of a felony. Utah Code § 9-9-404 (2015); Utah Code § 76-6-412 (2015).

Virginia

It is a felony if a person buys or sells a dead human body, or traffics, transmits, conveys, or procures a body for trafficking outside the state. Code of Virginia § 32.1-303 (2015).

Washington

Physicians and students under their authority may have human remains for instruction; otherwise, anyone who purchases or receives is guilty of a felony. Revised Code of Washington § 68.50.060 (2015). Revised Code of Washington § 68.50.140 (2015).

West Virginia

Anyone who (or through an agent) offers for sale or exchange human skeletal remains commits a misdemeanor. West Virginia Code § 29-1-8a (2015).

Canada, Federal Law

In Canada, the Criminal Code applies nationally, but jurisdiction for enforcing the Criminal Code lies with the provinces. The Criminal Code is very clear:

> Section 182: Everyone who (a) neglects, without lawful excuse, to perform any duty that is imposed on him by law or that he undertakes with reference to the burial of a dead human body or human remains, or (b) improperly or indecently interferes with or offers any indignity to a dead human body or human remains, whether buried or not, is guilty of an indictable offence and liable to imprisonment for a term not exceeding five years. (An Act respecting the criminal law, Revised Statutes of Canada 1985, c. C-46 s. 182. R.S.C., 1985, c. C-46 s. 182.)

Federally, Section 182 of the Canada Criminal Code would seem to cover the buying and selling of human remains. It is divided into two parts, where the first part covers what happens when the duty to bury a dead body is not followed, and the second part covers interfering or "offering an indignity" to a dead body. Cases brought so far under the second part of the law include instances of sexual misconduct, hiding the evidence of homicide, improper storage, or interference with monuments or caskets (Bolieiro 2010). While Section 182 does not explicitly state that buying or selling human remains is illegal, we would argue that these actions certainly lack dignity and so Section 182 it seems would be applicable.

The importation of human remains into Canada is covered by several federal acts, which are interpreted in "Memorandum D19-9-3: Importation and exportation of human remains and other human tissues," updated 1 April 2021 (Canadian Border Services Agency 2021). Germane to our discussion is the requirement that human remains (which explicitly includes skeletons, skulls, bones, and anthropological and archaeological "specimens") be accompanied by death certificates. Agents are directed to consider death certificates as valid unless there is a suspicion of fraud (Canadian Border Services Agency 2021). Importation without death certificates would be illegal.

Canadian Provincial Laws

Provincially, most provinces implement the same broad suite of laws regarding archaeological materials, where archaeological remains are claimed for the Crown by the Province. Manitoba is more explicit and claims property in and title right of possession for any human remains found by any person in Manitoba after 3 May 1967. Similarly, Saskatchewan claims all human remains found in a cemetery or otherwise as property of the Crown. For the other provinces, it is not clear how human remains *not* found archaeologically are to be treated. Ontario for instance, in its Funeral, Burial, and Cremations Services Act (formerly the Cemeteries Act), is concerned with identifying both marked and unmarked, official and "unofficial" grave sites, and who (or which community or First Nation) must be consulted (Ariss 2014: 46–50; Bolieiro 2010). The Heritage Resources Act, Continuing Consolidation of the Statutes of Manitoba 1986, c. H39.1 § 53. C.C.S.M. c. H39.1 § 53(1986); The Heritage Resources Act, Continuing Consolidation of the Statutes of Manitoba 1986, c. H39.1 § 45. C.C.S.M. c. H39.1 § 45(1986); The Heritage Resources Act, Continuing Consolidation of the Statutes of Manitoba 1986, c. H39.1 § 46. C.C.S.M. c. H39.1 § 46(1986); The Heritage Property Act, Statutes of Saskatchewan 1979–80, c. H-2.2 § 65–1. S.S. c. H-2.2 § 65–1; Funeral, Burial and Cremation Services Act, Statutes of Ontario 2002, c. 33 s. 94.S.O. 2002, c. 33 s. 94

The United Kingdom

The no property rule is the guiding rule in the UK. However, if "skill" is applied to transform the skull into something "new," then the bones do become something that can be owned (and thus dealt with under property laws). A confounding factor in this otherwise simple distinction is the age of the remains. Remains from the past one hundred years fall under the statutes of the Human Tissue Act of 2004, in which case various kinds of licenses come into play. It is an offence under the act to put human remains on display (which includes in a shop; see Schedule 1 of the Human Tissue Act of 2004). Whether this display now also extends to online exhibition, advertisement, or sale is, to the best of our knowledge, not yet tested. Buried remains require licensing to deal with (whether in archaeological or ecclesiastical contexts), and any that are disinterred require official plans for relocation (Human Tissue Act 2004 §30).

The Human Tissue Authority (HTA), part of the UK government's Department of Health and Social Care, states that all human remains "should be treated with respect and dignity," but the desecration or mutilation of a corpse is not against the law in England, Wales and Northern Ireland; Scotland is the exception. There is nothing to stop people from desecrating human remains in private, although a legal line in the sand is drawn regarding the sexual penetration of a corpse which is illegal under the Sexual Offences Act 2003 (§70). Tampering with human remains in public is also possible to be deemed an offense under outraging public decency (Jones 2017). Some laws may also affect the sharing of images of desecrated remains in the digital space. For example, according to the Obscene Publications Act 1959, the UK Crown Prosecution Service notes that prosecutors may consider whether public decency has been outraged first. The UK also has the Communications Act of 2003, which covers messages and other matters that are grossly offensive or of an indecent, obscene, or menacing character through a public electronic communications network. However, the interpretation of what constitutes obscenity under these laws is subjective.

Belgium and the Netherlands

Our research indicates that several of the major accounts on Instagram, Facebook, and other platforms buying and selling human remains are by individuals based in Belgium and the Netherlands. For more discussion of legislation in these two countries vis-à-vis the continued existence of sales on the widely used Dutch language platform Marktplaats.nl, see Huffer, Simons et al. (2022). The example of Belgium and the Netherlands gives us a useful summary of the problem of framing the human remains trade as a crime in Europe more generally. In general, human remains older than the 1950s are considered to be archaeological and are considered to be treated the same as other archaeological materials. The Kwaliteitsnorm Nederlandse Archaeologie (KNA) offers guidance on excavation and care of human remains, but there is no explicit guidance concerning the personal buying and selling of human remains. The Valetta Convention of 1992 guides most European legislation concerning cultural heritage, but it does not position human remains within cultural heritage (Waters-Rist, Schats, and Hoogland 2016). In Belgium, the relevant federal and regional laws are all predicated on the assumption that the human remains in question are recently dead (hiding a body after a murder, interfering with cemeteries, issues around organ donation and so on).

Regarding the Netherlands, most relevant legislation derives from the Wet op de Lijkbezorging (Funeral Services Act). Most articles refer to proper procedures for burials, cremations, autopsies, and the running of cemeteries. Articles 67, 71, 80, and 81 are some of the few that deal with the human remains themselves. Article 67 states that corpses may be dissected for science or scientific education purposes, providing that the deceased has consented pre-death (or that relevant others have consented on their behalf) (Wet 1 August 2018). Article 71 forbids the preservation of corpses beyond the circumstances discussed in the Wet op de Orgaandonatie (Organ Donation Act) (Wet 1 July 2020). Within Dutch legal context, once a corpse is donated to science, it is considered to have arrived "at its final destination" and is no longer considered to be human remains. There is no legislation regarding post-use disposal, though the remains are generally cremated by the body disposal program to which they were donated (Oostra et al., 2020). Articles 80 and 81 outline punishable offenses, including "the delivery, storage, disposal, transport, destruction, dissection, embalming or preserving treatment of a corpse in violation of law" (Wet 1 August 2018). The Wetboek van Strafrecht (Criminal Code) also provides some legislation surrounding the treatment of human remains. Section 150 of the Criminal Code makes it an offence to unlawfully disinter a body or move or transport a body while Section 151 makes it an offence to conceal the cause of death of a body (Wetboek van Strafrecht 2021). While disturbing a resting place/desecrating a grave is illegal (Section 149 of the Criminal Code), there are no specific corpse desecration or anti-necrophilia laws (*NLTimes* 2021). In Belgium, hiding the body of a murder victim or of someone killed through various injuries is an offense (Art. 340), and so is the breaking of burial laws (Art. 315), but issues concerning burial and cemeteries are left up to the various regions (e.g., Decreet 16 January 2004; Decreet 14 February 2019).

The Criminal Code, Organ Donation Act, and Funeral Services Act apply to human remains produced within the last fifty years. Pre-1950s, human remains are considered archaeological. In regard to archaeological legislation, the primary legislation comes from the Erfgoedwet (Heritage Law) and the Kwaliteitsnorm Nederlandse Archaeologie (KNA; Dutch Archaeology Quality Standard). The Dutch Heritage Law (Wet 9 December 2015) is more explicit about prohibiting the movement or sale of protected cultural heritage without prior approval (Art. 4.4-9; 5.1). Articles 4.10-16 further specify the procedure to follow for potential buyers of protected cultural heritage. However, the answer to a question asked by Ronald van Raak in 2009 in the Dutch Chamber of Representatives (Vraag en Antwoord Tweede Kamer 2009) revealed that there is no law specifically banning the trade in ancient human remains which might have been obtained a long time ago and potentially from abroad.

Within the most recent version of the KNA, there is some guidance on the excavation, cleaning, and storage of remains (Waters-Rist et al. 2016). However, there is no further guidance provided, ethical or otherwise. This is likely because most European cultural heritage legislation is derived from the European Convention on the Protection of the Archaeological Heritage/the Valetta Convention of 1992, which does not tacitly mention and include human remains of either local or extra-local origin as archaeological heritage, nor does it specifically discuss online trafficking under Article 10 on the prevention of the illicit circulation of elements of the archaeological heritage (Waters-Rist et al. 2016; Council of Europe n.d.). Similarly, there is no legislation against the use or display of human remains within a Dutch museum or collections context. According to the Museumvereniging/Museums Associations' Ethische Code voor Musea/Ethics Code for Museums, museums are allowed to collect human remains (Section 2.5), conduct research on remains (3.7), and exhibit remains (4.3), provided that these actions are done in a culturally and religiously respectful manner. Repatriation requests must be treated "with respect," but there is no mention of prohibiting the collection, research, or exhibition of culturally-sensitive human remains (Voorzitter Museumvereniging 2006).

Belgium has a federal law concerning the protection of underwater heritage (Wet 6 July 2013) which states human remains should be treated with respect (Art. 2§9) and that works should not unnecessarily disturb human remains (Bijlage I regel 5). A Flemish ministerial decision (Ministerieel Besluit 23 January 2009) concerning the documentation and registration of archaeological research provides practical norms for excavating and recording human remains (e.g., Art. 29.1-2; Art. 39) but does not concern the movement of (or trade in) human remains.

Australia and New Zealand

Australian Federal legislation defining what counts as human remains or cultural property and directed at curtailing import, export, and interstate/territory transport of the same includes the Biosecurity Act of 2015 and the Protection of Moveable Cultural Heritage Act (hereafter PMCHA) of 1986 (updated 2018). The PMCHA of 1986, regulation 1.3(c) includes human remains as Objects of Australian Aboriginal and Torres Strait Islander Heritage (Class A objects), making export illegal, along with archaeological artifacts and many categories of ethnographic and historical material culture. Regulations within the PMCHA 2018 should prohibit import of culturally significant items into Australia. Article 4 of the Act only mentions objects, but human remains can and have been included as sanctioned illegal imports (Forrest 2004; Arts.gov n.d.).

As currently listed on the website, there have been four repatriations of trafficked human remains under this Act since June 2000. They include a decorated Asmat skull to Indonesia returned in December 2006, sixteen incised Dayak skulls returned to Malaysia in May 2007, artifacts containing soil and human remains returned to Cambodia in March 2011 (as described in the Preface), and a set of four decorated skulls (two Dayak, two Asmat) returned to Indonesia in May 2018. Whether other repatriations under the Act also include human remains, but not as the item of focus, is unknown. At the state or territory level, most governments have also passed some version of a Human Tissue Act, usually in the 1980s. However, like in many other parts of the world, this legislation is concerned more with transplants, donations, transport of viable medical specimens, or funerary matters, and therefore does not specifically set down legislation or penalties to directly respond to private ownership, buying, selling, or shipping within or between states of the kinds of human remains talked about in this book. Biosecurity Act 2015(Cth) s. 110; Protection of Moveable Cultural Heritage Act 1986 (Cth) s. 1.3(c).

New Zealand's guiding federal-level legislation in relation to the treatment of the dead is very similar to that of Canada. Section 150 of the Crimes Act of 1961 concerns "misconduct in respect of human remains" (New Zealand Legislation 1961). As with the Canadian equivalent, the section is in two parts. Part A addresses individual responsibility to carry through with the burial or cremation of the deceased if this task is imposed on one. Part B, more pertinently, forbids improper or indecent interference with or the offering of an indignity to human remains, whether buried or not. Guilty parties face a two-year prison sentence, but as we have seen elsewhere, a loophole exists since private ownership, buying, or selling (online or offline) is not specifically codified.

On the New Zealand Customs website, the guidelines around the proper procedure to import, export, or otherwise manage the movement of human remains hinge on the key phrase "for interment." Regarding the importation of human remains, it states:

> An import entry is not required when human remains (for interment) are brought into New Zealand. However Customs clearance is required to obtain release from an airline or cargo storage facility. You will be asked to provide shipping documents and a death certificate to Customs. We will issue a delivery order for clearance purposes. There are no Customs charges. (New Zealand Customs Service n.d.)

Regarding export, it states:

> When human remains (for interment) are to be sent from New Zealand, the freight forwarder or airline will usually complete the required Customs formalities. An export entry is not required. (New Zealand Customs Service n.d.)

In general, an email address is provided to which one must send scanned copies of all relevant documents and note "Urgent—Human Remains" in the subject line.

A summary document brings together concise information on heritage legislation that might apply when Māori remains specifically have been "uncovered through accidental discovery or deliberately excavated/exhumed in emergency response situations, or as a result of natural processes, e.g., coastal erosion" (Heritage New Zealand Pouhere Taonga 2014). The Coroners Act of 2006 (§14(1)) requires any body discovered by accident to be reported to the police as soon as possible. Sections 51 and 55 of the Burial and Cremation Act of 1964 make it an offence to remove a body or parts of a body from any burial ground (Māori or Pakeha) without "licence under the hand of the minister."

Part 4 of the Heritage New Zealand Pouhere Taonga Act of 2014 (HNZPTA) requires a registry be kept of a wide range of archaeological sites, including every category of burial context previously or currently used by Māori communities. Finally, the Protected Objects Act of 1975 (POA) regulates export of protected objects, illegal import and export, and the sale, trade, and ownership of *taonga tuturu* (any finished item made or used by Māori). This would include items or modified remains removed from archaeological sites, as well as the export of *mokomokai/toi moko* (preserved heads).

It is these latter manifestations of sacred ancestral venerations that have been sought by collectors since the 1800s, that are slowly returning to Māori control after decades in foreign institutions, but that are also still sold and commercialized on the market (Fennell and Ross 2020; Yates 2013). To date, however, we have observed very few collectors or dealers of any type of remains openly indicating they are based in New Zealand or will ship to New Zealand. This might indicate that the abovementioned legislation is especially strong or likely to be enforced. Crimes Act 1961 s. 150; Coroners Act 2006 s. 14; Burial and Cremation Act 1964 § 51; Burial and Cremation Act 1964 § 55; Heritage New Zealand Pouhere Taonga Act 2014 s. 65; Protected Objects Act 1975 s.

Implications?

Although we have provided a substantial overview of state/province and federal legislation in several relevant demand (and also potentially source) countries, we need to clarify that we have not reviewed all possible relevant laws from all possible locations in which individuals participate in the trade as suppliers, middlemen, dealers, or collectors. Indeed, the flourishing of the bone trade online and its growth and spread across platforms has made any place a potential source of supply or demand. As with all categories of cultural heritage trafficking, legislation struggles to keep pace, given that collecting communities, especially within social media groups, forums, and chat rooms, teach each other how to evade what laws that do exist, where administrators can label themselves experts on not just what is being bought and sold, but on how to buy and sell it. This regularly includes information regarding real or perceived legal loopholes, asking community members for legal advice, giving instructions on how to bypass Customs in various locations, requesting specific ways to advertise, specific emojis or symbols to use to indicate location and price without risking algorithmic attention, and other tips and tricks of the trade. What is a certainty is that as social media and e-commerce platforms continue to rise and fall in popularity, change ownership (and therefore terms of service and community standards), and make future decisions about what is and is not permissible, traffickers of all types of goods will continue to find new ways to ply their trades.

The question, "Is it legal to buy or sell or own human remains?," is, as we have seen, extremely complex, with a wide variety of laws and approaches across multiple jurisdictions. Again, our purpose here is not to review every applicable law from every jurisdiction, or to explore what case law or precedent suggests for how current laws have been interpreted. We are pushing back against the common misperception that there is a kind of widespread lack of regulation across these many jurisdictions where we find many of the main traders active, that is on Instagram and other social media platforms.

In North American contexts, the *origin* of the human remains is often a key component when determining legality, especially whether the remains come from a cemetery. Case law is not much precedent, for aside from Louisiana, there have been few prosecutions under these existing laws about buying or selling. An interesting proviso concerning origin is demonstrated by Nebraska's statute (see above): the idea that it is the *purchaser's* state of knowledge that matters if an offense has occurred. The incentive for the dealer, clearly, is to obfuscate and otherwise set out to *not know* as much as possible about human remains to be purchased. Collectors do respond accordingly, and to immunize themselves against what law does exist, will routinely indicate that they have no reason to suspect any meaningful documentation might or should exist (with the exception of occasional museum labels attached to or written on bones that inevitably boost the "story" and price).

But if we, as researchers, *could* say something about the origin of human remains displayed in online photos, then perhaps we would have grounds to encourage the justice system to pursue legal options more often. If we can demonstrate that a reasonable person should automatically expect that the human remains come from a cemetery (recently or initially, regardless of how many collections they passed through before we observe them online), if we can demonstrate that there is no reasonable way one might expect to find an official death certificate (which is necessary for import in many jurisdictions remember), then there might be a way forward.

If we could say something about the origin and depositional context of remains offered for sale, from an archaeological perspective, we might be able to argue that any paperwork provided would be necessarily fraudulent. We might be able to demonstrate the indignity being committed. We might be able to suggest a better provenience (find spot) within a particular geographic location/legal jurisdiction. We might be able to bring some of these myriad laws to bear. These possibilities led us to wonder if the computer could see more in the photographs than we can, and so we tried another experiment.

Truth in Advertising

In June of 2017, we saw this post on Instagram:

> This little beauty of a skull was brought back from Vietnam by an American soldier. Uncut and in amazing condition. Message me for more information and if you want to buy it. . . . Worldwide shipping available.

How can we know if this purported origin is true? How can we actually *know* where human remains come from or from what peoples, when we see them online? In this section, we outline an experiment that *might* help in this regard. The first thing to keep in mind, is that we are dealing with probabilities, not certainties. In what follows, we present our attempts to narrow down the possibilities using a machine learning technique called "one-shot learning," trained on photographs of human skulls located in museum contexts.

When *forensic anthropologists* are presented with human remains they need to identify, the determination of "ancestry" and estimation of sex of unprovenienced human remains (i.e., remains for which the original scene of the crime, or place of deposition or burial is unknown) relies on the careful measurement of "landmarks" on the bones. These "landmarks" have themselves been determined by careful study of both provenienced and unprovenienced human remains from a wide variety of populations and time periods. The ones that seem to work best come from the skull or the pelvis (when suitably calibrated, standardized for population, and analyzed). There are software packages available like FORDISC 3.1 (Jantz and Ousely 2005) and CRANID (Wright 1992) that take the measurement of key points on the bones, and through statistical comparison with its reference data will suggest an affinity to a certain population within a certain probability range.

In recent years, researchers have begun to apply machine learning techniques to this data, with very good results (e.g., Navega et al. 2014a; 2014b; Ousley 2016; Maier et al. 2015) suggesting the potential to improve the accuracy of identifying unprovenienced remains at the population and individual levels (e.g., Nagpal et al. 2017). We use the term "ancestry" or "origin" in their forensic anthropological senses; "race" is a social construction, and we are not thereby implying that these categories are anywhere indicative of the lived experience of these individuals (and see the work of Ross and Williams discussed below).

Traditional forensic anthropological approaches to estimating ancestry, especially of remains recovered from crime scenes, clandestine graves, or sites of mass disaster, as well as unprovenienced remains recovered from the market, seek to quantify and qualify the complex interrelationship between skeletal morphology, genetics, geographic origin, and sociocultural constructs (Pilloud and Hefner 2016; Dunn et al. 2020). While various researchers have and continue to attempt to develop regression equations to estimate ancestry from a variety of different bones (e.g., Liebenberg, L'Abbé, and Stull 2015; Meeusen, Christensen, and Hefner 2015; Wescott 2005; Tallman and Winburn 2015; Ünlütürk 2017; Swenson 2013), it is the collection of a battery of metric measurements and non-metric (macromorphoscopic) trait data from ideally intact crania that are considered the most reliable.

Ideally, ancestry estimation would occur as part of a suite of interdisciplinary research performed in collaboration with anthropologists and/or law enforcement to fully establish the biological profile and (as much as possible) the life history of the individual whose cranium was recovered from the market (e.g., J. Watkins et al. 2017; Dodrill et al. 2016). Given the ephemeral nature of what appears and disappears online, the preferred situation of being able to assess the remains in person in controlled laboratory conditions is very rarely realized.

Even then, recent work has re-evaluated a decade's worth of papers from 2009 to 2019 in the *Journal of Forensic Sciences* and has demonstrated that forensic scientists do not use the various terms and concepts in consistent ways (Ross and Williams 2021). They point out that while "race" as a category has long been debunked, it continues in use (and misuse, and inconsistent application, for racial categorizations) by forensic anthropologists because of its continued applicability in law enforcement. Instead, Ross and Williams demonstrate that understanding the historical factors behind the often extremely fluid and historically contingent population formation processes is necessary to understand the morphological trends spotted in skeletal remains; labeling a set of remains as "African," or "European," or "Asian" ignores a great deal of history and human variability. Ross and Williams point out that ancestry, in forensic terms, is used so loosely that it is, more or less, a synonym for race. Instead, through a re-evaluation of nearly four hundred sets of human remains, Ross and Williams demonstrate that the "Asia, Europe, Africa" type of classification is ahistorical and, for the test case they explore, "biologically meaningless." They advocate instead for what they call a population structure approach, which

> allows us to understand how microevolutionary factors such as genetic drift act in concert with cultural factors (i.e., marriage patterns) and historical events (i.e., epidemics, colonization) to influence human variation . . . a major consideration

in the application of a population structure approach is to account for historical events such as population influxes and settlements, religious secularization, language differences, temporality, and spatial patterning that would be impacted by microevolutionary forces. (Ross and Williams 2021: 1)

If forensic anthropologists and geneticists are granted access to human remains being traded online after seizure by law enforcement, forensic methods of assessing population affiliation from cranio-facial and dental morphology and, perhaps more reliably, mtDNA analysis, can illuminate *something* about the lives and big-picture origins of these trafficked individuals.

We do not have that kind of evidence. We wondered instead if it would be possible to use computer vision to analyze the photographs. Remember, these photographs are the only evidence for these lives lived that we have. Once purchased, this person disappears again into someone's collection. How many people's remains are being bought and sold? From what populations, in the sense Ross and Williams discuss, have their remains been sourced? *If* it is possible to say something from this source of evidence, we might be able to start to answer those questions. *If* this computer vision/machine learning technique works. These are big ifs.

We designed an initial experiment using what we have—photographs from social media, and photographs from museums that have human remains in their collection from known populations. In this way we hoped to account for the population structure in a way that acknowledges the historic and contingent forces at work—to see if we could teach the computer to learn to *not* determine ancestry, but to say, "this image is different from what I have learned about human remains, along the following dimensions." If enough differences add up, we posit that we have learned something of the populations in these photographs. We turned to neural networks again. You will recall that neural networks, when shown enough data of a particular class of thing, learn to associate the way the various computational neurons and their linkages light up with that thing, and things that look similar. But for what we wanted to do, there were some rather serious problems with that approach.

More Ethics of Machine Learning

In this case, we do not really have the right kind of data, and enough of it, to try that kind of approach. Even if we did, there are certain ethical issues, not least of which is the close use of such technologies for what amounts to little more than digital phrenology and, like traditional phrenology, provides cover for more pernicious evils. The entrepreneur who made an app that determines if one is gay or not from a photo springs to mind (Hardwick 2019).

If we are "methodological individualists," that is, we believe that only humans are capable of moral actions, then there is no ethical problem with machine vision, only in how we use it. If, on the other hand, we take the view that the algorithms of machine vision are an extension of our ability to act, then the moral responsibility for what results is both with us *and* with the machine (A. Hanson 2009: 92). Risam argues that we must be attuned to the ways that many of our digital tools represent white, male, Global-North ways of knowing, in that the "human" imagined as the test case for achieving human-levels of acuity in image recognition is the same kind of human most often responsible for the design of these algorithms in the first place (Risam 2019: 124–36). In which case, we have to examine not only the results of the usage of these technologies but also *how* these technologies work and *to what* their attention is attuned. Hanson argues that the moral force in situations where there is joint responsibility, human and machine, also depends on the degree of harm that can be accomplished (A. Hanson 2009: 97–98).

The harms are several. Amazon famously created an artificial intelligence to help sort candidates for jobs and as such learned from its training data the biases of its own HR department towards male candidates (see for instance Reuters 2018). Similarly, a company called Predictim released an application that assesses potential babysitters from a variety of social media posts to determine their trustworthiness to work with clients' children (Lee 2018), just one such application of many. In this latter case, the founders of the company demonstrate a profound lack of awareness that the choice of reference materials embodies their own priorities, privileges, and perspectives on what constitutes a suitable candidate, with all of the racial and other systemic biases that exist within this legal grey area (Merrillees 2017). In which case, we need to ask, what, and how much harm can our research accomplish versus the good that we can accomplish? Is the application of these digital methods to understand the bone trade (and by extension, other categories of online trafficking) worth the risk?

There is first, a harm to the vendor. While we think that this way of making a living is morally and ethically wrong, as we have seen, it is not necessarily illegal in all jurisdictions or in all contexts. An AI that flags something for sale as suspect can interfere with the person's livelihood. Then there is the potential backlash against the researcher from the vendor community. There is the potential harm against descendant communities and the risk of re-traumatization. We acknowledge these risks, but think it is still worth pursuing to carefully develop a machine vision approach nevertheless, since so much of the law is framed around the origin of the remains in question; without some way of assessing this from the evidence that we have, there might not be any other way to flag remains for a deeper investigation.

Training a neural network model on a corpus of images, from scratch, is massively computationally intensive, requiring millions of images in order to be successful. The amount of energy required means that there are environmental harms. And then there are the source images used for training and the issue of representativeness. The Inception V3 model from Google was trained on the ImageNet corpus, which manually paired hundreds of thousands of images against the Wordnet hierarchy (Szegedy et al. 2014; Krizhevsky et al. 2012). For all its success at identifying and captioning images, when we tried it out on photographs that we collected, it did not recognize human remains at all, for these were not part of the training corpus. Perhaps transfer learning might solve that.

In transfer learning, you will recall, we start with a trained neural network that knows how to classify patterns into categories. If we throw out those categories and show the trained neural network new categories, it can transfer its high-level representation of how lines, edges, curves and so on go together to recognize the new categories with the new labels. If a researcher creates a corpus with one thousand images of human remains from one people and one thousand images from another, and show these to the network, the machine will duly find that every unknown image represents some combination of the two peoples' human remains because these are now the only two categories of images that it knows.

Whether or not the labeling is correct is conveyed by a probability estimate, but remember, it is not the probability of whether the image depicts X or Y. It is the probability that X or Y matches the aggregate characteristics of the images collected in the training data in the first place. It could well be that the classifier has picked up on some subtle bias in that original data—perhaps the images for the first category all have a particular backdrop, a texture in the wood platform supporting the remains (a function of what the photographer had handy that day) while the second set of images were all taken through museum vitrines.

In an experiment using a convolutional neural network against X-ray images from three different hospitals, to see if the neural network could diagnose disease, the researchers found that the CNN was picking up signals specific to the individual hospital systems. That is, the CNN learned what an X-ray from a portable X-ray machine looked like. Since portable X-ray machines are typically used in cases where the patient is already very sick and cannot be moved readily, images from portable machines tend to have a much higher rate of positive diagnoses (Zech 2018; Zech et al. 2018). The CNN learned *not* what signals of disease were discernible in the X-ray, but that X-rays sourced from a particular kind of machine signal disease.

When we collect images from social media posts, we must be attuned to the fact that the neural network might be picking up signals that have little to do with the ostensible subject of the photo. Archaeological users of neural network approaches to data need to be alert to and investigate the confounding information, and to work out what this is doing to how the computer *sees* or makes sense of the data. (Indeed, this is an active area of research in computer vision, with some results suggesting that the majority of the CNN algorithm's performance accounting for its accuracy seems to be correlated to low-level noise in the images, rather than in the more complex signals; Brendel and Bethge 2019.)

This applies to transfer learning as well: what extraneous signals are we introducing to our training dataset? Once the re-trained model is deployed in an app, the model acts as a black box, with no realistic way to know just what signals are being perceived. The resulting app carries the appearance and authority of machine learning, where we end up with an "official" result: 88 percent *this*; 93 percent *that* (see Dao 2018 for a curated list of artificial intelligence technologies deployed in ways that take advantage of this rhetoric). And that is a powerful story in the context of the trade in human remains, where it is as much the story about an image that sells the bones as it is anything inherent in the bones themselves.

Imagine a classifier that focuses on identifying carved or decorated crania allegedly of Dayak origin that was trained to recognize modern carvings on skulls (however obtained) as "authentic" nineteenth-century materials. We could easily create such a classifier by mistake. If we published our transfer-learning trained neural network in an open access venue, it would not be difficult to see it being used to support sellers' stories, to authenticate materials. We would have committed, in effect, an act of digital phrenology that enhances the violence already meted out to these individuals through removal from their place of origin, subsequent modification, trafficking, and transformation into a commercial object!

This technology is also being deployed by, for example, IBM and the NYC Police Department to obtain stills of individuals caught on closed-circuit TV footage and label the images with physical tags, such as ethnicity or clothing color, to allow police to search video databases for individuals matching a description of interest (Joseph and Lipp 2018). It is also being used in China to further marginalize the Uighur people and create "social credit scores" in a system of constant surveillance (Samuel 2018). Is it ethical for human remains trade research to employ the same technologies that are being deployed against basic human freedoms? An even more direct analogy is the increasing use of AI to detect child abuse images online, such as iCOP (a suite of automatic AI techniques that focuses on file metadata rather than images directly; Peersman et al. 2014; L. Clark 2016; Tarantola 2016). The major association of computing, the Association for Computing Machinery (ACM) has recently redone their code of ethics to foreground doing no harm (ACM 2018). Whatever we design, it must do no harm.

We set aside our initial experiments with neural networks (that used approaches like transfer learning), until we could figure out the balance between harm and benefit. We settled on an approach that makes a virtue of having little data.

An Experiment with One-Shot Learning

So-called one-shot learning approaches to computer vision do not rely on masses of data, but are predicated instead on the idea that we have only a few examples of the domain we are interested in—maybe even only one. Then, the trained model is presented with two images that the model has not encountered before—a person of interest—and a second photograph which may or may not contain that person, for instance. The model can determine whether that second photograph contains the person depicted in the first image. This approach uses *two* neural networks that have the same pattern of weights and activations. The two images are presented to the two networks, which convert each image to a vectorized representation (a list of measurements or numbers along 2,048 dimensions). The networks are joined together by a final loss function that determines the *dissimilarity* between the two vectors. (These kinds of networks were first introduced in 1993 for the purposes of signature verification; see Bromley et al. 1993.)

In plain English, we take an image and show the network another image and measure the degree of difference between how the network lit up for the first image versus the second. The smaller the degree, the more likely that the two images are of the same thing.

Because neural networks are potentially sensitive to other elements of the photograph aside from the human remains themselves such as boxes in the background, the edges of windows, labels and so on, we removed the backgrounds from all images using the https://www.remove.bg service from Kaleido AI GmbH, which itself is built on a neural network trained to recognize foreground versus background objects. The images used for training the neural network in the first place are not part of the subsequent test.

We augmented the training data set by adjusting the orientation, cropping, flipping the axes, and so on of that initial image (see for instance Shorten and Khoshgoftaar 2019). We automatically rotated, translated, and adjusted lighting so that we could account for the variability in the quality of target image, such that we build into the network knowledge of how skulls look under different conditions, both photographic and in terms of taphonomic condition that themselves are indicative of primary burial/deposition and/or secondary storage conditions or use (e.g., Pokines 2015a, 2015b; Pokines et al. 2017; Yucha, Pokines, and Bartelink 2017). We end up with thirty-three different views for each of the neural network training images, thus 363 images generated using standard data augmentation techniques (Tanner and Wong 1987; van Dyk and

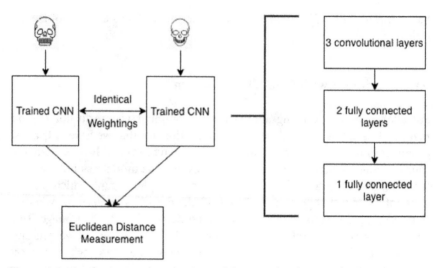

Figure 4.1. A schematic representation of the one-shot learning architecture, where two networks are used at once and a pair of images are evaluated. In practice, a single network where the images are evaluated in turn achieves the same effect at a great savings in memory. Skull icons by user "freepik" on flaticons.com, and user Jake Dunham, thenounproject.com. Originally published in Graham et al. 2020, figure 2, CC-BY 4.0.

Meng 2001). In this way, we can build a neural network representative of the very diverse category of "the human skull."

The images for training the neural network within this initial experiment were sourced by Huffer from his research within several ethnographic and osteological collections over the last several years, including at: the Gustavianum Museum (Uppsala, Sweden), the Ethnographic Museum (Stockholm, Sweden), the Musée de l'Homme (Paris, France), the Sarawak Museum (Kuching, Malaysia), the Smithsonian National Museum of Natural History (Washington, DC, USA), the Tropenmuseum (Amsterdam, Netherlands), the Volkenkunde Museum (Leiden, Netherlands), the Pitt-Rivers Museum (Oxford, UK), the Oxford Museum of Natural History (Oxford, UK), and the Duckworth Laboratory (Cambridge, UK). When training the network, we use a triplet loss function. We train the neural network on triplets where each triplet of images contains an "anchor" or target image and then a second image ("positive") of the same object depicted from a different view, and a third image depicting a view of a *different* object. The difference between the positives and the negatives are used to update the network's weights, which teaches the network to learn the subtle differences between different skulls.

Having trained the network, we moved onto the experiment. For this experiment, we culled through the thousands of images that we have collected and selected twenty-eight examples where the image showed a skull framed towards the camera *and* the vendor told a story about the skull's provenance and provenience. For our training data to *create* the network in the first place we used photographs from museum collections similarly framed (but augmented: it is possible to increase the amount of training data by flipping, rotating, and translating images so that we end up with several different kinds of views). For testing, we had another seventy images from forensic literature and museum collections where we had information about the broad origin of the remains. Then we started comparing pairs of images, all ninety-eight images, measuring the differences. That's 9,604 pairs to examine. We took the results for just the seventy images from museums, to see statistically (using two different techniques) if the patterns of differences for remains known to be from individuals who came from African, Asian, European, and Indigenous North American populations could be clearly differentiated. Despite the issues with these classifications discussed earlier, we used these broad-brush categories because these were the classifications used in the literature we were drawing from. (For the detailed technical discussions about the code and statistics, see the original article, Graham, Lane, et al. 2020.)

Then we tried it again with the human remains depicted in social media. Remember that we are taking the vendors at their word here, when they tell us that the remains came from Vietnam, or wherever else. We cannot claim, with this method, that particular human remains came from a particular part of the world or belong to a particular cultural group. They each are dissimilar across several dimensions. If we reduce those dimensions down to two (to make the broad differences legible to us), *these* skulls are differentiated enough from all of these other skulls, some of which we know something about their origin. And for the ones where we do know something *true* about their origin, they separate out *enough* that we might make a correlation. We are not taking averages or means or making "typical" groups. We are using a method that respects the individuality of each person's remains.

What Vendors Claim . . .

Remember that the story sells the skeleton. We have screen-captured (and have been sent) numerous examples of commentary on images of human remains for sale in which buyers/sellers also ask for help estimating the age, sex, or probable origins of the human remains they recently obtained, or else offer competing interpretations. These requests for help demonstrate that at least a proportion of those engaged in this trade are not well-versed in the osteological methods and techniques necessary to have at least a general concept of *who* they are collecting, and therefore cannot verify the claims of sellers before buying. In any event, testimony from collectors themselves in media outlets such as Wired UK demonstrate that an important concern is that the item should be *real bone*; provenance, provenience, and accurate demographic information are usually less important (O. Schwartz 2019).

There seem to be two main story tropes that are told by collectors and dealers in relation to the ancestries of the remains they acquire. The first is that many remains, especially whole skeletons or crania, were stolen or sourced from British-controlled and post-Independence India to supply medical students during the 1800s to as recently as the 1980s. The second, told by niche collectors interested in "tribal art" tends to argue that their authentic "ethnographic" specimens were somehow *meant* to be collected by the Western explorers, missionaries, or "natural historians" who first acquired them. These "ethnographic" materials tend to be crania or long bones or teeth modified by Indigenous people for ritual use in the past or present, or as part of early "curio" markets ca. 1800–1950. Twenty-first century osteoarchaeology can more readily acknowledge that many such collections now held by museums, but especially by private individuals, first came into global circulation for the purposes of "scientific racism" during the emergence of physical anthropology as a discipline (Redman 2016).

Neither of these stories ethically absolve participants in this trade, but the former is often presented as "ok" while the latter, since it involves the stealing of remains of First Nations, Native American, Aboriginal, and other Indigenous groups, is seen by traders as something to avoid, due to the existence of explicit legislation like NAGPRA, which most traders are aware of (see for instance the interviews with traders in O. Schwartz 2019 and Troian 2019a, 2019b). (With regard to the trade in human remains from India in the context of medical students' anatomical studies, as we noted in Chapter 1, we have observed that the trade continues in modern form for Indian and Bangladeshi students in both public and private Facebook groups.)

We will also note that there are many examples of remains being actively looted from known or unknown prehistoric and historic archaeological sites, more recent open-air cemeteries, recovered from clandestine burials or found by chance (Huxley and Finnegan 2004; Halling and Seidemann 2016; Seidemann et al. 2009). Vendors of course do not mention this as a venue for how remains come to be in their possession.

. . . And Why We Often Disbelieve Them

With the one-shot learning technique, we were able to measure the *dissimilarities* within the entire group of images. But this was only the first step. We used this matrix of dissimilarities to create models of the data that we could then compare the social media materials against. (And remember, it would take physically analyzing the human remains themselves in order to confirm conclusively what follows.)

This matrix of differences was represented as a 35-dimensional space using a technique called "non-metric multidimensional scaling" (and "35" because the 70 × 70 matrix containing dissimilarities within the training data are symmetrical, and so half the number of rows or columns will suffice to capture 100 percent of the variance). If you remember your introduction to statistics class (if you had that experience), this is similar to how principal components analysis reduces the variance in a data set to two dimensions; here each new dimension is the axis that represents most of the remaining dissimilarities between skulls.

We used those differences with two statistical approaches to create models of the data. Then, we could use the model to predict into which group a skull should be assigned. Knowing the original groups (our "grounded material") for some of them functioned as a kind of check on the model. We explored a variety of tests and found that MDA (Mixture Discriminant Analysis) was most suitable for our purposes—assessing whether a case belongs to a given category for our grounded materials. Since the subpopulations from which these materials are derived have different average metric dimensions and differing frequencies of macromorphoscopic trait expression, MDA is a good choice because MDA assumes each class is a mixture of subgroups following a Gaussian distribution, instead of a single Gaussian distribution per class as in a Linear Discriminant Analysis. That is to say, it works better for more complex data.

We took the same data and used a different approach to generate a model to see what its results implied. The idea here is to triangulate via a different method towards our same goal of prediction and explore how the predictions from the two methods coincide with each other and/or with vendor attributions of origin. In our second approach we fed the data to a neural network. The neural network attempts to learn a model from our square matrix of distances (every image compared to every other image), where it trains its model on our grounded materials. The grounded materials were divided at random into an 80–20 percent split into "training" and "validation" sets, and then the trained model was used to predict (test) the accuracy of the social media posts.

Of the unprovenanced images of human skulls:

- Thirteen images have a purported "ancestry" or origin that neither the MDA nor the neural network models predict.
- Seven images have a purported "ancestry" that both the MDA and the neural network model also predict.
- Eight images have a purported "ancestry" that both models predict but are different from what the vendors claimed.

- There are seven instances where the neural network model agreed with the claimed origin but not with the MDA prediction.
- There is one instance where the MDA predicted origin agreed with the claimed origin but not with the neural network suggested origin.

The models lend support to the vendor's story in fifteen of the twenty-eight cases, but only in seven of those cases does the vendor's story seem particularly strong, i.e., two different models predict the same origin (within all the usual caveats of this study). In eighteen cases, the models do not support the vendor, nor do they support each other, suggesting that those particular skulls might be worth further investigation, in that they have an origin not captured by our grounded examples. In eight cases, the two models agree with each other, but not the vendor, which perhaps suggests cases where the vendor is either unknowledgeable or is misrepresenting the origin of the skulls.

Truth in advertising? Well, at least as far as this experiment goes, you might not be getting what you think you are getting. Thirteen of the twenty-eight posts were better grouped into categories *other* than what the vendors suggested. That is to say, the models might not necessarily tell us what group the remains might *best* be categorized as, but they do tell us that they certainly *are not* what the vendors say. For nearly a quarter of the photographs we looked at our statistics suggested these would be better grouped as Indigenous North American.

We cannot prove that they are, but we can suggest that skulls with an Indigenous North American ancestry are circulating in this market far more than vendors either know or let on: indeed, vendors are often quite careful to state that they would never knowingly trade in skulls from Indigenous groups. These results suggest in part that *knowingly* is the key word here. Perhaps the correct synonym might be "openly." More skulls are claimed to be Asian than what the model predicts, as the historic trade in bodies from India and China perhaps provides moral cover. According to this experiment, *none* of the purportedly "European" skulls can be so classified.

Recall the Spirit Eye Cave human remains, which could be matched to an mtDNA haplogroup and could be connected to a living, lineal descendant. Our experiment here is not proof; but it should be enough to suggest that *all* human remains being bought and sold in the United States might be subject to far more laws than commonly understood *unless* other taphonomic, morphological, or mtDNA data demonstrates otherwise. Such evidence of course is usually only obtainable in full if the remains are seized and able to be assessed by experts. This is a bold claim, and hinges on the word "knowingly." We feel that the experiment demonstrates *a possibility* that at least some human remains bought, sold, and transported in the United States (perhaps more than known or admitted to by collectors) are of Indigenous peoples. If there is a chance that the human remains are Indigenous, then the only way to decisively confirm one way or another is through mtDNA, given that other categories of data obtainable from osteological or laboratory analysis (e.g., cranio-facial morphology, cultural modifications to cranial shape, evidence for specific modifications or decorations, soil or pollen analysis, isotope analysis) often paint a relatively broad picture (e.g., J. Watkins et al. 2017).

This has been an experiment. The mismatch between what the vendors *say* about the skulls and what the models *predict* also lends weight to the idea that at least some vendors/collectors misrepresent the origins and life histories contained within the remains of the once-living individuals they have now reduced to commodities (either through a lack of concern for such details or ignorance of how to discern such details from the bones themselves). And the image of the skull purportedly a war trophy from Vietnam? The statistics suggest an "African" ancestry, while the machine learning model suggests an "Asian" ancestry. The vendor's story cannot be confirmed and appears to use Vietnam and the cultural memories of that conflict to try to inflate the sale price.

An Aside: Building a Taphonomic Classifier

Knowing the taphonomic processes observable in images of human remains for sale, the marks and changes made to bones depending on whether they were at some point in wet ground, were burned, were gnawed on by animals, all of the changes that happen after death, could also give us a perspective on the truth in advertising of bone vendors. It would give us a sense of the scale of different routes through which human remains have been procured for market. Taphonomic processes are the ways that human remains decay over time. A skeleton buried in highly acidic soil (as in a pine forest) will show evidence of different kinds of processes than one buried in loamy farmer's fields. Tree roots and other plants, insects, rodents, and other creatures will all leave their own distinctive traces on the remains. Cultural modifications are also taphonomic processes—drilling with a stone drill or cutting with a bandsaw to add patterns to a skull will leave distinctive traces.

How many images show evidence of water damage? How many images show evidence of root damage or the specific coloration that can come only from exposure to soils with high copper content (green), or iron (dark red), or manganese (reddish-purple)? Such information might give us an indication of when "from a former medical collection" really means "removed from a grave." It is possible that computer vision could pick these traces out. Taphonomic processes are much clearer to spot in photographs (although not without issue—the process of preparing medical specimens removes much evidence).

Using computer vision to identify them is also less ethically fraught since the idea is to learn something of what has happened to the remains post-death, rather than trying to connect them to a living population. By focusing on taphonomic processes, we might have a tool that non-osteologists could use to pick out the osteologically real but culturally fake human remains that abound in these online spaces.

In this experiment, we used transfer learning to create a neural network image model that learned to recognize these taphonomic processes. Remember, a trained neural network that recognizes general images has already learned how to distinguish curves, lines, areas of color, angles, and myriad other dimensions of image data. If we show this neural network our images of human remains, it will light up in particular ways and then guess a label according to its last layer of labels (selecting the closest label to the pattern). With transfer learning, we feed in many examples of what we are looking for: hundreds of examples of "water damaged bone" or "fire damaged bone" or "canid tooth marks" and similar. (Building such a training set is itself an enormous challenge requiring thousands of images!) The former labels in the pre-trained network are removed, and the neural network now has new labels that it can associate with the modifications to bone or tooth enamel that the different taphonomic processes cause. We can show the neural network an image, and it will return a prediction on the kind(s) of taphonomic processes that it can see in the image.

We built such a classifier as a kind of computational sketch to work out what the issues would be. Even with data augmentation techniques, getting enough training data was difficult. Nevertheless, it *appears* to work well on the test images we fed it after training. On the few test images we fed it, it correctly labeled the major taphonomic process present. A trained professional of course spots these processes easily, but an advantage of getting the machine to do it is in terms of scale. It can process hundreds and thousands of pictures in mere minutes. But remember, once a neural network has learned a new domain through transfer learning, it *only* knows those categories that you have taught it, so of course it will make a prediction. Are the predictions right? Or rather, how wrong are they? This is the problem of *validation* and again, one would have to have the human remains in a lab somewhere to determine what taphonomic processes are *actually* present.

Until that happens, we do not have enough grounds to *use* this classifier to say anything about the human remains trade. But when our only evidence is a photograph, this might again be the only route we have to assess these processes. So why not build such a thing? Aside from the technical difficulties of obtaining enough training data and then validating the results, the mere existence of such a classifier could open up potential abuses ("no taphonomic processes present! 100 percent certified donated medical remains ethically sourced!"). While of course recognizing the potential for abuse, such a tool, if made user-friendly (and only available in appropriate circumstances) and trained on a sufficiently large and detailed dataset, could be useful for law enforcement and customs officials, since it could provide information about the remains in question that the trader might not be able to explain—those osteologically real but cultural fakes. The law might be porous on the actual buying and selling of human remains, but it has a lot to say about fraud.

Conclusion

We are not legal scholars, but we have recounted to the best of our understanding the nature and shape of current laws and principles. The legal situation concerning the buying and selling of human remains is complex and depends on where the vendor is located, where the buyer is located, how and across what borders are the remains shipped, the intent and state of knowledge for both the buyer and the seller about the remains, the cultural origin of the remains, and the manner in which the remains ceased to be human, becoming a mere "thing." The body of law in the English common law tradition, or even in the civil Roman law tradition has trouble understanding bones as something more than just leftovers from the process of life. Other traditions, as among the Huron-Wendat for instance, recognize that spirit remains with the bones after death (see for instance Durand 2020). (The integration of Indigenous legal traditions into English or Roman legal traditions is an area that we have not explored in this volume, but it is a concept that is gaining ground in some settler colonial societies, see e.g., Borrows 1996 and would have implications for the trade in human remains.)

If we could say something about where in the world human remains originated, or from what cultural group, or how the remains came to be something to be traded in the first place, we might be able to better understand which laws might apply, and how. It is not, contrary to what many bone vendors say, "perfectly legal!" It is complex and obfuscated, and the evidence we work with is not ideal. And to some extent, the most prolific vendors know and exploit these loopholes.

Computer vision and machine learning might enable us to say enough to cast doubt on the stories vendors tell. Photographs of human remains appear briefly on social media and disappear again once the remains are sold. A single photograph might be the only evidence of a life lived. One-shot learning holds potential for us to be able to map a landscape of sourcing or broad-strokes geographic populations. The results might be incorrect in terms of fine details but taken at a more macroscopic level as a relative positioning vis-à-vis other remains, they might be our best bet to understand the broad patterns when social media photos are all we have.

The initial experiment we summarize here and discuss in more detail in the relevant publication suggests that there might be something that can be done, if it is done ethically, carefully, and in full awareness of its limitations. It seems to us that there are grounds (and perhaps, with larger datasets and careful training, even a method) for challenging what vendors say about what they are selling. What is being sold, and the blanket statements of legality that often accompany sales, are not what they seem.

CHAPTER

5

Why Does It Matter?

"I don't care what happens to my remains after I'm dead, so I don't really see the problem," said the distinguished professor of archaeology. "That," I responded, "is precisely the problem. Other people do care about what happens to their ancestors, their relatives, their kin. And we as archaeologists need to respect that."

In this book, we have illustrated the depth and breadth of the human remains trade today as it is currently understood based on open posts and pages on a variety of social media. This trade exists in an ever-evolving sociocultural, historical, legal, and digital context. Why does it matter? It matters a great deal, because it constitutes the evidence of past social injustice, normalizes continuing injustice, and can directly relate to profiting from or obscuring the existence of crime.

You Are Closer to the Trade in Human Remains Than You Might Think

"I don't buy or sell human remains, so this doesn't really apply to me." Look at your mobile phone. It's an amazing constellation of technologies, all of which were invented at different times and places, and once were quite separate devices. Through Moore's law and advances in manufacturing, they have all merged into this one, magical thing in your pocket. And a lot of that phone—its components—find their way to you on actual blood and bone. The rare minerals inside the phone's components, for instance, come from mines in Africa, fought over in bloody conflicts and mined without regard for the safety, welfare, or liberty of the miners (Crawford and Joler 2018). But there's a connection here with the human remains trade as well.

Alexander Graham Bell and his collaborator Clarence J. Blake were working on a project trying to teach the Deaf how to speak. They were experimenting with a recently invented device called the phonautograph, a device that transmediated sound waves into the scratches of a needle onto a piece of paper covered with soot. The idea was that deaf people could see, in the scratchings, what sound looked like, then they could try to modulate their own voices and see the results, iterating closer and closer until they got to something that looked/sounded like the examples. It did not really work because the fidelity and sound quality just were not sufficient for the task. The original phonautograph, invented by the Frenchman Édouard-Léon Scott de Martinville, was directly inspired by the anatomy of the human ear. He experimented, with middling success, by using various kinds of animal skins as a tympanic membrane. Bell and Blake said, "well, why not use an actual human ear?" And so, they procured an actual human ear and its associated pieces of skull. This work directly led Bell to realize:

> I was struck with the remarkable disproportion in weight between the membrane and the bones that were vibrated by it. It occurred to me that if a membrane as thin as tissue paper could control the vibration of bones that were, compared to it, of immense size and weight, why should not a larger and thicker membrane be able to vibrate a piece of iron in front of an electro-magnet. (Quoted in Everett 2019)

Your telephone depends directly on the collection, dissection, and crafting of someone's flesh and bone onto an electrical-mechanical apparatus. Modern digital media technologies can be traced back to this moment (Everett 2019).

Maybe that is not real enough for you? Another way you are closer to the trade in human remains than you might think comes from the domain of statistics. The connections between Francis Galton, Karl Pearson, and Flinders Petrie, are well known in the history of archaeology. Galton and Pearson are the "fathers" of many statistical tests and approaches, while Flinders Petrie systematized field research in archaeology. Galton and Pearson wanted to demonstrate the scientific foundations for the Victorian world-system (where White men were on top). Petrie wanted to put archaeology onto a scientific foundation. Petrie provided the skeletal remains for Galton and Pearson, Galton and Pearson provided the math (Sheppard 2010; Challis 2016). The various statistical tests that Galton and Pearson developed are used all the time, and nobody now uses them to try to argue for racial superiority. But once we see people as things to be measured, there are always those who find that other people do not measure up. The latest incarnations of these approaches are predictive policing algorithms (see D'Ignazio and Klein 2020: 13; Angwin et al. 2016) or as we've seen, neural network image classification models trained on perceived gender, sexual orientation, or emotion. This work all ultimately rests on the foundations created by the original trade in human remains. The vendors on Instagram are in a way playing in the debris from this first moment.

What Do Human Remains *Do* for Those Who Collect Them?

Drawing on Césaire (1955), Fanon ([1961] 2002), and Mbembe (2019), Hicks (2020) argues that the ethnographic museum was a place of containment, a place where Africans could become dehumanized by being turned into things. The role of museums in particular in the institutional trade in human remains has been explored in depth by Redman (2016). Here, we want to think a bit more about what it means for every-day collectors to treat human remains as things, for one's own personal *Wunderkammer* or Do-It-Yourself Museum. A correspondent showed us a post from a bone collector Facebook group, where the person posting expressed a desire to create their very own personal museum. They framed this idea as a response to the way governments and archaeologists (in their view) hid "significant finds" from the public through a lack of funding or disinterest (which is a common trope in pseudoarchaeology; see for instance Dibble 2022). The image associated with the comment that began the thread shows a photo of an elongated skull (elongated through the practice of head binding, and thus from somewhere along the western edge of South America). Similar posts abound across multiple platforms. Leaving aside the notion that archaeologists are hiding anything, we ask, what kind of museum does this correspondent want to make? In the quotation above, the person wants to follow "correct collection procedures," in their words, but if they did that, they would not, in fact, have a museum. Our analysis of the composition of photographs from public Instagram accounts (summarized in Chapter 3) demonstrates that the platonic ideal of a "museum," as it emerges across the photographs they share, very much appears to harken back to the ethos of the ethnographic museums of the early twentieth century, and even the personal *Wunderkammer* tradition before that.

Redman (2016) discusses how many such bone rooms in museums were first put together, and the scientific racism that underpinned much of that early work. Hicks (2020) frames the emergence of the ethnographic museum as a tool of empire to justify colonization through creation of an Other that could be put safely on a shelf. It is no accident that the kind of museum that bone traders seem to emulate and desire mimics those late nineteenth-, early twentieth-century museums, and so perpetuates the ills of those museums, the racism, the colonialism, and the re-traumatization. But we will speculate that there's something else going on here, and it goes hand-in-glove with pushback against the work of repatriation in late twentieth and early twenty-first century museums.

Since the 1990s and the passing of NAGPRA in the US, attitudes towards displaying human remains have changed in US museums (and indeed across the world to a degree; see the papers in Williams and Giles 2016). This change was driven initially through having to comply with the law, and latterly by a sea-change in academic attitudes towards working with Indigenous communities. The relationship between the living and the dead in Indigenous communities is of paramount importance, but historically non-Indigenous scholars often treated Indigenous human remains as nothing more than data to pick over.

Settler-colonial scholars, administrators, and politicians approached the dead from a position grounded in Western Christianity and the Enlightenment: there is nothing in Christianity that implies that the everyday dead should be treated in any particular way, and the Enlightenment suggests a division between the mind and the world such that anything can be put on display and studied (Swain 2016). Most archaeologists now recognize that working *with* (rather than despite) descendant communities is morally and ethically the right thing to do, given the damage that our academic ancestors have done. Working with descendant communities also produces better archaeology and understanding. While NAGPRA obviously only applies to the United States, similar colonial histories have created similar kinds of conditions needing repatriation and restitution in Australia, Canada, New Zealand, South Africa, Namibia, Brazil, and many other countries besides.

In European museums and elsewhere, human remains continue to be displayed and are sometimes the subject of blockbuster exhibitions (in North America, especially if the remains are of mummies or early colonial inhabitants). We opened this section with a quote from a discussion at a conference, with an archaeologist colleague, which does encapsulate a view that remains current among a (fortunately dwindling) number of practitioners. Sometimes, such attitudes are couched in a similar paraphrase: "We didn't colonize anywhere, so why should we worry about repatriation?" (See Weiss-Krejci 2016 on Austrian attitudes towards the dead.) Stutz (2016) contrasts Scandinavian practices and attitudes towards displaying the dead, noting drily that exhibits of mummies or colonial Jamestown inhabitants in the US reflect "a different set of ethical guidelines appear to be put in motion, absolving the exhibition from the otherwise omnipresent problematization of the practice" (Stutz 2016: 286–87). Stutz also suggests that because archaeology emerges in Europe in a "nationalistic" context rather than a "colonial" context, displaying (European) human remains has thus been seen to be unproblematic. This of course ignores the display of human remains sourced from European colonies in the first place, or, as with Abraham Ulrikab and his family, from human zoos (see Chapter 1).

Many of the most prominent individuals in the bone trade (those most active on social media) are based largely in the UK, the United States, and Canada, with a second-tier based in Europe who seem to primarily trade within the EU. In this second tier, skulls from eighteenth- and nineteenth-century

Austrian ossuaries, with their gothic-script labels often fetch high prices. In Austria, it is not uncommon for cemeteries to be cleared and human remains disinterred, as there is neither a societal expectation nor a legal requirement for graves to remain in the ground (see Weiss-Krejci 2016). We have discussed earlier how much of the human remains and antiquities trades flows from source countries that suffered the effects of colonization, through the hands of people living in a context where there is no inherent recognition of the dignity or importance of ancestors to descendant communities, to consumer countries where there is currently right-wing political push-back against the gains Indigenous and First Nations groups have made in reclaiming their agency. (Even in 2022, where the evidence of thousands of deaths of children in Canada's Indian Residential Schools was *already known* from survivor testimony, and confirmed through archaeological ground-penetrating radar analysis, a major right-wing newspaper felt confident publishing op-eds that suggested these are not *really* graves of children [Kay 2022]. We will also note that there are frequently skulls and articulated skeletons of children for sale in the online markets.)

All of that to say: the creation of Do-It-Yourself-museums by some of the most well-healed and high-profile collectors appears to us to be happening in a way that tries to delegitimize Indigenous autonomy and agency over their communities and their own Ancestors. But do bone traders do this consciously?

The Power of Absences

We do not think so. We think it emerges because of what Williams and Giles (writing in the context of mortuary archaeologists and their engagement with contemporary society) call the "mnemonic and social power of . . . absences" (Williams and Giles 2016: 10). In this case, there are two sources of absence. Firstly, it is evident that the majority of human remains collectors and dealers simply do not know what they have. Bone enthusiasts might *have* some bones, but everything else is absent, and the power of that absence is that it demands their imagination to fill it. Secondly, the writings of archaeologists are not aimed at the broader population; we write for each other, we publish behind paywalls, and in the absence of accessible (in every sense) writing, people turn to the material that is available. Google "elongated skull" and you won't be met with quality academic research for the most part. Instead, you will instead learn a lot about "mysteries" that science cannot solve, and other pseudoarchaeology. Using Google Scholar might serve a search for peer-reviewed information better, but to what extent would the public know about the resource or use it? We (the archaeological community) have created this second absence through our publication practices and through a habit of not rewarding public-facing work.

The connection with pseudoarchaeology is especially pernicious. Pseudoarchaeology today often relies on archaeological theory of the late nineteenth and early twentieth century (since that is often the material most easily accessed, being out-of-copyright and abounding across the web; Card and Anderson 2016), and in those days, diffusionism was a core explanatory mechanism. The researcher looked for parallels between different cultures, and where they found them, they assumed the earlier one transmitted the idea to the latter one. These cultures were determined by looking at assemblages of material culture and deciding that patterns within these sets could be equated with a people (Siapkas 2016: 4). This essentialism was also a core tenet of scientific racism:

> The epistemological convergences between culture-historical archaeology and scientific racism resides instead in the common adherence to essentialism. That is, despite variations in detail, both culture-historical archaeology and scientific racism are founded on the assumption that people have deep-seated immutable inner traits which are articulated in their culture. Furthermore, these perspectives are also governed by the assumption that somatic traits correspond with inner characteristics. (Siapkas 2016: 6)

Pseudoarchaeology is built on a foundation of hyper diffusionism, driven to ascribe all civilization to *someone else* (be that Atlantis, Lemurians, Solutreans, or aliens). In addition to the actual racism of assuming that non-European/settler-colonial societies were not capable of the feats that archaeologists attribute to them, the assumption that everything within the non-Western past is explainable by diffusion from a lost civilization or from beyond the stars ultimately bolsters the underlying racism of holding one race to be biologically, culturally, and morally superior to others.

As a digital, modern-day, reflection of this phenomenon, the Do-It-Yourself "museums" of the wealthiest or best-networked collectors operating online and offline today, we suggest draw on whatever literature or resources are at hand that enables the trader or collector to fill the gaps, to fill the absences. The material at hand comes from archaeology's early years, and as a result of archaeology's professional, largely inward and closed, gaze. It also comes from the amplification of these views by mainstream and non-mainstream media outside of social media. Think *Ancient Aliens*, a long-running History Channel hit, for example. The stories that having a Do-It-Yourself museum enables the collector to tell themselves and tell others who come to view their prowess in person or online are echoes of this colonial epic. They allow the collector to cast themselves as the hero.

Echoes of Colonial Manliness

It would be conventional here to discuss the impact of Indiana Jones and his well-known cry, "It belongs in a museum!," but a better exemplar would be a hero who was contemporary with the emergence of archaeology and culture-historical approaches, who was contemporary with the intellectual (such as they are) foundations of pseudoarchaeology, whose imperial souvenirs might very well have ended up in those early ethnographic museums: Allan Quatermain.

Quatermain was the creation of H. Rider Haggard, writing towards the end of the nineteenth century. A big game hunter, Quatermain was the epitome of Victorian values as expressed in Britain's African colonies. Merrick Burrow (2013) explores Allan Quartermain and Haggard's work to show how masculinity is constructed in these adventures. The short answer is that this vision of nineteenth-century manliness is done through fusing the "qualities of the gentleman with those of the barbarian" (Burrow 2013: 74). The gentleman had to be capable of barbarism when out in the colonies and then show the potential for this capability at home; the key to demonstrating this barbarism upon return to Britain was via imperial souvenirs, which could be artifacts, hunting trophies, or human relics.

These souvenirs required the creation or transformation of other humans and animals into things, and then juxtaposing these in British contexts. These things become tokens of manly violence, and so their display in a civilized context demonstrates a gentleman's ability to restrain themselves in polite company, but to do whatever is necessary at any other time. Such values were communicated to the larger population through the construction of over-the-top dioramas, like Rowland Ward's "The Jungle" at the Colonial and Indian Exhibition of 1886. This spectacle was constructed from hunting trophies provided by the Prince of Wales, and it was arranged to suggest the obvious violence of life in Britain's colonies. It has been suggested that Ward's composition of the trophies was based on the diorama "Arab Courier Attacked by Lions" at the 1869 Exposition Universelle in Paris (Burrow 2013: 83). This diorama is now on display at the Carnegie Museum of Natural History in Pittsburgh; during restoration it was discovered that the head of the courier actually contains a human skull (Pellicer 2021).

The imperial souvenirs of Haggard's stories, the animal and human trophies, are familiar to readers now as *the* visual tropes of colonial fantasy (see the "hunter" character in the original Jumanji 1995 film, for instance to see how legible the trope remains). Today, these imperial souvenirs are readily findable online under the term oddities or curiosities. These *things* that Ward created are the precursors to the "art" many collectors of human remains make of the skulls and bones they trade, also labeled as oddities or curiosities. The other aspects of these tropes lie not just in what these characters do or say, but in how these characters adorn their homes in England. In Burrow's reading, the taking of souvenirs from the colonial "little wars" in which these adventures are situated, becomes a way through which the masculinity of these characters can be expressed. "Each novel constitutes a fantasy within which the protagonist's masculinity is redeemed and elevated through immersion into 'barbarian' experience within [the] 'lost' worlds in the African interior" (Burrow 2013: 75). The barbarism of the European adventurer or military administrator is not metaphorical. Denver A. Webb explores at some length the way that Victorian military theorists and officers (British in particular) constructed their identities in this manner, around ideas of barbarism and trophy hunting, and differentiating the rules of war according to whether the enemy was "civilized" or "savage" (Webb 2015: 46–48). Hicks calls this "white projection" or accusing the enemy of acts of savagery so as to excuse European acts of barbarism (Hicks 2020: 37–48; Webb 2015: 47). A trade in Xhosa heads emerged over the nineteenth century; Webb quotes one Ensign Whittle, who wrote to his father in 1847, "I have seen a [Xhosa] head for sale, I would have bought it but it was too dear so I shall wait till I can kill one myself." Later, he wrote again: "I intend trying to make some money by selling [Xhosa] heads, which are very expensive in Cape Town" (Quoted in Webb 2015: 47).

Webb goes on to draw out how war and trophy hunting were intimately linked as parts of the dominant masculine identity of the European military. Couple this identity with a rhetorical frame that casts savage enemies as subhuman, and the result was the taking of human body parts as trophies as an integral part of creating European rule in Africa (Webb 2015: 48–49).

> Skulls, ears, and testicles were also collected widely by many who professed no interest in phrenology. Such collection occurred within a culture of hunting that was a strong component of masculine identity, and where the enemy were seen as subhuman and aligned with animal attributes in military and settler discourses. Taking heads and other body parts as "trophies" was a way colonists exerted power over the Xhosa—by possessing them, literally and figuratively. It was, at least partially, an extension of the collection of mementoes. (Webb 2015: 55)

Eventually, these mementoes were transported to Britain, Germany, Belgium, and beyond, to be displayed in country houses and personal and public museums. The meaning of these nineteenth-century oddities, whether animal or human, emerges from how they are placed in relationship with each other around the houses of upper-class beneficiaries of Empire. They celebrate the manly violence done at the edges of Empire, in the name of Empire and bring them back to the domestic sphere, making it a bit more wild but successfully dominated. Buying a human skull *today* is a continuation of the imperial souvenirs of the nineteenth and early twentieth century practice—in many cases, skulls bought today might very well have originally *been* imperial souvenirs. Owning such a souvenir allows the person to participate in fantasies of control and "thingification" of people who are not White. It is the wielding of one's private museum as both status symbol and metaphorical weapon, an at-home version of what the ethnographic museums did for Empire. To buy human remains is to assert a kind of control, a kind of virile masculinity that harkens back to the "good old days," which can be read as racist as you might imagine.

To see that these tropes still have currency, we only have to look at the garb of Melania Trump while on visit to Kenya (wearing khaki trousers and a pith helmet), or the self-presentation of "Vintage Egyptologist" (VE) Colleen Darnell on Instagram, where "vintage" harkens to the 1920s and British-ruled Egypt:

> The highly curated, and professional, pictures and videos produced by VE are the result of conscientious, deliberate choices. These testify to a vision of Egyptology that is intimately tied to the reproduction of colonial imageries. (Blouin, Hanna, and Bond 2020)

Blouin, Hanna, and Bond go on to say that VE's success emerges

> *Because* it occludes: the colonial violence that, under British rule, made possible the *ideas* of Egypt and Egyptology they are celebrating; the complexity, multifaceted identity, and shifting nature of Egypt's land, peoples, and histories; and many (Egyptian, American) pasts, and presents. By doing so, it stages and celebrates a white-supremacist type of vintage Egyptology. (Blouin, Hanna, and Bond 2020)

On 13 March 2022, the *Toronto Star* (a major Canadian newspaper) published a profile of the owner of a store that sells human remains and other portable antiquities, fossils, and oddities (Percy-Beauregard 2022). The banner image? A photograph of the owner sitting on a Victorian-era stool made from an elephant's foot, the very picture of the imperial souvenir in action. The imperial souvenir allows a person to participate in fantasies of control and "thingification," a performance of the museum as a weapon, and domestication of what the ethnographic museums did for the Empire. Human remains function as tokens of manly barbarism (as Burrow 2013 calls it), and the photos on Instagram continue the duration of the original "taking" (of life, of land . . .). Photographs and their sharing enhance a particular kind of imperial masculinity for the collector. This appears to be regardless of whether the collector appears or identifies as male, female, or non-binary.

Haggard's stories demonstrate for us that the meaning of trophies shifts away from whatever they purportedly "are," to the way in which they are assembled: "in practices of public exhibition and domestic display alike, the origin of an object is displaced by the production of a general effect whose meaning is determined not by lived experience but by the aesthetics of arrangement" (Burrow 2013: 80).

A Do-It-Yourself museum assembled by a collector draws on the absences around what can be known of the remains to create a space for a personal epic of manly barbarism. It draws on pseudo-archaeological understandings of what human remains are, and what human remains do. It depends on understanding human remains not as Ancestors, not as humans, but as things that can be contained. Hicks writes,

> The Euro-American anthropology museum constitutes a further space of *containment*, in Fanon's terms, of *chosification* in Césaire's terms, of *mummification*, *statuefication* and *fetishisation* in those of Mbembe. In this transformation of life and substance museums became a key regime of practice through which Africans were dehumanised. (Hicks 2020: 180)

Indigenous peoples and First Nations in North America, Australia, New Zealand, and several other countries are actively engaged in trying to return Ancestors home from public institutions. This, to the logic of the bone trade, is intolerable because it insists on seeing human remains not as things, but as people. Again, the Do-It-Yourself museum is the resurrection of the ethnographic museum of the late nineteenth and early twentieth century. As such, it has a "chronopolitics," in that it continues the violence that turned the dead into things in the first place, a process "memorialised, through the technology of the anthropology museum" (Hicks 2020: 180; see also the film by Aïsha Azoulay, *Un-documented: Unlearning Imperial Plunder*, 2021). Instagram, as the infrastructure of these Do-It-Yourself museums, is implicated again in the colonialism that dehumanized these remains in the first place. The digital technology of photo sharing and photo finding presents us with spectacles that teach us how to view the dead, in every way similar to the great expositions of the nineteenth century that taught Europeans how to view Empire. Instagram, as a technology, works actively against the interests of repatriation.

Social Media Is the Dealer

Studying the underlying network or graph of connections gives us lenses to look at and think through the network effects of connection—that is, the core mechanics that give social media value. When you click on something on social media, you leave a little breadcrumb of metadata, an information point demonstrating interest. These breadcrumbs of metadata, when aggregated over time, device, geolocation, co-location with *other people* whether in online spaces or physical spaces (your phone keeps notes on what other phones are *nearby*), services you have agreed to, cross-referenced email addresses . . . all this information builds up a profile that is bundled with other similar profiles and bought and sold by data brokers online. When Facebook or Instagram's algorithms interact with this rich data trail, they begin to surface posts for you that other similar data profiles have shown an interest in.

Traditionally, if you were interested in purchasing antiquities or human remains, you would go through a broker or a middleman. That role has been usurped by digital media. Facebook's Groups feature will push posts into your feed from groups you do not follow: show an interest in looted antiquities, and Facebook will happily, automatically, hook you up with more groups where you can obtain antiquities directly. As Siva Viyandath (2018) put it, the problem with Facebook is Facebook. It is working correctly when it actively promotes such materials into people's feeds. Human networks on-the-ground intersect with algorithmic networks, and the effect is to supercharge the antiquities trade. The Athar Project (*athar* is Arabic for "antiquities") led by Katie Paul and Amr Al-Azm has been studying and tracking the role Facebook has been playing in the funneling of antiquities from the Middle East and North Africa (among other places, such as Thailand and Ukraine) to consumers in North America and Western Europe. By tracking the presence or absence of administrators in these groups, it is possible to generate a mapping of the interconnections of groups to groups, containing nearly two million individual accounts, spanning the globe (Paul and Al-Azm 2019).

As with antiquities, so with human remains. *Social media is the dealer.* The people who buy human remains online are participating in networks that are both *on* the web and *of* the web. Without social media platforms, the trade would be significantly smaller than it currently is. The machine will connect a person who demonstrates an interest in this material to others who are willing to sell it in a matter of seconds. But sometimes, people want to help things along, and for that, they use hashtags. And it is through hashtags that we, as outsiders, first approached the trade.

The Act of Observation

That we can spot some changes from 2017 in the discourses surrounding human remains that seem connected to our own work is in some ways heartening (see Chapter 2). But in other ways, it is troubling. When we do non-digital archaeology, the materials do not push back at us, they do not change because we are looking at them, in the way that digital materials do. Dealers that we have observed for some time now take pains to not mention explicit prices (they instead direct communications into private direct messaging applications). When we do work on the image data itself, we notice individuals overlaying text into the images to evade metadata trawls (Huffer and Graham 2018;

Huffer, Wood, and Graham 2019). The nature of the data seems to be changing because of our and others' observations and reporting.

Not only does the act of observation change that which we observe, it also triggers a kind of red-queen effect, where we have to keep modifying what we do to stay ahead of that which we study, and why replication/reproducibility is a necessary part of our work. This opens up another dimension to the ethical considerations of digital archaeology around replicability—or at least, the *reporting* of replicable research. The episode that led to our brief moment of media attention in 2019 triggered much sensational reporting. The major inflection point was when our research was paired with interviews with bone traders in *Wired* magazine (O. Schwartz 2019). After that moment, the story was repackaged and reprinted in other outlets like the UK's *The Sun*. As we tracked these iterations, our academic view was filtered, diluted, and reduced while the bone traders' perspectives continued to be showcased.

How much new traffic was pushed towards bone traders as a result? We do not believe that it is possible to quantify, since if one is interested in human remains, it is easy enough to find them on Instagram, Facebook, or elsewhere. It takes but a moment to find public and private groups on Facebook dedicated to trading human remains. Joining closed groups almost always requires appearing to have the correct sort of profile and/or satisfactorily answering the gatekeeping questions of the group's administrators—something a passingly curious individual, reading our research but not actively collecting, would likely be able to do. Whether or not someone's curiosity is sparked enough to search for human remains due to reading newspaper articles that quote us or our published work, or indeed having read this book, examples of human remains (or many other categories of) trafficking on these platforms are hiding in plain sight, and not hiding all that well. Indeed, having shown the machine such an interest, the platform's recommendation algorithms will facilitate further connections.

An article that appeared on *LiveScience.com* (Jarus 2020) quoted us and several law enforcement officials. The reporter described what he saw during several months of clandestine observing of several private human remains trading groups on Facebook (and then what happened when he approached Facebook officials). After publication, two of the largest groups at the time dedicated solely to human remains were removed. Almost immediately, however, the admins of these groups formed new ones, as did prominent collectors who had been active in the now-removed groups. In the "about" information publicly stated for these new groups, a key requirement for membership is that prices not be stated at all. Note that many other groups also exist that are older and have not markedly changed policy, save for using emojis, numbers or symbols to state prices or willingness to ship, misspelling human, and numerous other tricks. It is arguable that these slight changes of discourse in the language of the posts on both platforms reflect a greater concern for the apparent legality of the trade than there once perhaps was.

What We Have Learned

The trade in human remains is growing substantially each time we look, even if dealers are moving the actual financial details or transactions to more private services that cannot be studied. The trade in human remains transitions from one platform to the next, when terms-of-service change, or are enforced. Dealers make ready use of the affordances of the platforms both as advertising and to promote the trade as morally neutral (or even, a net positive, "saving" material for study). Some platforms enable push back and engagement in ways that other platforms do not, and on these platforms, we can see scholars and students and other members of the public leveraging the affordances of the platform to address the harms and ethics of the trade directly. People who pushback on the trade compose their videos and photographs in ways that visually oppose traders.

Vendors can often be quite cagey in their use of language to signal when something is for sale. Vendors and enthusiasts visually compose their photographs in ways that suggest both the conscious and unconscious need to demonstrate authority through appropriating a very particular moment in museology and public display of the dead. A kind of *digital* colonialism is at play. Networks of taste formation and visual influence can be discerned and identified through computer vision cross-referenced with the metadata in posts and photographs, which helps to homogenize the visual language of the trade.

It may be possible in broad strokes to identify patterns of visual dissimilarities that speak to the population affinity of human remains (skulls) in photographs. There are historical and, via computer vision and neural networks, analytical reasons to believe that a portion of the human remains being bought and sold *and marketed* as being obtained legally are actually of Indigenous peoples. Many human remains on the market are osteologically real but culturally fake, having been modified to meet a perceived desire for remains from particular cultures. There is a panoply of laws that make it (on paper) very difficult to buy, sell, and transport human remains, but these are not widely enforced (with most vendors assuming that as long as human remains in the United States are not obviously of Indigenous origin, they are fair game).

The tools that we have used to study this trade are powerful but could also have unintended side effects of legitimizing or authenticating remains, and so critical ethical engagement must be foregrounded at every step. Publishing most of our research as open access work has made our research and our findings better known than perhaps they might otherwise have been (especially outside of academia), but this might also have had an effect of changing the way vendors do business. It has certainly led to our work being mentioned in popular media, but sometimes when newspapers and media pick up these initial items, reprinting and reworking the story, we see our voice diminished with each iteration, while the messaging of the bone traders remains loud and clear.

Connections with Other Kinds of Illicit Trades

Earlier, we said that "social media is the dealer." The patterns that we observe with regard to human remains are also present on social media across all manner of illicit and illegal goods and services. In 2018, this led us to come together with an alliance of researchers and activists, all concerned with the unintended consequences of Section 230 of the Communications Decency Act in the United States, to found the *Alliance to Counter Crime Online* (www .counteringcrime.org). By sharing our research, we are starting to see the interconnections between platform affordances and techniques of exploiting these platforms across a myriad of areas of concern. The more that we understand the human remains trade at scale and how it relates to other categories of trafficking, the more we can provide the intelligence that law enforcement needs when it seizes and investigates cases. Ultimately, we all seek to restore as much dignity to the dead as we can by taking them off the market (and, wherever possible, disrupting the market while we do it). They have already been reduced to things several times since they died; we hope our work can help to return them to the status of Ancestors.

We also believe that the work we discuss here, and future work to come, is crucial given how relatively understudied the human remains trade is compared to other categories of antiquities trafficking (and indeed most research and law enforcement time and effort devoted to illicit trafficking focuses on wildlife, drugs, weapons, and child sexual assault material). Even though we have only really begun to investigate today's online bone trade, it has already become clear that it really is the story that sells the skeleton, and that law enforcement, prosecutors, descendant communities, and all other stakeholders need to know the right story and need to use every tool available to do so.

As traditional markets for art, antiquities, and "oddities" continue to grapple with where to draw the line between legality and desire, peer pressure and one's personal ethical boundaries, what we have learned especially is that the human remains trade occupies a special place within this milieu. No one, not us nor collectors nor dealers deny that these were people once. The question is, what are they now? Are they still people, still Ancestors? We say, yes. In which case, to actively participate in this trade really seems to require a much higher degree of cognitive dissonance than many other categories of antiquities collecting. It is a special kind of living person who can thing-ify (Yates 2022) the deceased and their parts, or on the other hand, proclaim to cherish and learn from their collection as caretakers while ignoring or downplaying how and why most remains entered the market in the first place.

What You Can Do

The current pandemic has had some minor effect on the trade in human remains. Many of the larger vendors represent themselves as idealized small businesses, a kind of anchor on a traditional Main Street, a Mom-and-Pop operation just trying to make a living selling bones to pay the bills. Such posts are a very small percentage of the overall volume, but are interesting, rhetorically, for the moves that they are making. One states that they will "remove pieces from the website once we reopen," which implies that they do not really see the online aspect of this trade as central to their own practice. Other similar posts talk of selling off "prized pieces" to make ends meet. Still others gloat that with more people working online during the pandemic, there will be more opportunities to sell to new customers—or to *create* new customers. Many of the posts in this vein carry a #supportlocal hashtag, in conjunction with tags or phrases like "medically prepared," "research quality," or "ethically sourced" to remove the whiff of something morally unsound. The sense created is that these sellers are gosh-darned aw-shucks pillars of the community, working hard to make a living. If you encounter this sort of thing, what should you do?

If you encounter human remains at a flea market or antique store, casually inquire about them and then mentally record as much information as possible, such as price, general number and condition of remains for sale, and any other information the vendor might offer (true or not). Importantly, it is best to not arouse too much suspicion or ask too many pointed questions regarding source or legality. Those are questions that can come only during the course of a professional investigation. Asking such questions might cause the vendor to end the conversation prematurely.

When human remains are encountered online, remember that social media companies themselves are reticent to enforce their own community standards when it comes to human remains (but see Jarus 2020 for developments as far as Facebook is concerned). Remember that the legal landscape at all levels is uneven and complex (see Chapter 4). If the remains are encountered for sale online, whether in public or private social media pages administered by individuals, businesses, or groups, or on e-commerce platforms, the first step should be to take thorough screen-captures of the post itself, including group and individual poster URLs, all associated metadata (such as the number of likes and shares and who liked and shared), and the number of individuals who commented on the post, including their individual page URLs and the nature of the comment. On a Mac, a screenshot can be captured by pressing the shift, cmd, and 4 keys at the same time; the mouse will turn into a crosshair and you can then click and drag to define the area of the screen you wish to capture. On a Windows machine, you can either press the PrtScn key, or press the Windows key and the G key, or search for the "Snipping Tool" from the Start menu.

If you have a degree of technical ability, you might try to turn the relevant page into a web archive file (also known as a WARC file). These are something like zip files, and once created will contain all of the necessary pieces to rec-reate a website without having to load it from the internet. There are a variety of ways of doing this, but one way is to use the Webrecorder app for a desktop (https://webrecorder.net/tools).

The next step is to make backup copies of all records and then reach out to relevant authorities to the extent possible in one's location. This can include contacting one's local police precinct, Medical Examiner's office, museum curators (in those instances in which a museum with anthropological/oste-ological collections exists in your area), or University faculty or researchers in forensic anthropology, osteoarchaeology, or related disciplines who them-selves might be well-connected to various state and Federal level law enforce-ment agents who can investigate matters further. In many instances, the phone numbers or email addresses of relevant individuals can be found online. Given that professionals cannot be in all places at once, it is increasingly crucial that the monitoring of this trafficking and the damage it does becomes a shared responsibility, one in which the public can begin to feel invested in helping to end the exploitation of the bodies of Ancestors, and of humanity's shared heritage.

You might wish to engage with people buying and selling human remains on various platforms. We would suggest you think carefully about your own security and safety before doing this. We are two white North American ac-ademics. What we are able to do and say online is not the same for every-one else. We would suggest reading "A DIY Guide to Feminist Cybersecurity" (https://hackblossom.org/cybersecurity/) to be aware of some of the issues one might face. On the other hand, some platforms are designed for the kind of engagement that *can* change minds and push back. With regard to TikTok, if you feel so moved and safe enough to do so:

- Compose response videos that are calm and collected in tone, that high-light the issues.
- Engage in the comments to provide the hooks on which counter narra-tives can be hung.

- Use strategies of peer-to-peer learning to discuss contentious material in a way that removes the oxygen from the original post.
- Look up the laws in one's own jurisdiction and when appropriate/safe, draw attention to these in the comments.
- Make it easy for TikTokers to find other good quality information to draw on. Publish open-access research and/or point to that research in the comments (and if discussing a TikTok video on another platform that permits it, link directly to the research).
- Leverage the power of peer-to-peer learning; support students and colleagues who engage on the platform.

Conclusion

Here at the end, we offer a final plea: do not buy human remains online. Do not buy human remains offline. Tell everyone you know who might be considering it that to participate in this trade is to continue the cycles of violence that turned people into things in the first place, including the rhetorics of white supremacy and pseudoarchaeology that continue to support it. Participating in the trade fosters demand and vendors will meet that demand. While there are many human remains already circulating in the market, new thefts from ossuaries, churches, abandoned or poorly guarded graveyards, and archaeological sites continue (see for instance Chandler 2018), even within those Western countries that serve as epicenters of demand today and in the past. Removal of remains from archaeological contexts destroys the relationships from which knowledge of the past is constructed. Removal of human remains breaks relationships between the living and the dead. Some vendors will modify the skull to increase its sale value. Some vendors will traffic in archaeological and ethnographic remains, which is also cultural property theft. Encourage local authorities to step in and try to identify the appropriate descendant communities.

The skulls and bones we see online are not things. They were people, their remains bought and sold, often far from where they lived, and where they should be allowed to rest.

They were people: Abraham Ulrikab. Ulrike. Sara. Maria. Tobias. Tigianniak. Paingu. Nuggasak. Mangi Meli.

They *remain* people.

A

A Walk-through of the InstagramCLI Python Package

Collecting data from social media is not easy. There are ethical, logistical, and legal concerns. We provide this appendix to show one way that one could collect hashtag metadata from Instagram, from the information Instagram provides whenever you visit a page. It is entirely possible that by the time you read this, this information or elements of it will be out of date. It is provided for educational purposes; use at your own risk.

If you go to any Instagram account—let's say the Instagram account for Ottawa's professional hockey team, the Senators (https://www.instagram.com/senators/) you'll be presented with the familiar Instagram layout—a banner with an avatar image, the number of posts, number of followers, following, perhaps some more links, and then a grid of photos. But there's more information available than what meets the eye.

In the address bar of your browser, append: /?__a=1&__d=1 (that's two underscores between the ? and the a, and two underscores between the & and the d) so that the full address reads: https://www.instagram.com/senators/?__a=1&__d=1 and hit enter. Depending on your browser, the browser will reload and you'll either see a mass of text that looks something like this:

```
"seo_category_infos":[["Beauty," "beauty"],["Dance &
Performance," "dance_and_performance"],["Fitness,"
"fitness"],["Food & Drink," "food_and_drink"],["Home
& Garden," "home_and_garden"],["Music," "music"],
["Visual Arts," "visual_arts"]], "logging_page_id":
"profilePage_306267297"
```

Or a series of headings with dropdown arrows beside them, looking something like this:

```
seo_category_infos              [. . .]
logging_page_id                 "profilePage_306267297"
show_suggested_profiles         false
show_follow_dialog              false
graphql                         {. . .}
toast_content_on_load           null
show_view_shop                  false
profile_pic_edit_sync_props     {. . .}
always_show_message_button_
to_pro_account                  false
```

What you are seeing are the *metadata* that Instagram loads up behind every page it displays to you. The interaction of this metadata with the code that governs the layout and styling of the page is what eventually makes the page you normally see. The metadata are arranged as a *graph*. That is to say, instead of tables connected to each other by primary keys (as in a "regular" database), the information that Instagram holds is represented like a *network* where there are nodes and edges. If you click on the dropdown beside "graphql," and continue to dive into the data, you'll start to see headings (nodes) like "edge_media_to_ caption"—every time the Senators add a new photograph, a new link (edge) is drawn to their account from that photo. Information is added as properties to that edge describing things like comments, captions, the url to the photo, and so on.

When we talk about scraping metadata, we mean that we speed up the process of paging through this underlying data that Instagram provides. Instagram *used* to provide a lot more data through a more formal process (using an open API or "application programming interface," a way of actually requesting data), but they turned that off years ago (unless you're a business willing to pay them for access to the data).

Now, if you are interested in following our process, you will need to configure your computer with some software, and you should also create a "dummy" account for Instagram, so as not to affect your regular Instagram experience. (The IP address of your machine can be tracked and blocked if you're not careful. We encourage you to read "A DIY Guide to Feminist Cybersecurity" at https://hackblossom.org/cybersecurity/ for a number of general issues to take into account before you embark on any of this kind of research.)

Step One. Install Python on your machine from Anaconda or Miniconda, selecting Python 3.

You will need Python installed on your machine. Macs come with Python 2.7 installed by default, but you will need Python 3. There are a variety of ways of doing this, but we will suggest you use the Anaconda distribution, available at: https://www.anaconda.com/distribution/#download-section.

We recommend Anaconda because it also comes with a wide variety of tools to make data science work easier; an alternative is Miniconda if you don't want the extras of the full Anaconda installation: https://docs.conda.io/en/latest/miniconda.html.

Another advantage of Anaconda and Miniconda is that installing them allows you to use the `conda` command to create environments or install additional helper Python packages (more on this in a moment).

Step Two. Create a new environment for your data collection.

Now, when you are working with Python, you can think of it as being a bit like working with Lego building blocks. These "legos" are called "packages" and different packages make doing different tasks much easier. Unfortunately, there can sometimes be conflicts *between* packages, so we avoid this by creating "environments" for doing different tasks. On our machines, we have environments just for collecting data, and environments for doing neural network image similarity work, and environments for doing text analysis. An "environment" is actually nothing more complex than a folder with all of the various Python bits and pieces for your task collected together *and an injunction to your machine to only use those bits and pieces while the environment is "activated."*

We're now going to use the `conda` command to create a new environment *just* for collecting Instagram metadata. If you are on a Mac, open the spotlight search and type in "terminal." On a windows machine, search for "Anaconda Command Prompt" (n.b. this is different than just "Command Prompt," which is another program. **When we say "command prompt" hereafter, we mean the *Anaconda command prompt***). The "terminal" or the "command prompt" are programs that allow you to interact with your computer by typing in commands (rather than by clicking on icons as you're no doubt most used to). By convention, when there is a command for you to run in the terminal or at the command prompt, we signal this by the use of the $ sign—you do not type the $, just the things that come after.

Run this command:

```
$ conda create -n scrape python=3.8
```

When the machine asks if you want to install the packages, select y. Your machine is now downloading and arranging all of the bits and pieces for a new environment called `scrape`. If you need to recall the names of environments you've created, you can get the list with:

```
$ conda env list
```

Step Three. Activate the environment you just created.

The `conda activate` command will tell your machine that you want it to understand that any Python it hereafter runs should come from the environment you just created. The complete command in this case is:

```
$ conda activate scrape
```

When you're finished working, you can set things back to normal with $ conda deactivate.

Step Four. Install the package for working with Instagram into your environment.

We're going to use a package created and maintained by Suyash Jawale, called "InstagramCLI." The code is made available through the "Python Package Index," https://pypi.org. (You can also find its source code at https://github.com/suyashjawale/InstagramCLI, if you wish to have a look.) Run this code at your terminal or command prompt (but remember, do not type in the $ symbol!):

```
$ pip install InstagramCLI
```

This is going to enable us to write some code to grab the underlying metadata that we are interested in.

Step Five. Write our code!

Python code is just a text file, which conventionally uses `.py` as the extension (extensions just tell your machine what kind of program is used to open the file, so here, Python). You can write code then in any text editor. We use Atom (https://atom.io) or Sublime Text 3 (https://www.sublimetext.com/3). **Do not use** Word, wordpad, or notepad; these add hidden codes and characters that will interfere.

Open your editor and create a new empty file. Into it, write the following code (**without the line numbers!**):

```
1 from InstagramCLI import InstagramCLI
2 hashtag="tag-of-interest"
3 this_many=10
4
5 # go scrape
6
7 cli = InstagramCLI(username="USERNAME,"
password="PASSWORD")
8 data= cli.get_hashtags(hashtag_name=hashtag,save_
urls=True,save_to_device=False,tag_count=this_
many,hashtag_type="recent")
9
10 # save as json
11 cli.close()
```

Change `tag-of-interest` to whatever you're interested in, keeping the quotations but without using a # symbol. Where it says USERNAME and PASSWORD, use the username and password for the account you created for this process.

Note where it says `save_to_device=False`. This means, "don't download the images/videos." If you change this to `True`, it will save the media, and write all of the metadata to file once all of the media are downloaded. Change `this_many=10` to the upper maximum of material you want to select but be careful: too much, too quickly, can get your account blocked.

Save your file via the `save as` dialogue, and make sure to save it with .py at the end, e.g., `tagscrape.py`. **Save this file into a dedicated folder for this experiment and make a note of its location on your machine (e.g., the full file path/address).**

In general, when you run code, sometimes you might get an error to the effect that there is a missing module. If you do, search for the module's name. Most times, all that has gone wrong is that there is a package that your code uses that isn't currently in your environment, and you can rectify this by running $ `pip install put_name_of_module_here`. You could also try $ `conda install put_name_of_module_here`.

Step Six. Run your code.

We now have to make sure that the terminal/command prompt is open in the same location as where you saved your tagscrape.py program.

There are a couple of ways of doing this. If you know the full file path to that folder (on our machine, it's called "scrape-experiment"), you can use the `cd` (change directory) command to do it, like so (your exact path or the sequence of folders and subfolders will be slightly different, of course):

`$ cd /Users/username/Documents/scrape-experiment` on a Mac;

`$ cd C:\Users\username\documents\scrape-experiment` on a Windows machine.

On Windows, use the file explorer to find the exact path; click through until you have the folder you want to work on displayed in the explorer. Then, click on the address bar. It will change so that you see the full path (starting with C:\ etc). Copy this. In the Anaconda command prompt, type `cd` and then paste the path (with ctrl + v). Hit enter; you're now in the correct location. Now run `$ conda activate scrape` to turn on that environment for that instance of the command prompt window. On a Mac, you can also set the preferences of the finder window so that you can see the full path for a folder, and enable the right-click option "services -> new terminal at folder." Then you'd run the conda activate command again as well, for the same reason.

You can make sure that you're in the right location by running the `$ pwd` command (on Mac) or the `$ chdir` command (on Windows). This will print out the full path of the folder you are in. You can also check to make sure your tagscrape.py program is present in a folder by using the `$ dir` command on Windows, and the `$ ls` command on Mac. **And now, the big moment: run your program with `$ python tagscrape.py`.**

If your program is set to download the media, via your file explorer/finder you'll see images and videos begin to fill up your folder. If you're only down-loading the metadata (which is much faster), you'll see a new file created using your hashtag, with the json file extension (this will also appear if you're down-loading media too, once all the media are downloaded). That's your metadata! You *will* get an email instantly from Instagram alerting you to a new login to your account from "Chrome Mobile on Google Pixel 2"; you might not have such a device, but that's what InstagramCLI looks like to Instagram.

A json file is another kind of text file, where all of the information is ar-ranged in key-value pairs, just like we saw when we first were looking at the Ottawa Senators' Instagram account. This can be a useful format if you're do-ing other kinds of computational analysis. You can open this file using your text editor. You might find it easier to parse using a spreadsheet, and so to convert it to csv format (which is a text file where the information is arranged in columns, separated by commas), we often use https://www.convertcsv.com/ json-to-csv.htm. You can open the csv in Excel or some other spreadsheet program. (Some readers might want to check out what can be accomplished with OpenRefine, which can work happily with json or csv files; see Dougherty and Ilyankou [2022] for an introduction at https://handsondataviz.org/open-refine.html.) The InstagramCLI package that we have just walked you through using can also collect other kinds of information from the basic metadata that Instagram provides. If you consult the Github page, you'll see example code that will work for other situations.

B

A Walk-through of the PixPlot Python Package

In this walk-through, we use the PixPlot package from the Yale DH Lab to visualize the similarity of images, using a neural network.

The Yale DH Lab has written and bundled together all of the code necessary to run thousands of images through a neural network trained for image recognition from Google. But instead of putting labels on the images, the code looks at how each image causes the neural network to light up in different ways (as a list of numbers, or scores, along each dimension that the neural network looks at). The mathematical distance between each list can be measured, and the result can be visualized using various clustering algorithms. You can visit http://pixplot.yale.edu/v2/loc/ to see for yourself the result (in this case, over 24,000 images from the George Grantham Bain Collection at the Library of Congress). The source code is available at https://github.com/YaleDHLab/pix-plot and a description of the entire process (before it was bundled into PixPlot) by Douglas Duhaime is available at https://douglasduhaime.com/posts/identifying-similar-images-with-tensorflow.html.

Step One. Set up a new environment.

Using what you learned in Appendix A, create a new folder, open the terminal/command prompt there, and create a new environment with Python 3.7. Let's call it `viz-sim`:

```
$ conda create -n =viz-sim python=3.7
$ conda activate viz-sim
```

(Notice that we're using a different version of Python in this environment.)

Step Two. Install PixPlot.

You can install everything PixPlot needs like this:

```
$ pip uninstall pixplot
$ pip install https://github.com/yaledhlab/pix-plot/
archive/master.zip
```

(The first command, to "uninstall" something we haven't installed yet, is a habit to just make sure everything is clean and ready to go.)

Step Three. Analyze and create the visualization.

Let's assume you have a folder of images somewhere on your machine. Find the complete path (location) of those images. You can do this using the file explorer or finder on your Windows/Mac machine. The command to enter at the terminal/command prompt is:

```
$ pixplot --images "path/to/images/*.jpg"
```

So if we had images on a Mac at this location: /Users/username/Docu ments/images-to-analyze/, the command would be

```
$ pixplot --images "/Users/username/Documents/
images-to-analyze/*.jpg"
```

If on a PC we had images at this location:

```
C:\Users\SGComputer\Documents\images-to-analyze
```

The command would be:

```
$pixplot --images "C:\Users\SGComputer\images-to-
analyze\*.jpg"
```

The asterisk at the end means, "every file that has a .jpg extension."

PixPlot will run its analysis, creating subfolders in the location where you're working. It will also build a website for you, and arrange the data and results appropriately, into a subfolder called "output."

Step Four. Examine the results.

Python comes with a built-in webserver. That means if you have all of the files for a website on your machine, Python's webserver can load those up so that your browser interprets the code correctly and displays the results as if you were loading up html from the web. At the command prompt, let's turn on the server:

```
$ python -m http.server 5000
```

That "5000" is a port; think of it like a channel that your browser will have to tune to, to "hear" the results. In your web browser, go to this location: http://localhost:5000/output.

To stop the server, hit ctrl+c in the command prompt/terminal. If you wish to have your visualization provide additional metadata on the images, see the "Adding Metadata" section of the PixPlot repository at https://github.com/YaleDHLab/pix-plot#adding-metadata.

Congratulations, you're now able to take a distant look at patterns of visual similarity in your materials. Look at the automatic "hotspots" in the centers of the largest clusters that PixPlot finds. What unites them? What makes them different? Pan from one cluster to another—what seems to account for the spatial change? These observations might provide you with new insights about visual tropes, patterns in composition, maybe even change over time or the spread of visual influence from early creators to later ones.

C

Text Analysis with Python and Jupyter

What large-scale patterns are present in the language of the posts you collected? This walk-through will demonstrate two approaches you might use.

At this point, you now have a lot of material you can work with. We will use two separate techniques to look for these patterns: "word vectors," and "topic models." There is a lot of information out there on how precisely these two techniques work, but the short answer is, the first imagines that words are laid out on a landscape, and words that "go together" are found in closer proximity. The second imagines that writers write by picking words out of x number of separate buckets, and so knowing the number of buckets, we can decompose a text probabilistically to those buckets to see what's in them. (On word vectors, see for instance Ryan Heuser's 2016 series of blog posts, at https://ryanheuser .org/; on topic models, see Melanie Walsh's interactive textbook on cultural analytics and the section on topic modeling at https://melaniewalsh.github.io/ Intro-Cultural-Analytics/05-Text-Analysis/05-Topic-Modeling.html.)

In Appendix A we wrote our own program and ran it. In this appendix we will show you how to create a computational "notebook" where you will be able to scrape information, and then explore linguistic patterns within the captions that you've scraped. In a computational notebook, we interact with Python through a page in our browser. We can add "code blocks" for Python and add "comment blocks" where we can annotate what we are doing, comment on the results, ask ourselves questions, and so on. Any code block can be run by selecting it and hitting the "run" icon, but it's generally a good idea, when you're starting out, to run the blocks in sequence. Think of it like a cake recipe. If you did steps 1 to 5, and then jumped back to step 3, then step 7, your cake would be pretty . . . awful. Computational notebooks are broadly similar in that regard. If this is your first foray into them, just remember that you start at the beginning and work your way to the end. For an excellent introduction to Jupyter notebooks, see Dombrowski (2019; https://programminghistorian .org/en/lessons/jupyter-notebooks).

This will make more sense in a moment.

Step One. Install and start a Jupyter notebook.

In Appendix A you created an environment called "scrape." Open your terminal/command prompt in the folder you were working in (the one that contains your "tagscrape.py" program, though we won't be using that program this time) and activate your environment. At the command prompt, run

```
$ conda install jupyter
```

Once that has installed, you can start up the notebook with

```
$ jupyter notebook
```

"Jupyter" is an amalgamation of "julia," "python," and "r," which are three different programming languages. You can use Jupyter with a wide variety of languages, but we'll use just Python for now. Your browser will open and the address in the address bar will be `localhost:8888/tree`. Since you started this from the folder you had been working in before, the page will display a list of the files and any subfolders in that location.

At the right-hand side, there is a dropdown menu labeled `new`. Select that, then choose "Python 3" from the dropdown menu.

A new page will open, with an empty notebook. You can click on where it says "Untitled" to give it a filename. The cursor will be blinking inside an empty code block. The code block also has a dark outline to indicate that it's the *active* code block. Finally, notice the tool bar with its "Run" button, the "Stop" button (a black square), and a dropdown that currently says "Code." If you change that to "markdown," the first code block will become a text block where you can write your comments and observations. There is also a "save" icon in that tool bar. While the notebook will autosave, do save it periodically. The tool ribbon also has a + icon and a scissors icon. The plus icon will add a new code block, while the scissors will cut the highlighted block.

Step Two. Install the packages we'll need.

For technical reasons related to how Jupyter works, we're going to install packages from within the notebook to make sure that the notebook knows exactly where to find them, rather than how you did it in the other walk-throughs. Into the first code block, write this code:

```
import pandas as pd
import csv
import json
```

```
import sys
!{sys.executable} -m pip install InstagramCLI
!{sys.executable} -m pip install gensim
!{sys.executable} -m pip install pyLDAvis
```

Then, hit the "Run" button. The [ ] at the left hand side of the code block will change to [*] to show that the code is running; when it is finished it will change to [1] to show that this block was the first block that ran.

The pandas package makes working with tabular data a bit easier; Instagram-CLI is our old friend for recovering metadata from Instagram, gensim will allow us to do the text analysis, and pyLDAvis will enable us to visualize the results in a way to facilitate exploration. The "csv" and "json" packages let us work with those file formats. The "sys" package enables us to do the pip install commands such that those packages are in the correct places. We do not need sys for json and csv since those ones are "baked in" to the generic Python 3 installation.

Step Three. Obtain some data and put it into a dataframe.

Hit the + button to make a new code block underneath the one that just ran. (By the way, you can shift a block up or down by selecting it—clicking on it—and then hitting the up or down arrows in the tool bar.) Add the following code, which should look familiar:

```
from InstagramCLI import InstagramCLI
hashtag="humanskullsforsale"
this_many=100
```

Run that code block. Since you are only declaring variables (that is, creating them and putting information into them), it will almost instantly change from [ ] to [2].

Add another code block. Into this block, put:

```
1 cli = InstagramCLI(username="username,"
password="password")
2 data= cli.get_hashtags(hashtag_name=hashtag,save_
urls=True,save_to_device=False,tag_count=this_
many,hashtag_type="recent")
3 cli.close()
```

(Ignore line numbers. Remember, since we're trying to put quite a long line of code into the confines of a printed book, there is no line break after save_;

that particular line ends with `hashtag_type="recent"`. We numbered the lines above to make that clearer.)

Change "username" and "password" to whatever you use (but again, use a burner account). Run this block. Underneath the code block you'll shortly start seeing messages about `Initiating`, `Authenticating` and so on, culminating with `Saved: humanskullsforsale_hashtag/humansk ullsforsale_recent_hashtag.json`. The [ ] will change to [*] while the code is running, and to [3] once it's finished.

Add another code block. Into this block, put:

```
with open(str(hashtag)+'_hashtag/'+str(hashtag)+'_
recent_hashtag.json', 'r') as f:
    filedata = json.loads(f.read())

df = pd.json_normalize(filedata, record_path =
['image'])

df.to_csv(str(hashtag)+'_hashtag/'+str(hashtag)+'_
recent_hashtag.csv')
```

Notice how the word "filedata" is indented underneath the line that began `with open`. In Python, indentation matters. You can *either* use the space bar to indent, or the tab key to indent, *but not both*. The first line of code is opening that json file we just saved and reading it into a new variable called "filedata." The next line of code is reading that json file into a table (or "data-frame," hence "df") but grabbing the data that exists within the "key" called "image" (see Appendix A about how Instagram organizes its metadata). The third line writes the df "to_csv." (Whenever you see a variable that you've created followed by a period, the command after the period is applied to the variable.) Now you have a copy of the data in a handy tabular format as well, for safekeeping.

Step Four. Preprocess the text from the captions to prepare for text analysis.

Add another code block. Into this code block we are going to import some of the functions or modules from Gensim that will allow us to preprocess the text. This preprocessing will remove "stop words" (the little words like "the," "and," "of" that occur very frequently in English but do not help our present, macroscopic analysis) and stem the words so that forms of a word are all considered tokens of the same word.

```
from gensim.parsing.preprocessing import preprocess_
string
df['new_caption'] = df.caption.apply(preprocess_
string)
```

Note: you should have two lines of code. Run that code block. The first line here loads up the gensim code to clean up our text. The second line says, "take the column of data containing our captions and preprocess it, and then create a new column of data called "new_caption" into which write the list of tokens.

If you'd like to see the result, add a new code block and put into it:

```
df
```

And run it. The notebook will give you a view of the first and last few rows, and the first and last few columns. If you scroll the result to the right, you'll see how the caption has been turned into a list of words in the new column.

Step Five. Word vectors.

Now we're going to use gensim to create a "word vector" model. This is a model that imagines words occupying a kind of two-dimensional spectrum, where words that are used more similarly in your source documents are closer together. Thus "river" and "bank" will turn up very close to one another in a model trained on a series of poems about summer holidays but very far apart in a model trained on a series of articles from the *Wall Street Journal*. In a new code block, we can do this in a single line of code after we tell it which extra bits from gensim we'll need:

```
from gensim.models import Word2Vec,KeyedVectors

wv_model = Word2Vec(sentences=df['new_caption'],
sg=0, min_count=10, workers=4, window =3, epochs =
20)
```

Run that code. It will take a bit of time before the [*] changes to signal that the operation has completed.

We're creating a model called "wv_model." We use the Word2Vec command to tell it to use the preprocessed text from the new_caption column. The other options are all "hyperparameters" that define how the model works (technically, we're using the "continuous bag-of-words" or CBOW approach. A search for "gensim cbow word2vec" will provide ample background on how this works and how you might tune it further).

Now let's see the result! We can ask the model for the words most similar to a target word. This can give us a sense of how words are being phrased. Try this—add a new block, and put this code in it:

```
wv_model.wv.most_similar("bone")
```

You'll be presented with a list of words, and a measurement (between 0 and 1) of their similarity. If a word isn't present in the model, you'll get an error; just change the word between the quotation marks and try again. Word vectors also let you explore the concept of "word analogies," where you can create lists of words to represent different concepts, and then by adding or subtracting those lists from other concepts, get a sense of how words are being used in your original data. Search for "word analogies gensim" for more information.

Step Six. Topic models.

Finally, let's create a model of the different topics to be found in our data. Create a new code block, and place this code into it:

```
import gensim
from gensim import corpora
dictionary = corpora.Dictionary(df['new_caption'] )

bow_corpus = [dictionary.doc2bow(text) for text in
df['new_caption'] ]
```

Here, "bow" means "bag of words," which we originally called "buckets." The first line here tells the notebook that we want the "corpora" set of tools from gensim. The next line uses those tools to create a matrix to represent all of the individual tokens and their frequencies, from the new_caption column.

Run that code block.

Now we'll actually create a topic model, using the "latent Dirichlet allocation" approach. We'll initially make a guess of fifteen topics. Make a new code block, and place this code into it:

```
ldamodel = gensim.models.ldamodel.LdaModel(bow_
corpus, num_topics=15, id2word = dictionary,
passes=20)

for index, topic in ldamodel.show_topics(formatted=
False, num_words=10):
    print('Topic: {} \nWords: {}'.format(index,
    [w[0] for w in topic]))
```

Run that code; once the [*] disappears, you will have a trained topic model ready to visualize! The second line of code loops through the complete list of topics and prints out the topics from most prominent to least, and then lists the top ten most prominent words in each topic. Note that the word "print" is indented to show that it is part of the loop.

To visualize the model, we invoke the pyLDAvis command, and tell it explicitly we're using a model built with gensim. Make a new code block and place this into it:

```
import pyLDAvis.gensim_models

pyLDAvis.enable_notebook()
vis = pyLDAvis.gensim_models.prepare(ldamodel, bow_
corpus, dictionary)
vis
```

Run that code. After a few moments (and perhaps a warning from Python about labels eventually being keyword-only, which we can ignore), an interactive visualization will appear in your notebook (Figure A.1). The left-hand side uses principle components analysis to show the relative size of the different topics and their relative similarity. Where topics overlap, perhaps we have selected too many topics in num_topics. If you mouse-over the various topics, the list of keywords and their relative contribution to the topic will change on the right.

For instance, in our data, there is a topic where the top words are "wunderkammern, darkinterior, cabinetdecuriosit, exotica, humanbonesforsaleuk."

There is no "right" number of topics; you can go back to the code block where we defined num_topics=15 and change that number, then rerun that code block. A new topic model will be created, and you can then rerun the visualization to see the results. Alternatively, you can add a new code block, and create a new topic with a new name:

```
ldamodel_2 = gensim.models.ldamodel.LdaModel(bow_
corpus, num_topics=7, id2word = dictionary, passes
=20)
vis2 = pyLDAvis.gensim_models.prepare(ldamodel_2,
bow_corpus, dictionary)
vis2
```

And run it so that you can compare the two models. If you wanted a third one, you could copy that block and change the 2 to a 3.

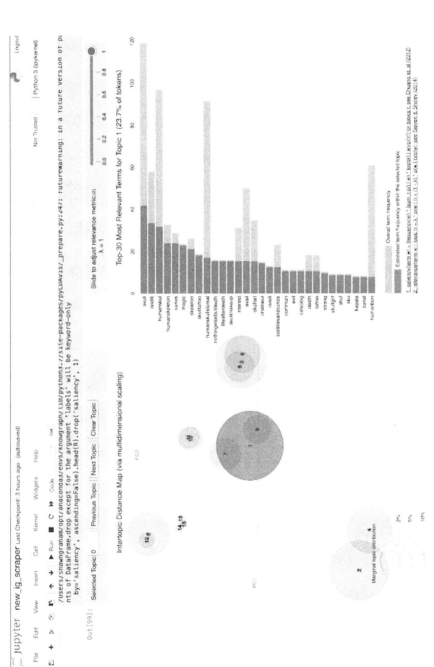

Figure A.1. A screenshot of the visualization of topic model distances using pyLDAvis. CC-BY 4.0.

Note that topic models are probabilistic, and so will be slightly different, even if you start from the same data.

If you'd like to see which topic is most prominent for which document, we can do that with this code block:

```
array_length = len(bow_corpus)

for i in range(array_length):
    print(i, ldamodel.get_document_topics(bow_
    corpus[i],minimum_probability=0.8))
```

The results will print out a list where the first row is labeled something like: 0 [(3, 0.958234]. This means the first post in our corpus of Instagram posts (document 0) has a caption that is 95% composed from Topic 3.

Happy exploring!

One more thing—your notebook autosaves periodically, but make sure to explicitly save it via the save button (or file -> download as -> notebook .ipynb). To shut everything down, close the browser tabs that are open, and then at the command prompt/terminal hit ctrl+c, and select "y" to shut down. When you want to resume work, remember to activate the environment first.

Package Versions

These appendices were written in February 2022. By the time you read them, various packages might be updated and not necessarily play nice together anymore. For reference's sake, here are the version numbers of the critical packages.

```
InstagramCLI==1.0.14
PixPlot==0.0.1.1
pandas==1.3.2
pyLDAvis==3.3.1
gensim==4.1.2
```

Glossary of Terms

Note: this glossary assumes no prior knowledge in the various fields from which these terms are drawn. Further readings are suggested for some entries.

aDNA (ancient DNA): a field of research using new techniques to recover and sequence minute amounts of DNA from archaeological, museological, or other samples. (Earlier approaches to DNA research required larger sample sizes and could not generally deal with DNA degraded by time.)

Application Programming Interface (API): a way of accessing data from a website formatted for computational use.

Betweenness centrality (network analysis, metric): a measurement of how "in between" a node is, by virtue of its positioning along the highest number of shortest paths between all pairs of nodes in a graph.

Chronopolitics: in general, the use of time to control a population or culture.

Computer vision: a field of artificial intelligence (AI) that enables computers and automated systems to make sense of visual inputs (images or videos) at scale.

Convolutional Neural Network: a kind of neural network optimized for image processing. The image data are processed by a "convolutional" layer first, where a "convolution" is a particular kind of mathematical operation that uses a "filter" to identify or highlight different kinds of features in an image—horizontal lines, vertical lines, curves, areas of flat color, and so on. The net effect is to create a kind of "visual field" that overlaps such that the neural network builds up layers that "see" different kinds of image data. (See also Karkare 2019; Mishra 2020)

Digital humanities: an academic field that studies the implications of humanities approaches to understanding the world applied to our current digital world. At the same time, the field uses digital tools (often developed for other purposes) to explore traditional questions of humanities research on new kinds or scales of information. (See whatisdigitalhumanities.com for a rotating series of possible definitions.)

Eigenvector centrality: a measurement of a node's centrality or influence in a network by virtue of being connected to other high-ranking nodes. The "Page-Rank" algorithm used by the Google search engine is a variant of this.

Gaussian distribution: also known as "normal distribution." When graphed, appears as a bell curve. Indicates that the probability of some result is distributed equally around the mean.

Generative Adversarial Network: a kind of neural network where *two* networks are used in opposition to one another (hence, adversarial). The one network learns to classify, while the other network tries to generate images. The second network takes the feedback it receives from the first network and uses it to adjust its learning so that it produces images that the first network can recognize. (See also Google, Generative Adversarial Networks, https://devel opers.google.com/machine-learning/gan.)

Inception V3: a pre-trained Convolutional Neural Network used for image and object classification, the third iteration of Google's Inception Convolutional Neural Network.

Isotope analysis, stable, radiogenic: humans and animals take up various chemical elements through what they eat and drink; isotopes of these elements (most often strontium or oxygen) can become fixed in the bones or teeth. By analyzing samples for certain isotopes, it is possible to draw conclusions about diet and to a degree, origin (or region inhabited for a prolonged period).

JSON: acronym for JavaScript Object Notation. A human-readable format specification for storing data as text in attribute-value pairs, e.g., dessert : cake.

Linear discriminant analysis: a statistical method that finds a linear combination of features that separates and distinguishes between two classes of objects.

Machine learning: *see also* Convolutional Neural Network. A wide variety of techniques and approaches fall under the rubric of "machine learning." In our work, we mean the ways neural networks can be exposed to inputs and gradually adapt their underlying pattern of nodes and edges to recognize these inputs.

Macromorphoscopic traits: as used in forensic anthropology, the slight variations in the shape of the skull including the shape of cranial bones, the shape of sutures, and the presence or absence of features, or protrusions. (See Plemons and Hefner 2016.)

Matrix: a way of representing pair-wise data as a square.

Microsoft Azure: a service from Microsoft to access high-end computing infrastructure for a variety of machine learning tasks including automatic scene description, via an API.

Mixture discriminant analysis: an extension of linear discriminant analysis, based on mixtures of "normal" distributions.

Modularity (network analysis, metric): a measurement of clusters of nodes in a graph that are interconnected more similarly to each other than they are to the rest of the graph.

mtDNA analysis: a method to trace an individual's maternal lineage using the relatively stable DNA found in the mitochondria of cells, extracted from bone, hair, or teeth collected from living or deceased people.

Network analysis: a series of techniques that measure the formal structural properties of a network or *graph* depicting pairs of entities and relationships.

Neural network: a machine learning technique that is loosely modeled on the way that the human brain learns. In the brain, neurons activate at a given level of stimulus, and in turn fire along connections to other neurons which may or may not fire in their turn (given the strength of connection which mitigates the signal). In an artificial neural network, the "neurons" are mathematical functions whose inputs and outputs are connected to other mathematical functions. These neurons are arranged in "layers"; the connections between layers have varying weights (and thus only pass inputs forwards or backwards if certain conditions are met). "Learning" is said to occur when the network's weights and activations are tuned. There are many varieties of neural networks.

Non-metric multidimensional scaling: a way of visualizing levels of similarity for individual data points within a complex dataset. It is an attempt to represent the dissimilarities of pairs of objects in two dimensions.

One-shot learning: in our work, an image classification approach using paired neural networks that are identical. Pairs of images are shown to the networks where one is known and the other is unknown, and the perturbation of the networks caused by the images is measured, giving a measurement of how much image 1 differs from image 2.

Orthorectification: a process applied to photographs to remove the effects of perspective. This means that the x and y axes in an orthorectified photograph are in the same scale. Measurements and plans can be taken directly from an orthorectified photograph of e.g., buildings, archaeological sites.

Osteology: the study of human skeletal remains in general, foundational to investigating skeletal data in its larger sociocultural and temporal context. Generally known as bioarchaeology, the study of animal skeletal remains from archaeological contexts is known as zooarchaeology.

Parasocial: a one-sided relationship between an individual and someone else not personally known to that individual, as with a fan to a celebrity, that influences that individual's behavior.

PixPlot: a package of python code that enables the use of a pre-trained convolutional neural network for image classifying, by the Yale Digital Humanities Lab. (For a discussion of what is happening under the hood, see Duhaime 2017.)

Population: in the context of human biology, the whole number of inhabitants occupying a specific area, and continually being modified by increases (births and immigrations) and losses (deaths and emigrations).

Principal Components Analysis: a way to reduce the complexity of a dataset by the creation of summary indices that can then be visualized.

Provenance: the history of ownership of an object.

Provenience: the precise in-situ archaeological context from which an object was recovered.

Scraper: a computational tool meant to automate the process of paging through web pages and downloading data from those pages. The resulting data are sometimes called a **scrape**. (See also Kurschinski 2013 for a walk-through of building a scraper to retrieve archival materials.)

Social network analysis: *see also* Network analysis. A series of techniques that focus on the shape of relationships between individual people or other social data. In social network analysis, it is important that all of the actors (*nodes*) are of the same kind of actor—all individual people, or all individual auction houses—and the relationships (*edges*) should all be of the same kind (the *graph is unimode*). Mixing different kinds of nodes and edges into a single network (the graph is *multimode*) is not recommended, as the various metrics are predicated on having such "unimode" data. (See the variety of lessons at the *Programming Historian* on network analysis, especially in historical contexts, at http://programminghistorian.org/en/lessons/?topic=network-analysis.)

t-SNE plot: t-distributed Stochastic Neighbor Embedding. An iterative, probabilistic approach used to reduce high-dimensional data into a low-dimensional space (2 or 3 dimensions). It is used particularly in cases where there are non-linear relationships in the data. (For more, see Vidiyala 2020.)

Taphonomy: the events and processes that occur to remains after death.

Topic model: a technique that takes unstructured text and tries to organize documents within a corpus in terms of their constituent topics. A topic model assumes that documents are mixtures of a set number of topics, thus within a corpus of text similarities across documents can be probabilistically assigned to those topics. There are a variety of algorithms which fall within the general method. One of the most common is "Latent Dirichlet Allocation" (LDA) (Blei, Ng, and Jordan 2003), and is the technique we use in Appendix C.

Vector: a list of numbers that describe different dimensions for some category of interest.

Word embedding models: a statistical technique that treats the relationships between word co-occurrences across a body of text as spatial. (See also Schmidt 2015d, 2015e.)

Word vector: *see also* Word embedding model. A representation of a word's *positioning* in a text or corpus according to multiple dimensions. (See also Prabhu 2019.)

References

Alfonso, Marta P., and Joseph Powell. 2007. "Ethics of Flesh and Bone, or Ethics in the Practice of Paleopathology, Osteology, and Bioarchaeology." In *Human Remains: Guide for Museums and Academic Institutions*, ed. Vicki Cassman, Nancy Odegaard, and Joseph Powell, 5–21. Walnut Creek: Altamira Press.

Altaweel, Mark. 2019. "The Market for Heritage: Evidence from eBay Using Natural Language Processing." *Social Science Computer Review* 39(3): 391–415.

Alterauge, Amelie, Thomas Becker, Brigitta Berndt, Christian Jackowski, and Sandra Lösch. 2016. "Testing 'Saintly' Authenticity: Investigations on Two Catacomb Saints." *Radio-Graphics* 36(2): 573–79.

Angeleti, Gabriella. 2022. "Anthropologist Opposed to Indigenous Repatriation Sues University for Alleged Threats to Her Free Speech." *The Art Newspaper.com*, 28 October. Retrieved 17 November 2022 from https://www.theartnewspaper.com/2022/10/27/elizabeth-weiss-anthropologist-san-jose-state-university-lawsuit-freedom-speech.

Angwin, Julia, Jeff Larson, Surya Mattu, and Lauren Kirchner. 2016. "Machine Bias." *ProPublica*, 23 May. Retrieved 25 March 2022 from https://www.propublica.org/article/machine-bias-risk-assessments-in-criminal-sentencing.

Aranui, Amber. 2020. "Restitution or a Loss to Science? Understanding the Importance of Returning Māori Ancestral Remains." *Museum & Society* 18(1): 19–29.

Aranui, Amber, Cressida Fforde, Michael Pickering, Paul Turnbull, Gareth Knapman, and Honor Keeler. 2020. "'Under the Hammer': The Role of Auction Houses and Dealers in the Distribution of Indigenous Ancestral Remains." In *The Routledge Companion to Indigenous Repatriation: Return, Reconcile, Renew*, ed. Cressida Fforde, Timothy C. McKeown, and Honor Keeler, 335–60. London: Routledge Press.

Ardia, David. 2010. "Free Speech Savior or Shield for Scoundrels: An Empirical Study of Intermediary Immunity Under Section 230 of the Communications Decency Act." *Loyola of Los Angeles Law Review* 43: 373.

Argyropoulos, Vasilike, Kyriaki Polikreti, Stefan Simon, and Dimitris Charalambous. 2011. "Ethical Issues in Research and Publication of Illicit Cultural Property." *Journal of Cultural Heritage* 12(2): 214–19.

Ariss, Rachel. 2014. "'Bring out Your Dead': Law, Human Remains and Memory." *Canadian Journal of Law and Society* 19(1): 33–54.

Arnold, Taylor, and Lauren Tilton. 2019. "Distant Viewing: Analyzing Large Visual Corpora." *Digital Scholarship in the Humanities* 34(1): i3–i16.

Artemis Gallery. n.d. "Artemis Gallery." *Artemisgallery.com*, https://www.artemisgallery.com/.

Arts.gov. n.d. "Returns of Foreign Cultural Property." *Arts.gov.au*. Retrieved 25 March 2022 from https://www.arts.gov.au/what-we-do/cultural-heritage/movable-cultural-heritage/importing-cultural-heritage-objects-australia/returns-foreign-cultural-property.

Association for Computing Machinery. 2018. "ACM Code of Ethics and Professional Conduct." *ACM.org*. Retrieved 25 March 2022 from https://www.acm.org/code-of-ethics.

Atwood, Robert. 2007. *Stealing History: Tomb Raiders, Smugglers, and the Looting of the Ancient World*. New York: St. Martin's Press.

Azoulay, Aïsha. 2021. *Un-documented: Unlearning Imperial Plunder*. Retrieved 25 March 2022 from https://vimeo.com/490778435.

Baber, Tessa T. 2016. "Ancient Corpses as Curiosities: Mummymania in the Age of Early Travel." *Journal of Ancient Egyptian Interconnections* 8(1): 60–93.

Barbera, Paul. 2015. "instaR: access to Instagram API via R." *Github*. Retrieved 17 September 2015 from https://github.com/pablobarbera/instaR/releases.

Barford, Paul. 2010. "But Is It Art? Collecting Human Body Parts, Legal? Ethical?" *Paul-barford.blogspot.com*. Retrieved 21 March 2020 from http://paul-barford.blogspot.com/2010/02/what-collectors-collect-human-body.html.

Bartlett, Alison. 2015. "Male Professors are 'Genius': Female Professors are 'Nice.'" *The New Republic*, 10 February. Retrieved 21 March 2020 from https://newrepublic.com/article/121024/heres-one-way-gender-discrimination-plays-out-academia.

BBC News. 2018a. "The Search in Germany for the Lost Skull of Tanzania's Mangi Meli." *BBC News.com*, 18 November. Retrieved 25 March 2022 from https://www.bbc.com/news/world-africa-45916150.

———. 2018b. "Executed Tanzanian Hero's Grandson Takes DNA Test to Find Lost Skull." *BBC News.com*, 20 November. Retrieved 25 March 2022 from https://www.bbc.com/news/world-africa-46277158.

Begley, Patrick. 2019. "'Box of Human Bones' Pulled from Auction Sale." *The Sydney Morning Herald*, 7 July. Retrieved 25 March 2020 from https://www.smh.com.au/national/nsw/box-of-human-bones-pulled-from-auction-sale-20190706-p524qj.html.

Bishara, Haim. 2020. "Penn Museum to Remove Skull Collection of Enslaved People." *Hyperallergic*, 23 July. Retrieved 24 March 2020 from https://hyperallergic.com/577941/penn-museum-to-remove-skull-collection-of-enslaved-people/.

Blakey, Michael. 1988. *The W. Montague Cobb Skeletal Collection: First Report*. Washington, DC: Department of Sociology and Anthropology, Howard University.

———. 1995. *The W. Montague Cobb Skeletal Collection and Biological Anthropology Laboratory at Howard University: Special Report and Announcement*. Washington, DC: Department of Sociology and Anthropology, Howard University.

Blei, David M., Andrew Ng, and Michael Jordan. 2003. "Latent Dirichlet Allocation." *Journal of Machine Learning Research* 3(4–5): 993–1022. https://doi.org/10.1162/jmlr.2003.3.4-5.993.

Blouin, Katherine, Monica Hanna, and Sarah E. Bond. 2020. "How Academics, Egyptologists, and Even Melania Trump Benefit from Colonialist Cosplay." *Hyperallergic*, 22 October. Retrieved 24 March 2020 from https://hyperallergic.com/595896/how-academics-egyptologists-and-even-melania-trump-benefit-from-colonialist-cosplay/.

Bogenschneider, Bret, and Arkadiusz Mironko. 2021. "eBay Frauds: Specific Illustrations and Analysis." *Loyola Consumer Law Review*, 31 July. https://ssrn.com/abstract=3939644.

Bolieiro, Andrea. 2010. "The Dead Body Offence in Canada: How Courts Interpret and Apply Section 182 of the Criminal Code." *Canadian Law Library Review* 35(3): 125–31.

Bonilla, Yarimar, and Jonathan Rosa. 2015. "#Ferguson: Digital Protest, Hashtag Ethnography, and the Racial Politics of Social Media in the United States." *American Ethnologist* 42(1): 4–17.

Borrows, J. 1996. "With or Without You: First Nations Law (in Canada)." *McGill Law Journal* 41: 629–65.

Bourdieu, Pierre. 1984. *A Social Critique of Judgement of Taste: Classes and Classifications.* London: Routledge.

boyd, danah, and Kate Crawford. 2012. "Critical Questions for Big Data: Provocations for a Cultural, Technological, and Scholarly Phenomenon." *Information, Communication & Society* 15: 662–79. https://doi.org/10.1080/1369118X.2012.678878.

Brants, Thorsten, and Alex Franz. 2006. "Web 1T 5-gram Version 1." *Linguistic Data Consortium*, 19 September. https://catalog.ldc.upenn.edu/LDC2006T13.

Braun, Christopher. 2020. "Equipped with Shovels, Pickaxes, and Books: Treasure Hunters and Grave Robbers in Medieval Egypt." In *Living with Nature and Things: Contributions to a New Social History of the Middle Islamic Periods*, ed. Bethany J. Walker and Abdelkader Al Ghouz, 79–102. Göttingen: Vandenhoeck & Ruprecht.

Brendel, Wieland, and Matthias Bethge. 2019. "Approximating CNNs with Bag-of-Local-Features Models Works Surprisingly Well on Imagenet." *OpenReview*, 8 February. Retrieved 24 March 2022 from https://openreview.net/forum?id=SkfMWhAqYQ.

Brenna, Connor T. 2022. "Bygone Theatres of Events: A History of Human Anatomy and Dissection." *The Anatomical Record* 305(4): 788–802.

British Association for Biological Anthropology and Osteoarchaeology [BABAO]. 2018. "Ethics and Standards." *Babao.org.uk.* Retrieved 24 March 2022 from http://www.babao.org.uk/publications/ethics-and-standards/.

Brodie, Neil. 2002. "Illicit Antiquities." In *Illicit Antiquities: The Theft of Culture and the Extinction of Archaeology*, ed. Neil Brodie and Katherine W. Tubbs, 1–22. Routledge: London.

———. 2011. "Congenial Bedfellows? The Academy and the Antiquities Trade." *Journal of Contemporary Criminal Justice* 27(4): 408–37.

———. 2014. "Auction Houses and the Antiquities Trade." In *Third International Conference of Experts on the Return of Cultural Property*, ed. Souzana Choulia-Kapeloni, 63–74. Athens: Archaeological Receipts Fund.

———. 2015. "Archaeological and Criminological Approaches to Studying the Antiquities Trade: A Comparison of the Illicit Antiquities Research Centre and the Trafficking Culture Project." *Cuadernos de Prehistoria y Arqueología de la Universidad de Granada* 25: 99–105.

———. 2019. "Through a Glass, Darkly: Long-Term Antiquities Auction Data in Context." *International Journal of Cultural Property* 26(3): 265–83.

Bromley, Jane, James W. Bentz, Léon Bottou, Isabelle Guyon, Yann LeCun, Cliff Moore, Eduard Säckinger, and Roopak Shah. 1993. "Signature Verification Using a Siamese Time Delay Neural Network." *International Journal of Pattern Recognition and Artificial Intelligence* 7(4): 669–88. https://doi.org/10.1142/S0218001493000339.

Bull, Anna Cento, and Daniela De Angeli. 2021. "Emotions and Critical Thinking at a Dark Heritage Site: Investigating Visitors' Reactions to a First World War Museum in Slovenia." *Journal of Heritage Tourism* 16(3): 263–80.

Burrow, Merrick. 2013. "The Imperial Souvenir: Things and Masculinities in H. Rider Haggard's *King Solomon's Mines* and *Allan Quatermain*." *Journal of Victorian Culture* 18(1): 72–92.

Campsie, Alison. 2021. "Medieval Skull Removed from Edinburgh Auction Given Concerns over Sale of Human Remains." *The Scotsman*, 9 March. Retrieved 14 March 2021 from https://www.scotsman.com/heritage-and-retro/heritage/medieval-skull-removed-from-edinburgh-auction-given-concerns-over-sale-of-human-remains-3158751.

Canadian Border Services Agency. 2021. "Importation and Exportation of Human Remains and Other Human Tissues. Memorandum D19-9-3." *Government of Canada.*

Retrieved 24 March 2022 from https://www.cbsa-asfc.gc.ca/publications/dm-md/d19/ d19-9-3-eng.html.

Caplan, Robyn, and Philip M. Napoli. 2018. "Revisiting Section 230 of the Communications Decency Act: Using Legislative History to Understand and Evaluate the Evolution of Social Networks." Retrieved 24 March 2022 from https://papers.ssrn.com/sol3/ papers.cfm?abstract_id=3136036.

Card, Jeb B., and David S. Anderson, eds. 2016. *Lost City, Found Pyramid: Understanding Alternative Archaeologies and Pseudoscientific Practices*. Tuscaloosa: University of Alabama Press.

Carney, Scott. 2007. "Inside India's Underground Trade in Human Remains." *Wired*, 27 November. Retrieved 25 March 2022 from https://www.wired.com/2007/11/ff-bones/.

———. 2011. *The Red Market: On the Trail of the World's Organ Brokers, Bone Thieves, Blood Farmers, and Child Traffickers*. New York: William Morrow.

Carter, Christopher, Flora Vilches, and Calogero M. Santoro. 2017. "South American Mummy Trafficking: Captain Duniam's Nineteenth-Century Worldwide Enterprises." *Journal of the History of Collections* 29(3): 395–407.

CBC Radio. 2021. "Story about Florida Man's Skeleton Guitar Appears to Be a Hoax, Say Local Reporters." *CBC Radio As It Happens*, 15 February. Retrieved 24 March 2022 from https://www.cbc.ca/radio/asithappens/as-it-happens-monday-edition-1.59146 19/story-about-florida-man-s-skeleton-guitar-appears-to-be-a-hoax-say-local-re porters-1.5914782.

Césaire, Aimé. 1955. *Discours sur le colonialisme*. Paris: Editions Presence Africaine.

Challis, Debbie. 2016. "Skull Triangles: Flinders Petrie, Race Theory and Biometrics." *Bulletin of the History of Archaeology* 26(1): Art 5. https://doi.org/10.5334/bha-556.

Chandler, Oscar. 2018. "Macabre Theft of Skulls in Kent." *Church Times*, 3 August. Retrieved 25 March 2022 from https://www.churchtimes.co.uk/articles/2018/3-august/news/uk/ macabre-theft-of-skulls-in-kent.

Chappell, Duncan, and Damien Huffer. 2013. "Quantifying and Describing the South and Southeast Asian Antiquities Trade: Australia as an Overlooked Destination?" *ARC Centre of Excellence in Policing and Security*, Briefing Paper 24. Retrieved 24 March 2022 from https://www.researchgate.net/publication/299656737_Quantifying_and_ describing_ the_South_and_Southeast_Asian_illicit_antiquities_trade_Australia_as_ an_overlooked_destination.

Chartier, Daniel, Marie Mossé, Sharon Rankin, Aaju Peter, Renée Hulan, Robert Fréchette, Bob Mesher, Laura Perez-Gauvreau, Béatrice Archambault, Éloïse Lamarre, Andréanne Sylvain, Patrice Viau, Yannick Legault, Marianne Stenbaek, and Lisa Qiluqqi Koperqualuk. 2021. "Ulrikab, Abraham." *Littératures Inuites / Inuit Literatures*. Retrieved 24 March 2022 from https://inuit.uqam.ca/en/person/ulrikab-abraham.

Chaykowski, Kathleen. 2016. "Instagram Reaches 600 Million Monthly Users, Doubling in Size in Two Years." *Forbes.com*, 15 December. Retrieved 24 March 2022 from https:// www.forbes.com/sites/kathleenchaykowski/2016/12/15/instagram-reaches-600-mil lion-monthly-users-doubling-in-size-in-two-years/?sh=1032d921b24b.

Chesler, Adam. 2004. "Open Access: A Review of an Emerging Phenomenon." *Serials Review* 30(4): 292–97. https://doi.org/10.1080/00987913.2004.10764926.

Clark, Liat. 2016. "AI Is Being Used to Hunt out Child Porn and Sexual Abuse Images across the Web." *Wired*, 12 January. Retrieved 24 March 2022 from https://www.wired.co.uk/ article/ai-interpol-track-child-abuse.

Clark, Peter A. 2003. "Prejudice and the Medical Profession." *Health Programs* 84(5): 12–23.

Claverie, Pierre-Vincent. 2008. "Les acteurs du commerce des reliques à la fin des croisades." *Le Moyen Age* CXIV: 589–602. https://doi.org/10.3917/rma.143.0589.

Conde, Ximena. 2021. "Health Official Resigns over Mishandling of MOVE Bombing Remains." *National Public Radio*, 14 May. Retrieved 24 March 2022 from https://www.npr.org/2021/05/14/996760426/health-official-resigns-over-mishandling-of-move-bombing-remains.

Council of Europe. n.d. Details of Treaty no. 143. Retrieved 22 November 2022 from https://www.coe.int/en/web/conventions/full-list?module=treaty-detail&treatynum=143.

Cox, Caroline, and Alan Collins. 2020. "Selective Liability, Regulated Digital Commerce, and the Subversion of Product Trading Bans: The Case of Elephant Ivory." *Human Dimensions of Wildlife: An International Journal* 26(3): 245–61.

Crawford, Kate, and Vladen Joler. 2018. "Anatomy of an AI System." *Anatomyof.ai*. Retrieved 24 March 2022 from https://anatomyof.ai/.

Crockett, Richard, Thomas Pruzinsky, and John A. Persing. 2007. "The Influence of Plastic Surgery 'Reality TV' on Cosmetic Surgery Patient Expectations and Decision Making." *Plastic and Reconstructive Surgery* 120: 316–24.

Cusumano, Michael A. 2021. "Technology Strategy and Management: Section 230 and a Tragedy of the Commons." *Communications of the ACM* 64(10): 16–18.

Cyca, Michelle. 2022. "24 Important TikTok Stats Marketers Need to Know in 2022." *Hootsuite*, 9 March. Retrieved 24 March 2022 from https://blog.hootsuite.com/tiktok-stats/.

Dahan, Michel. 2018. "From Rome to Montreal: Importing Relics of Catacomb Saints through Ultramontane Networks, 1820–1914." *Social History* 51(104): 255–77.

Daley, Jason. 2018. "After More Than 90 Years, Looted Mummy Parts Repatriated to Egypt." *Smithsonian Magazine*, 9 January. Retrieved 24 March 2022 from https://www.smithsonianmag.com/smart-news/mummy-parts-repatriated-egypt-90-years-after-being-looted-180967760/.

Dao, David. 2018. "Awful AI Is a Curated List to Track Current Scary Usages of AI: Hoping to Raise Awareness." *Github*. Retrieved 10 May 2023 from http://github.com/daviddao/awful-ai.

Davidson, James M. 2007. "'Resurrection Men' in Dallas: The Illegal Use of Black Bodies as Medical Cadavers (1900–1907)." *International Journal of Historical Archaeology* 1: 193–220.

Davidson, Katherine, Shawn Graham, and Damien Huffer. 2021. "Exploring Taste Formation and Performance in the Illicit Trade of Human Remains on Instagram." In *Crime and Art: Sociological and Criminological Perspectives of Crimes in the Art World*, ed. Naomi Oosterman and Donna Yates, 29–44. Cham: Springer Press.

Davis, Tess. 2011. "Supply and Demand: Exposing the Illicit Trade in Cambodian Antiquities through a Study of Sotheby's Auction House." *Crime, Law and Social Change* 56(155): 155–74.

Decreet. 2004. Betreffende begraafplaatsen en de lijkbezorging. Belgisch Staatsblad, 10 February. Retrieved 28 June 2021 from http://www.ejustice.just.fgov.be/eli/decreet/2004/01/16/2004035175/staatsblad.

———. 2019. Betreffende wijziging van Hoofdstuk II van Titel III van Boek II van Deel I van het Wetboek van de plaatselijke democratie en de decentralisatie betreffende de begraafplaatsen en de lijkbezorging (1). Belgisch Staatsblad, 14 February. Retrieved 28 June 2021 from http://www.ejustice.just.fgov.be/eli/decreet/2019/02/14/2019201258/staatsblad.

Deleuze, Gilles, and Felix Guattari.1980. *Mille Plateaux*. Paris: Minuit.

Denadai, Rafael, Karin Milleni Araujo, Hugo Samartine Jr., Rodrigo Denadai, and Cassio Eduardo Raposo-Amaral. 2015. "Aesthetic Surgery Reality Television Shows: Do They Influence Public Perception of the Scope of Plastic Surgery?" *Aesthetic Plastic Surgery* 39: 1000–9. https://doi.org/10.1007/s00266-015-0577-6.

Dennis, L. Meaghan. 2020. "Digital Archaeological Ethics: Successes and Failures in Disciplinary Attention." *Journal of Computer Applications in Archaeology* 3(1): 210–18. https://doi.org/10.5334/jcaa.24.

Dery, Mary. 2010. "Embalmed on eBay." *Photofile* 90: 56–63.

Dezuanni, Michael L. 2021. "Tiktok's Peer Pedagogies—Learning about Books through #Booktok Videos." *AoIR Selected Papers of Internet Research*. https://doi.org/10.5210/spir.v2021i0.11901.

Diaz, Johnny. 2020. "Penn Museum to Relocate Skull Collection of Enslaved People." *The New York Times*, 7 July. Retrieved 24 March 2022 from https://www.nytimes.com/2020/07/27/us/Penn-museum-slavery-skulls-Morton-cranial.html.

Dibble, Flint. 2022. "With Netflix's *Ancient Apocalypse*, Graham Hancock Has Declared War on Archaeologists." *The Conversation*, 18 November. https://theconversation.com/with-netflixs-ancient-apocalypse-graham-hancock-has-declared-war-on-archaeologists-194881.

D'Ignazio, Catherine, and Lauren F. Klein. 2020. *Data Feminism*. Cambridge, MA: MIT Press.

Dobson, Eleanor. 2017. "Sleeping Beauties: Mummies and the Fairy-Tale Genre at the Fin De Siècle." *Journal of International Women's Studies* 18(3): 19–34.

Dodrill, Taylor N., Greg C. Nelson, Jessica H. Stone, and Scott M. Fitzpatrick. 2016. "Determining Ancestry of Unprovenienced Human Remains from the Grenadines, Southern Caribbean: Dental Morphology and Craniometric Analyses." Paper presented at Undergraduate Research Symposium 2016, University of Oregon. Retrieved 28 March 2022 from https://scholarsbank.uoregon.edu/xmlui/bitstream/handle/1794/19937/Dodrill_UGRS_2016.pdf.

Duhaime, Douglas. 2017. "Identifying Similar Images with TensorFlow." douglasduhaime.com. Retrieved 28 March 2022 from https://douglasduhaime.com/posts/identifying-similar-images-with-tensorflow.html.

Dundler, Lauren. 2019. "'Still Covered in Sand.looked Very Old.'—Legal Obligations in the Internet Market for Antiquities." *Heritage* 2(3): 2311–26.

———. 2021. "#antiquitiesdealers" In *Crime and Art: Sociological and Criminological Perspectives of Crimes in the Art World*, ed. Naomi Oosterman and Donna Yates, 45–62. Cham: Springer Press.

Dunn, Rhian R., Micayla C. Spiros, Kelly R. Kamnikar, Amber M. Plemons, and Joseph T. Hefner. 2020. "Ancestry Estimation in Forensic Anthropology: A Review." *WIREs Forensic Science* 2(4): e1369. https://doi.org/10.1002/wfs2.1369.

Durand, Yves Sioui. 2020. *Okhoüey Atisken—L'esprit des os. Écrits théoriques, poétiques et polémiques*. Québec: Les Presses de l'Université Laval.

eBay. n.d. "Human Remains and Body Parts Policy." *eBay.com*. Retrieved 28 March 2022 from http://pages.ebay.com/help/policies/remains.html.

———. n.d. "Our History." *eBay.com*. Retrieved 28 March 2022 from https://www.ebayinc.com/company/our-history/.

Etsy. 2017. "Prohibited Items Policy." *Etsy.com*. Retrieved 28 March 2022 from https://www.etsy.com/legal/prohibited/#Q2.

Everett, Tom. 2019. "Reconstructing Bell and Blake's 1874 Ear Phonautograph." *Science Museum Group Journal*, September 11. Retrieved 28 March 2022 from http://journal.sciencemuseum.org.uk/browse/issue-12/writing-sound-with-a-human-ear/.

Fanon, Frantz. (1961) 2002. *Les Damnés de la terre*. Paris: La Découverte.

Farley, Patrick. 2019. "Quickstart: Computer Vision Client Library—Azure Cognitive Services." *Microsoft*. Document updated 2022, retrieved 24 March 2022 from https://docs.microsoft.com/en-us/azure/cognitive-services/computer-vision/quickstarts-sdk/client-library.

Fay, Elizabeth. 2011. "Virtual Artifacts: eBay, Antiquities, and Authenticity." *Journal of Contemporary Criminal Justice* 27(4): 449–64.

———. 2013. "Trading in Antiquities on eBay: The Changing Face of the Illicit Trade in Antiquities." PhD diss., Keele University.

Feddema, Kim, Paul Harrigan, and Shasha Wang. 2021. "The Dark Side of Social Media Engagement: An Analysis of User-Generated Content in Online Wildlife Trade Communities." *Australasian Journal of Information Systems* 25: 1–35. https://doi.org/10.3127/ajis.v25i0.2987.

Fennell, Marc, and Monique Ross. 2020. "The Headhunters: Tattooed, Severed and Mummified Māori Heads Were Once a Prized Collector's Item in Britain. New Zealand Wants Them Back." *Abc.net.au*, 15 December. Retrieved 28 March 2022 from https://www.abc.net.au/news/2020-12-14/mokomokai-maori-heads-stuff-the-british-stole-repatriations/12771180.

FERIARTE. 2019. "A Mummy's Head from Imperial Egypt, One of the Main Showpieces at FERIARTE 2019." *Ifema.es*, 21 October. Retrieved 28 March 2022 from https://www.ifema.es/en/feriarte/news/feriarte-mummy-19.

Fforde, Cressida, Timothy C. McKeown, and Honor Keeler, eds. 2020. *The Routledge Companion to Indigenous Repatriation: Return, Reconcile, Renew*. London: Routledge.

Floridi, Luciano. 2002. "On the Intrinsic Value of Information Objects and the Infosphere." *Ethics of Information Technology* 4: 287–304.

Forrest, Craig. 2004. "Australia's Protection of Foreign States' Cultural Heritage." *University of New South Wales Law Journal* 27: 605–30.

Fradley, Michael, and Nicole Sheldrick. 2017. "Satellite Imagery and Heritage Damage in Egypt: A Response to Parcak et al. (2016)." *Antiquity* 91(357): 784–92. https://doi.org/10.15184/aqy.2017.25.

Franchi, Violette. 2022. "A Paris Museum Has 18,000 Skulls: It's Reluctant to Say Whose." *The New York Times*, November 28. Retrieved 29 November 2022 from https://www.nytimes.com/2022/11/28/arts/design/france-human-remains-restitution-skulls.html?smid=nytcore-ios-share&referringSource=articleShare.

Francis, Deepa. 2001. "Bodysnatching in Canada." *Canadian Medical Association Journal* 164(4): 530.

Francis, Tracy, and Fernanda Hoefel. 2018. "'True Gen': Generation Z and Implications for Companies." *McKinsey & Company*, 12 November. Retrieved 28 March 2022 from https://www.mckinsey.com/industries/consumer-packaged-goods/our-insights/true-gen-generation-z-and-its-implications-for-companies.

Frerking, Christopher, and Heather Gill-Frerking. 2017. "Human Remains as Heritage: Categorisation, Legislation, and Protection." *Art, Antiquity and Law* 22(1):49–73.

Friedan, Jonathan D., and Sean Patrick Roche. 2007. "E-commerce: Legal Issues of the Online Retailer in Virginia." *Richmond Journal of Law and Technology* 13(2): 1–16.

Frieman, Catherine, and Mark Gillings. 2007. "Seeing Is Perceiving?" *World Archaeology* 39(1): 4–16. https://doi.org/10.1080/00438240601133816.

Froehlich, Heather. 2015. "Corpus Analysis with Antconc." *The Programming Historian*. https://doi.org/10.46430/phen0043.

Funk, Kellen, and Lincoln A. Mullen. 2018. "The Spine of American Law: Digital Text Analysis and U.S. Legal Practice." *American Historical Review* 123(1): 132–64. https://doi.org/10.1093/ahr/123.1.132.

Gans, Herbert. 1999. *Popular Culture and High Culture: An Analysis and Evaluation of Taste*. New York: Basic.

Garcia, Nilda M. 2021. *Mexico's Drug War and Criminal Networks: The Dark Side of Social Media*. Routledge: New York.

Geary, Patrick J. (1978) 1990. *Furta Sacra: Thefts of Relics in the Central Middle Ages*, rev. ed. Princeton: Princeton University Press.

———. 1994. *Living with the Dead in the Middle Ages*. Ithaca: Cornell University Press.

Gefen, David. 2000. "E-commerce: The Role of Familiarity and Trust." *Omega* 28(6): 725–37.

Gibbs, Martin, James Meese, Michael Arnold, Bjorn Nansen, and Marcus Carter. 2014. "#Funeral and Instagram: Death, Social Media, and Platform Vernacular." *Information, Communication & Society* 18(3): 255–63.

Gillespie, Tarleton. 2017. "Governance of and by Platforms." In *The SAGE Handbook of Social Media*, ed. Jean Burgess, Alice Marwick, and Thomas Poell, 254–78. Thousand Oaks: SAGE Press.

Gillingham, Paul. 2010. "The Strange Business of Memory: Relic Forgery in Latin America." *Past & Present* 206(5): 199–226.

Goldman, Eric. 2017. "The Ten Most Important Section 230 Rulings." *Tulane Journal of Technology and Intellectual Property* 20: 1–9.

———. 2020. "An Overview of the United States' Section 230 Internet Immunity." In *The Oxford Handbook of Online Intermediary Liability*, ed. Giancarlo Forsio, 154–71. Oxford: Oxford University Press.

Goodwin, Danny. 2022. "TikTok Videos Can Now Be 10 Minutes." *Search Engine Land*, 1 March. Retrieved 28 March 2022 from https://searchengineland.com/tiktok-10-minute-video-length-381434.

Graham, Shawn, and Damien Huffer. 2020. "Reproducibility, Replicability, and Revisiting the Insta-Dead and the Human Remains Trade." *Internet Archaeology* 55. https://doi.org/10.11141/ia.55.11.

Graham, Shawn, Damien Huffer, and Jaime Simons. 2022. "When TikTok Discovered the Human Remains Trade: A Case Study." *Open Archaeology* 8(1): 196–219. https://doi.org/10.1515/opar-2022-0235.

Graham, Shawn, Damien Huffer, and Jeff Blackadar. 2020. "Towards a Digital Sensorial Archaeology as an Experiment in Distant Viewing of the Trade in Human Remains on Instagram." *Heritage* 3(2): 208–27. https://doi.org/10.3390/heritage3020013.

Graham, Shawn, Ian Milligan, and Scott Weingart. 2015. *Big Historical Data: The Historian's Macroscope*. London: Imperial College Press.

Graham, Shawn, Alex Lane, Damien Huffer, and Andreas Angourakis. 2020. "Towards a Method for Discerning Sources of Supply within the Human Remains Trade via Patterns of Visual Dissimilarity and Computer Vision." *Journal of Computer Applications in Archaeology* 3(1): 253–268. https://doi.org/10.5334/jcaa.59.

Gross, Daniel A. 2018. "Tanzania Joins International Movement Demanding Return of Human Remains in Germany." *Hyperallergic*, 16 March. Retrieved 28 March 2022 from https://hyperallergic.com/433003/tanzania-repatriation-human-remains-germany/.

Guzzardi, Nicole. 2012. "New Etsy Rules: Bones, Hazardous Materials and Other Things You Can No Longer Sell." *Huffpost*, 11 October. Retrieved 28 March 2022 from http://www.huffingtonpost.com.au/entry/new-etsy-rules-no-longer-sell_n_1778310.

Halcrow, Sian, Amber Aranui, Stephanie Halmhofer, Annalisa Heppner, Norma Johnson, Kristina Killgrove, and Gwen Robbins Schug. 2021. "Moving beyond Weiss and Springer's *Repatriation and Erasing the Past*: Indigenous Values, Relationships, and Research." *International Journal of Cultural Property* 28(2): 211–20. https://doi.org/10.1017/S0940739121000229.

Halling, Christine L., and Ryan M Seidemann. 2016. "They Sell Skulls Online?! A Review of Internet Sales of Human Skulls on eBay and the Laws in Place to Restrict Sales." *Journal of Forensic Sciences* 61(5): 1322–26. https://doi.org/10.1111/1556-4029.13147.

Hamilakis, Yannis. 2013. "Afterword: Eleven Theses on the Archaeology of the Senses." In *Making Senses of the Past: Toward a Sensory Archaeology*, ed. Jo Day, 409–19. Carbondale: Southern Illinois University Press.

———. 2014. *Archaeology and the Senses: Human Experience, Memory, and Affect*. Cambridge: Cambridge University Press.

———. 2017. "Sensorial Assemblages: Affect, Memory and Temporality in Assemblage Thinking." *Cambridge Archaeology Journal* 27(1): 169–82.

Hanson, Allen F. 2009. "Beyond the Skin Bag: On the Moral Responsibility of Extended Agencies." *Ethics and Information Technology* 11(1): 91–99. https://doi.org/10.1007/s10676-009-9184-z.

Hanson, Jeffery R. 2011. "Looting of the Fort Craig Cemetery: Damage Done and Lessons Learned." *American Antiquity* 76(3): 429–45. https://www.jstor.org/stable/41331901.

Hardwick, Courtney. 2019. "The Latest Bad Idea: An App That Tells You How Gay You Are." *IN Magazine*, 22 October. Retrieved 28 March 2022 from https://inmagazine.ca/2019/10/the-latest-bad-idea-an-app-that-tells-you-how-gay-you-are/.

Harper, Douglas. 2002. "Talking about Pictures: A Case for Photo Elicitation." *Visual Studies* 17(1): 13–26.

Harris, Katie A. 2014. "Gift, Sale, and Theft: Juan De Ribera and the Sacred Economy of Relics in the Early Modern Mediterranean." *Journal of Early Modern History* 18(3): 193–226.

Häubl, Gerald, and Kyle B. Murray. 2001. "Recommending or Persuading? the Impact of a Shopping Agent's Algorithm on User Behavior." In Proceedings of the 3rd ACM Conference on Electronic Commerce October 2001, New York, 163–70.

Hefner, Joseph T., Brian F. Spatola, Nicholas V. Passalacqua, and Timothy P. Gocha. 2016. "Beyond Taphonomy: Exploring Craniometric Variation among Anatomical Material." *Journal of Forensic Sciences* 61(6): 1440–49. https://doi.org/10.1111/1556-4029.13177.

Heritage New Zealand Pouhere Taonga. 2014. *Koiwi Tangata Human Remains*. Archaeological Guidelines Series 8. *Heritage.org.nz*, 25 August. Retrieved 28 March 2022 from https://www.heritage.org.nz/protecting-heritage/archaeology/archaeological-guidelines-and-templates.

Herva, Vesa-Pekka, Eerika Koskinen-Koivisto, Oula Seitsonen, and Suzie Thomas. 2016. "'I Have Better Stuff at Home': Treasure Hunting and Private Collecting of World War II Artefacts in Finnish Lapland." *World Archaeology* 48(2): 267–81.

Hicks, Dan. 2020. *The Brutish Museums: The Benin Bronzes, Colonial Violence and Cultural Restitution*. London: Pluto Press.

History.com. n.d. "Pawn Stars." *History.com*. Retrieved 28 March 2022 from https://www.history.com/shows/pawn-stars.

Horowitz, Karen Alexander. 2007. "When is § 230 Immunity Lost?: The Transformation from Website Owner to Information Content Provider." *3 Shilder Journal of Law Communications & Technology* 14. Available at: https://digitalcommons.law.uw.edu/wjlta/vol3/iss4/2.

Hu, Chuanbo, Minglei Yin, Bin Liu, Xin Li, and Yanfang Ye. 2021. "Identifying Illicit Drug Dealers on Instagram with Large-Scale Multimodal Data Fusion." *ACM Transactions on Intelligent Systems and Technology (TIST)* 12(5): 1–23.

Huffer, Damien. 2018. "The Living and the Dead Entwined in Virtual Space: #Bioarchaeology and Being a Bioarchaeologist on Instagram." *Advances in Archaeological Practice* 6: 267–73. https://doi.org/10.1017/aap.2018.24.

Huffer, Damien, and Duncan Chappell. 2014. "The Mainly Nameless and Faceless Dead: An Exploratory Study of the Illicit Traffic in Archaeological and Ethnographic Human Remains." *Crime, Law and Social Change* 62(2): 131–53. https://doi.org/10.1007/s10611-014-9528-4.

Huffer, Damien, Duncan Chappell, Nathan Charlton, and Brian F. Spatola. 2019. "Bones of Contention: The Online Trade in Archaeological, Ethnographic and Anatomical Human Remains on Social Media Platforms." In *The Palgrave Handbook on Art Crime*, ed. Saskia Hufnagel and Duncan Chappell, 527–56. London: Palgrave Macmillan.

Huffer, Damien, and Nathan Charlton. 2019. "Serious Enquiries Only, Please: Ethical Issues Raised by the Online Human Remains Trade." In *Ethical Approaches to Human Remains*, ed. Kirsty Squires, David Eriksson, and Nicholas Marquez-Grant, 95–129. Cham: Springer Press.

Huffer, Damien, and Shawn Graham. 2017. "The Insta-Dead: The Rhetoric of the Human Remains Trade on Instagram." *Internet Archaeology* 45(2). https://doi.org/10.11141/ia.45.5.

———. 2018. "Fleshing Out the Bones: Studying the Human Remains Trade with Tensorflow and Inception." *Journal of Computer Applications in Archaeology* 1(1): 55–63.

Huffer, Damien, Anthony Guerreiro, and Shawn Graham. 2021. "Osteological Assessment of a Seized Shipment of Modified Human Crania: Implications for Dayak Cultural Heritage Preservation and the Global Human Remains Trade." *Journal of Borneo-Kalimantan* 7(1): 67–93.

Huffer, Damien, Jaime Simons, Tom Brughmans, and Shawn Graham. 2022. "'Alleen voor studiedoeleinden' [For study purposes only]: The human remains trade on Marktplaats.nl." *Anthropologica et Praehistorica* 131: 37–53.

Huffer, Damien, Cristina Wood, and Shawn Graham. 2019. "What the Machine Saw: Some Questions on the Ethics of Computer Vision and Machine Learning to Investigate Human Remains Trafficking." *Internet Archaeology* 52. https://doi.org/10.11141/ia.52.5.

Hugo, Kristin. 2016. "Human Skulls Are Being Sold Online, but Is It Legal?" *National Geographic*. Retrieved 28 March 2022 from https://www.nationalgeographic.com/science/article/human-skulls-sale-legal-ebay-forensics-science.

Huxley, Angie K., and Michael Finnegan. 2004. "Human Remains Sold to the Highest Bidder! A Snapshot of the Buying and Selling of Human Skeletal Remains on eBay®, an Internet Auction Site." *Journal of Forensic Sciences* 49(1): 1–4. https://doi.org/10.1520/JFS2002222.

Ifergan Gallery. 2021. "Ancient Egyptian Female Mummy Head, New Kingdom, 18th Dinasty, 1000 BC." *Ifergangallery*. Retrieved 28 March 2022 from https://ifergangallery.com/piece/ancient-egyptian-female-mummy-head-new-kingdom-18th-dinasty-1000-bc/.

Iken, Katja. 2021. "Wo steckt der Kopf des Mangi Meli?" *Spiegel*, 28 March. Retrieved 25 March 2022 from https://www.spiegel.de/geschichte/deutscher-kolonialismus-in-afrika-wo-steckt-der-kopf-des-mangi-meli-a-1e5ab093-222a-4453-93d3-597e8aea417c.

Immonen, Visa, and Jussi-Pekka Taavitsainen. 2011. "Finger of a Saint, Thumb of a Priest: Medieval Relics in the Diocese of Turku, and the Archaeology of Lived Bodies." *Scripta Instituti Donneriani Aboensis* 23(1): 141–73.

Instagram. n.d. "Permissions Review Instagram Developer Documentation." Retrieved 24 March 2022 from https://www.instagram.com/developer/review/.

———. n.d. "Terms of Use." Retrieved 24 March 2022 from https://help.instagram.com/478745558852511/.

Jahng, Mi Rosie. 2019. "Watching the Rich and Famous: The Cultivation Effect of Reality Television Shows and the Mediating Role of Parasocial Experiences." *Media Practice and Education* 20(4): 319–33.

Jantz, Richard, and Stephen Ousely. 2005. "FORDISC 3.1." Retrieved 28 March 2022 from https://fac.utk.edu/fordisc-3-1-personal-computer-forensic-discriminant-functions/.

Jarus, Owen. 2020. "Looted Skulls and Human Remains Are Being Sold in Black Markets on Facebook." *Live Science*, 2 July. Retrieved 28 March 2022 from https://www.live science.com/human-bone-trade-facebook.html.

Jibréus, Dan. 2014. "The Long Journey of White Fox." *Nebraska History* 95: 100–23.

Jones, Imogen. 2017. "A Grave Offence: Corpse Desecration and the Criminal Law." *Legal Studies* 37(4): 599–620.

Joseph, George, and Kenneth Lipp. 2018. "IBM Used NYPD Surveillance Footage to Develop Technology That Lets Police Search by Skin Color." *Theintercept.com*, 6 September. Retrieved 28 March 2022 from https://theintercept.com/2018/09/06/nypd-surveillance-camera-skin-tone-search/.

Kang, Gaobi, Jian Wang, Xuejun Yue, Guofan Zeng, and Zekai Feng. 2021. "Transfer Learning Based Crop Disease Identification Using State-of-the-Art Deep Learning Framework." *2021 IEEE International Performance, Computing, and Communications Conference (IPCCC)*, 1–6. https://doi.org/10.1109/IPCCC51483.2021.9679406.

Karkare, Prateek. 2019. "Convolutional Neural Networks: Simplified." *AI Graduate*, 15 February. https://medium.com/x8-the-ai-community/cnn-9c5e63703c3f.

Kapishev, Raiym. 2016–22. "'Instagram-php-scraper' v0.4.5." *Github*. Retrieved 28 March 2022 from https://github.com/postaddictme/instagram-php-scraper/.

Kay, Barbara. 2022. "Barbara Kay: What We Don't Know about Unmarked Graves at Residential Schools." *National Post*, 17 January. Retrieved 28 March 2022 from https://nationalpost.com/opinion/barbara-kay-what-we-dont-know-about-unmar ked-graves-at-residential-schools.

Kersel, Morag M. 2008. "The Trade in Palestinian Antiquities." *Jerusalem Quarterly* 33: 21–38.

Kersel, Morag M., and Austin Hill. 2019. "The (W)Hole Picture: Responses to a Looted Landscape." *International Journal of Cultural Property* 26(3): 305–29. https://doi.org/10.1017/S0940739119000195.

Kinkopf, Katherine M., and Jess Beck. 2016. "Bioarchaeological Approaches to Looting: A Case Study from Sudan." *Journal of Archaeological Science: Reports* 10: 263–71. https://doi.org/10.1016/j.jasrep.2016.09.011.

Kirkegaard, Emil O. W., and Julius D. Bjerrekaer. 2016. "The OKCupid Dataset: A Very Large Public Dataset of Dating Site Users." *Open Differential Psychology* 46: 1–10. https://doi.org/10.26775/ODP.2016.11.03.

Kjellström, Anna. 2017. "Tangible Traces of Devotion: The Post-Mortem Life of Relics." *Current Swedish Archaeology* 25(1): 151–75.

———. 2022. "From Saint to Anthropological Specimen: The Transformation of the Alleged Skeletal Remains of Saint Erik." In *Interdisciplinary Explorations of Postmortem Interaction: Dead Bodies, Funerary Objects, and Burial Spaces through Texts and Time*, ed. Elizabeth Weiss-Krejci, Sebastian Becker, and Philip Schwyzer, 167–89. Cham: Springer Press.

Klein, Holger A. 2004. "Eastern Objects and Western Desires: Relics and Reliquaries between Byzantium and the West." *Dumbarton Oaks Papers* 48: 283–314.

Klevnäs, Alison. 2013. *Whodunnit? Grave Robbery in Anglo-Saxon England and the Merovingian Kingdoms*. Oxford, UK: Archaeopress, BAR International Series.

Knapman, Gareth, and Cressida Fforde. 2020. "Profit and Loss: Scientific Networks and the Commodification of Indigenous Ancestral Remains." In *The Routledge Companion to Indigenous Repatriation: Return, Reconcile, Renew*, ed. Cressida Fforde, C. Timothy McKeown, and Honor Keeler, 361–80. London: Routledge.

Kosseff, Jeff. 2016. "The Gradual Erosion of the Law That Shaped the Internet: Section 230's Evolution over Two Decades." *The Columbia Science & Technology Law Review* 18(1): 1–3.

———. 2019. *The Twenty-Six Words That Created the Internet*. Ithaca: Cornell University Press.

———. 2022. "A User's Guide to Section 230, and a Legislator's Guide to Amending It (or Not)." *Berkeley Technological Law Journal* 37(2): 2–40.

Kozlowska, Iga. 2018. "Facebook and Data Privacy in the Age of Cambridge Analytica." *Jsis. washington.edu*, 30 April. Retrieved 28 March 2022 from https://jsis.washington.edu/news/facebook-data-privacy-age-cambridge-analytica/.

Kramer, Adam D. I., Jamie E. Guillory, and Jeffrey T. Hancock. 2014. "Experimental Evidence of Massive-Scale Emotional Contagion through Social Networks." Proceedings of the National Academy of Science USA 111(24): 8788–90. https://doi.org/10.1073/pnas.1320040111.

Krizhevsky, Alex, Ilya Sutskever, and Geoffrey E. Hinton. 2012. "Imagenet Classification with Deep Convolutional Neural Networks." In *Advances in Neural Information Processing Systems 25*, ed. Peter Bartlett, Fernando Pereira, Chris J. C. Burges, Léon Bottou, and Kilian Q. Weinberger, 1097–1105. Red Hook: Curran Associates, Inc. Retrieved 28 March 2022 from https://papers.nips.cc/paper/4824-imagenet-classification-with-deep-convolutional-neural-networks.

Kurschinski, Kellen. 2013. "Applied Archival Downloading with Wget." *Programming Historian*, 13 September. http://programminghistorian.org/en/lessons/applied-archival-downloading-with-wget.

Laestadius, Linnea, and Yang Wang. 2018. "Youth Access to JUUL Online: eBay Sales of JUUL Prior to and Following FDA Action." *Tobacco Control* 28: 617–22.

Laramée, François Dominic. 2018. "Introduction to Stylometry." *The Programming Historian*. https://doi.org/10.46430/phen0078.

Lasaponara, Rosa, Maria Danese, and Nicola Masini. 2012. "Satellite-Based Monitoring of Archaeological Looting in Peru." In *Satellite Remote Sensing: Remote Sensing and Digital Image Processing*, vol 16, ed. Rosa Lasaponara and Nicola Masini, 177–93. Dordrecht: Springer Press.

Lee, Dave. 2018. "Predictim Babysitter App: Facebook and Twitter Take Action." *BBC. com*, 27 November. Retrieved 28 March 2022 from https://www.bbc.com/news/technology-46354276.

Lewis, Ben. 2021. "Kim Kardashian and the Mystery of the Golden Coffin." *The Times. co.uk*, 17 July. Retrieved 28 March 2022 from https://www.thetimes.co.uk/article/kim-kardashian-and-the-mystery-of-the-golden-coffin-2vvl3gbwg.

Liebenberg, Leandi, Erika N. L'Abbé, and Kyra E. Stull. 2015. "Population Differences in the Postcrania of Modern South Africans and the Implications for Ancestry Estimation." *Forensic Science International* 257: 522–29. https://doi.org/10.1016/j.forsciint.2015.10.015.

Liu, Hugo. 2007. "Social Network Profiles as Taste Performances." *Journal of Computer-Mediated Communication* 13(1): 252–75.

Live Auctioneers. 2016. "Important Ancient Egyptian Mummy Head." *Liveauctioneers. com*, 12 September. Retrieved 28 March 2022 from https://www.liveauctioneers.com/item/47172147_important-ancient-egyptian-mummy-head.

———. 2017. "Important Ancient Egyptian Mummy Head." *Liveauctioneers.com*, 16 October. Retrieved 28 March from 2022 from https://www.liveauctioneers.com/item/56172381_an-important-egyptian-mummy-head.

Lueck, Jennifer A. 2012. "Friend-Zone with Benefits: The Parasocial Advertising of Kim Kardashian." *Journal of Marketing Communications* 21(2): 91–109. https://doi.org/10.1080/13527266.2012.726235.

Lutz, Hartmut, ed. 2005. *The Diary of Abraham Ulrikab: Text and Context.* Ottawa: University of Ottawa Press.

MacBeath, Alastair. 2022. "Disruptive Endeavours: Ethical Guidance for Civil Society Organizations Monitoring and Responding to Online Trafficking in Endangered Species." *GITOC Global Initiative Against Transnational Organized Crime.* Retrieved 28 March 2022 from https://globalinitiative.net/analysis/ethical-guide-cso-iwt/.

Mackenzie, Simon, Neil Brodie, Donna Yates, and Christos Tsirogiannis. 2020. *Trafficking Culture: New Directions in Researching the Global Market in Antiquities.* New York: Routledge.

Maier, Christopher A., Kang Zhang, Mary H. Manhein, and Xin Li. 2015. "Palate Shape and Depth: A Shape-Matching and Machine Learning Method for Estimating Ancestry from Human Skeletal Remains." *Journal of Forensic Sciences* 60(5): 1129–34. https://doi.org/10.1111/1556-4029.12812.

Malm, Sara. 2017. "The Vatican Bans Sales of Saints' Body Parts, Including Hair Strands and Teeth, to Stop Them Being Sold for Thousands on Online Auctions." *Daily Mail Online*, 18 December. Retrieved 28 March 2022 from http://www.dailymail.co.uk/news/article-5191219/The-Vatican-banning-sales-relics-saints.html.

Márquez-Grant, Nicholas, and Linda Fibiger. 2011. *The Routledge Handbook of Archaeological Human Remains and Legislation: An International Guide to Laws and Practice in the Excavation and Treatment of Archaeological Human Remains.* New York: Routledge.

Márquez-Grant, Nicholas, and Kirsty Squires. 2018. *Ethical Challenges in the Analysis of Human Remains.* London: Springer Press.

Marsh, Tanya D. 2012. "Rethinking Laws Permitting the Sales of Human Remains." *Huffpost.com*, 13 October. Retrieved 28 March 2022 from https://www.huffpost.com/entry/laws-permitting-human-remains_b_1769082.

———. 2015. *The Law of Human Remains.* Wake Forest: Wake Forest Law School.

Mashburg, Tom. 2020. "Facebook, Citing Looting Concerns, Bans Historical Artifact Sales." *The New York Times*, 23 June. Retrieved 28 March 2022 from https://www.nytimes.com/2020/06/23/arts/design/facebook-looting-artifacts-ban.html.

Mayallah, Elisha. 2020. "Marking 120 years of Mangi Meli's Death." *The Citizen*, 3 May. Retrieved 28 March 2022 from https://www.thecitizen.co.tz/tanzania/magazines/sound-living/-marking-120-years-of-mangi-meli-s-death-2708628.

Mbembe, Achille. 2019. *Necropolitics.* Durham: Duke University Press.

McCorristine, Shane. 2015. "The Dark Value of Criminal Bodies: Context, Consent, and the Disturbing Sale of John Parker's Skull." *Journal of Conservation and Museum Studies* 13(1): 1–7.

McCouat, Philip. 2013. "The Life and Death of Mummy Brown." *The Journal of Art in Society.* Retrieved 28 March 2022 from http://www.artinsociety.com/the-life-and-death-of-mummy-brown.html.

Meeusen, Rebecca A., Angi M Christensen, and Joseph T. Hefner. 2015. "The Use of Femoral Neck Axis Length to Estimate Sex and Ancestry." *Journal of Forensic Sciences* 60(5): 1300–4. https://doi.org/10.1111/1556-4029.12820.

Merrillees, Louise. 2017. "Is 'Uber for Babysitters' App Gobi the Future of Childcare or a Step Too Far?" *ABC.com*, 5 November. Retrieved 28 March 2022 from https://www.abc.net.au/news/2017-11-05/uber-for-babysitters-future-of-childcare-or-step-too-far/9063068.

Mickel, Allison. 2016. "Tracing Teams, Texts, and Topics: Applying Social Network Analysis ot Understand Archaeological Knowledge Production at Çatalhöyük." *Journal of Archaeological Method and Theory* 23: 1095–126. https://doi.org/10.1007/s10816-015-9261-z.

Milligan, Ian. 2019. *History in the Age of Abundance? How the Web Is Transforming Histori-cal Research*. Montreal: McGill-Queen's University Press.

Milovanovic, Selma. 2008. "Egypt Could Jail Australian Dealer for 15 Years." *The Syd-ney Morning Herald*, 2 December. Retrieved 28 March 2022 from https://www.smh.com.au/world/egypt-could-jail-australian-dealer-for-15-years-20081226-gdt7rc.html.

Mimnagh, Louise M. 2017. "The Disposition of Human Remains and Organ Donation: Increasing Testamentary Freedom While Upholding the No Property Rule." *Western Journal of Legal Studies* 7(1): article 3. Retrieved 28 March 2022 from https://ir.lib.uwo.ca/uwojls/vol7/iss1/3.

Ministerieel Besluit. 2009. Ter uitvoering van het Cultureel-erfgoeddecreet van 23 mei 2008, voor wat betreft de toekenning van een kwaliteitslabel aan collectiebeherende cultureel- erfgoedorganisaties en de indeling van musea en culturele archiefinstellin-gen bij het Vlaamse niveau. Belgisch Staatsblad. Retrieved 23 November 2022 from http://www.ejustice.just.fgov.be/eli/besluit/2009/01/23/2009035133/staatsblad.

Mishra, M. 2020. "Convolutional Neural Networks, Explained." *Towards Data Science*, 26 August. https://towardsdatascience.com/convolutional-neural-networks-explain ed-9cc5188c4939.

Montrose, Tamara V., Lori R. Kogan, and James A. Oxley. 2021. "The Role of Social Media in Promoting Organised Dog Fighting." *The Veterinary Nurse* 12(8): 386–91.

Nafte, Myriam. 2014. "Trophies and Talismans: The Traffic of Human Remains." Ph.D. diss., McMaster University.

Nagpal, Shruti, Maneet Singh, Arushi Jain, Richa Singh, Mayank Vatsa, and Afzel Noore. 2017. "On Matching Skulls to Digital Face Images: A Preliminary Approach." *IEEE International Joint Conference on Biometrics (IJCB)*, 813–19. https://doi.org/10.1109/BTAS.2017.8272775.

Nahon, Karine, and Jeff Hemsley. 2013. *Going Viral*. Cambridge, UK: Polity Press.

Nash, Stephen E., and Chip Colwell. 2020. "NAGPRA at 30: The Effects of Repatriation." *Annual Review of Anthropology* 49: 225–39.

Navega, David, Catarina Coelho, Ricardo Vicente, Maria Teresa Ferreira, Sofia Waster-lain, and Eugénia Cunha. 2014a. "AncesTrees: Ancestry Estimation with Random-ized Decision Trees." *International Journal of Legal Medicine* 129: 1145–59. https://doi.org/10.1007/s00414-014-1050-9.

Navega, David, Ricardo Vicente, Duarte N. Vieira, Ann H. Ross, and Eugénia Cunha. 2014b. "Sex Estimation from the Tarsal Bones in a Portuguese Sample: A Machine Learning Approach." *International Journal of Legal Medicine* 129: 651–59. https://doi.org/10.1007/ s00414-014-1070-5.

New Zealand Customs Service. n.d. "Human Remains." *Customs.govt.nz*. Retrieved 28 March 2022 from https://www.customs.govt.nz/covid-19/personal/human-remains/.

New Zealand Legislation. 1961. "Crimes Act 1961." *Legislation.govt.nz*. Retrieved 28 March 2022 from https://www.legislation.govt.nz/act/public/1961/0043/137.0/DLM329287.html.

Nilsson, Martina, Göran Possnert, Hanna Edlund, Bruce Budowle, Anna Kjellström, and Marie Allen. 2010. "Analysis of the Putative Remains of a European Patron Saint–St. Birgitta." *PLoS ONE* 5(2): e8986. https://doi.org/10.1371/journal.pone.0008986.

NLTimes. 2021. "Grapperhaus Does Not Want to Make Corpse Desecration Punishable by Law." *NLTimes.nl*. Retrieved 28 June 2021 from https://nltimes.nl/2021/03/13/grapperhaus-want-make-corpse-desecration-punishable-law.

Nord, Andrew. 2020–22. "TikTok Scraper." *Github*. Retrieved 28 March 2022 from https://github.com/drawrowfly/tiktok-scraper.

Norvig, Peter. 2008. "Google Web Trillion Word Corpus." *Natural Language Corpus Data: Beautiful Data*. Retrieved 28 March 2022 from http://norvig.com/ngrams/.

Oostra Roelof-Jan, Tamara Gelderman, W. J. Mike Groen, H. Gepke Uiterdijk, Erik L. H. Cammeraat, Tristan Krap, Leah S. Wilk, Mark Lüschen, W. Elly Morriën, Frans Wobben, Wilma L. J. M. Duijst, and Maurice C. G. Aalders. 2020. "Amsterdam Research Initiative for Sub-surface Taphonomy and Anthropology (ARTISTA)—A Taphonomic Research Facility in the Netherlands for the Study of Human Remains." *Forensic Science International* 317(110483). https://doi.org/10.1016/j.forsciint.2020.110483.

Ousley, Douglas S. 2016. "Forensic Classification and Biodistance in the 21st Century: The Rise of Learning Machines." In *Biological Distance Analysis: Forensic and Bioarchaeological Perspectives*, ed. Marin A. Pilloud and Joseph T. Hefner, 197–212. New York: Elsevier. https://doi.org/10.1016/B978-0-12-801966-5.00010-X.

Parcak, Sarah, David Gathings, Chase Childs, and Greg Mumford. 2016. "Satellite Evidence of Archaeological Site Looting in Egypt: 2002–2013." *Antiquity* 90(349): 188–205.

Parke, Erin. 2021. "Online Black Market Bone Trade under Scrutiny as Researchers Investigate." *Abc.net.au*, 15 September. Retrieved 28 March 2022 from https://www.abc.net.au/news/2021-09-15/black-market-bone-trade-online-under-scrutiny/100461008.

Paul, Katie A. 2018. "Ancient Artifacts vs. Digital Artifacts: New Tools for Unmasking the Sale of Illicit Antiquities on the Dark Web." *Arts* 7(2): 1–19. https://doi.org/10.3390/arts7020012.

Paul, Katie A., and Amr Al-Azm (with contributions by Shawn Graham). 2019. "Facebook's Black Market in Antiquities: Trafficking, Terrorism, and War Crimes." *Athar Project*. Retrieved 28 March 2022 from http://atharproject.org/report2019/.

Paul, Katie A., Kathleen Miles, and Damien Huffer. 2020. "Two Clicks Away: Wildlife Sales on Facebook." *Alliance to Counter Crime Online*. Retrieved 28 March 2022 from https://www.counteringcrime.org/wildlife-sales-on-facebook.

Pawn Stars Fan. 2021a. "Pawn Stars Season 17 Episode 1 | Asmat Ancestor Skull." *YouTube*. Retrieved 28 March 2022 from https://www.youtube.com/watch?v=LXdeYaN51Qo.

———. 2021b. "Pawn Stars Season 17 Episode 17 | Tibetan Kapala." *YouTube*. Retrieved 28 March 2022 from https://www.youtube.com/watch?v=XmjU-fQXvrQ.

Peckham, Deborah L. 2005. "The Internet Auction House and Secondary Liability—Will eBay Have to Answer to GROKSTER?" *Trademark Rep.* 95: 977.

Peersman, Claudia, Christian Schulze, Awais Rashid, and Margaret Brennan. 2014. "iCOP: Automatically Identifying New Child Abuse Media in P2p Networks." *2014 IEEE Security and Privacy Workshops*, 124–31. https://doi.org/10.1109/SPW.2014.27.

Pellicer, Marlene Pardo. 2021. "The Dead Man Trapped Inside a Mannequin." *Marlene's Newsletter*, 27 December. Retrieved 28 March 2022 from https://marlenepardopellicer.substack.com/p/the-dead-man-trapped-inside-a-mannequin?s=r.

Penn Museum. 2021. "Towards a Respectful Resolution." *Penn Museum*, 25 August. Retrieved 28 March 2022 from https://www.penn.museum /towards-respectful-resolution/.

Percy-Beauregard, Celeste. 2022. "Bone Home: Why Skullstore and the Prehistoria Museum on Dundas East Make up the 'World's Weirdest Recycling Center.'" *Toronto Star*, 13 March. Retrieved 28 March 2022 from https://www.thestar.com/life/together/places/2022/03/13/bone-home-why-skullstore-and-the-prehistoria-museum-on-dundas-east-make-up-the-worlds-weirdest-recycling-center.html.

Perdue, Robert Todd. 2021. "Who Needs the Dark Web? Exploring the Trade in Critically Endangered Plants on eBay." *American Journal of Criminal Justice* 46: 1006–17.

Perez, Sarah. 2021. "TikTok Adds Creator Monetization Features, Including Tips and Video Gifts." *Tech Crunch*, 2 December. Retrieved 28 March 2022 from https://tech

crunch.com/2021/12/01/tiktok-adds-creator-monetization-features-including-tips-and-video-gifts/.

Perry, Sara. 2019. "The Enchantment of the Archaeological Record." *European Journal of Archaeology* 22(3): 354–71.

Pester, Patrick. 2022. "Desecrated Human Skulls Are Being Sold on Social Media in UK's Unregulated Bone Trade." *LiveScience.com*, 7 October. Retrieved 17 November 2022 from https://www.livescience.com/human-skulls-desecrated-uk-human-remains-trade.

Petersen, Margit Anne, Ida Lund Petersen, Camilla Poulsen, and Lotte Stig Nørgaard. 2021. "#Studydrugs–Persuasive Posting on Instagram." *International Journal of Drug Policy* 95: 103100. https://doi.org/10.1016/j.drugpo.2020.103100.

Pilkington, Ed. 2020. "Philadelphia City Council Apologises for Deadly 1985 MOVE Bombing." *The Guardian.com*, 14 November. Retrieved 28 March 2022 from https://www.theguardian.com/us-news/2020/nov/13/philadelphia-1985-move-bombing-apology.

———. 2021. "Bones of Black Children Killed in Police Bombing Used in Ivy League Anthropology Course." *The Guardian*, 23 April. Retrieved 28 March 2022 from https://www.theguardian.com/us-news/2020/nov/13/philadelphia-1985-move-bombing-apology.

Pilloud, Marin A., and Joseph T. Hefner, eds. 2016. *Biological Distance Analysis: Forensic and Bioarchaeological Perspectives*. New York: Elsevier.

Piombino-Mascali, Dario, and Heather Gill-Frerking. 2019. "The Mummy Autopsy: Some Ethical Considerations." In *Ethical Approaches to Human Remains*, ed Kirsty Squires, David Errickson, and Nicholas Márquez-Grant, 605–25. Cham: Springer. https://doi.org/10.1007/978-3-030-32926-6_29.

Plemons, Amber, and Joseph T. Hefner. 2016. "Ancestry Estimation Using Macromorphoscopic Traits." *Academic Forensic Pathology* 6(3): 400–12. https://doi.org/10.23907/2016.041.

Pokines, James T. 2015a. "Taphonomic Characteristics of Former Anatomical Teaching Specimens Received at a Medical Examiner's Office." *Journal of Forensic Identification* 65(2): 173–95.

———. 2015b. "A Santería/Palo Mayombe Ritual Cauldron Containing a Human Skull and Multiple Artifacts Recovered in Western Massachusetts, U.S.A." *Forensic Science International* 248: e1–7. https://doi.org/10.1016/j.forsciint.2014.12.017.

Pokines, James T., Nicollette Appel, Corey Pollock, Christopher J. Eck, Amanda G. Maki, Skylar A. Joseph, Lindsey Cadwell, and Christina D. Young. 2017. "Anatomical Taphonomy at the Source: Alterations to a Sample of 84 Teaching Skulls at a Medical School." *Journal of Forensic Identification* 67(4): 600–32.

Prabhu. 2019. "Understanding NLP Word Embeddings—Text Vectorization." *Towards Data Science*, 11 November. https://towardsdatascience.com/understanding-nlp-word-embeddings-text-vectorization-1a23744f7223.

Purbrick, Louise. 2013. "Trading the Past: Material Culture of Long Kesh/Maze, Northern Ireland." *Journal of War & Cultural Studies* 6(1): 58–74.

Rachwani, Mostafa. 2021. "Western Australia Auction House Pulls Human Skull from Sale after Complaint." *The Guardian*, 7 January. Retrieved 24 March 2022 from https://www.theguardian.com/australia-news/2021/jan/07/western-australia-auction-house-pulls-human-skull-from-sale-after-complaint.

Ray, Sanjana. 2018. "Decoding India's Secret Trade of Bone Smuggling". *The Quint*, 5 December. Retrieved 24 March 2022 from https://www.thequint.com/explainers/decoding-indias-secret-trade-in-bone-smuggling.

Redman, Samuel J. 2016. *Bone Rooms: From Scientific Racism to Human Prehistory in Museums*. Cambridge, MA: Harvard University Press.

Reinhard, Andrew. 2018. *Archaeogaming: An Introduction to Archaeology in and of Video Games.* New York: Berghahn Books.

Reuters. 2018. "Amazon Ditched AI Recruiting Tool That Favored Men for Technical Jobs." *The Guardian.com*, 10 October. Retrieved 28 March 2022 from https://www.theguardian.com/technology/2018/oct/10/amazon-hiring-ai-gender-bias-recruiting-engine.

Richardson, Lorna-Jane. 2018. "Ethical Challenges in Digital Public Archaeology." *Journal of Computer Applications in Archaeology* 1(1): 64–73.

Riggs, Christina. 2014. *Unwrapping Ancient Egypt.* London: Bloomsbury Press.

Risam, Roopika. 2019. *New Digital Worlds: Postcolonial Digital Humanities in Theory, Praxis, and Pedagogy.* Evanston: Northwestern University Press. https://doi.org/10.2307/j.ctv7tq4hg.

Rivet, France. 2014. *In the Footsteps of Abraham Ulrikab: The Events of 1880–1881.* Gatineau, Quebec: Polar Horizons.

———. 2018. "Ethnographic Objects Associated with the Labrador Inuit Who Were Exhibited in Europe in 1880" [Objets ethnographiques associés aux Inuit du Labrador exhibés en Europe en 1880]. *Études Inuit Studies* 42(1–2): 137–59.

Rohrlich, Justin. 2022. "Americans Are Buying Souvenirs Online from Ukraine War." *The Daily Beast*, 18 June. Retrieved 29 November from https://www.thedailybeast.com/ukrainians-are-selling-war-trophies-on-ebay-and-americans-are-buying-russian-items.

Rooney, Shannon McLaughlin. 2020. "Memory, Margins and Materiality: The Philadelphia MOVE Bombing." PhD diss., Temple University.

Roque, Ricardo. 2010. *Headhunting and Colonialism: Anthropology and the Circulation of Human Skulls in the Portuguese Empire, 1870–1930.* London: Palgrave Macmillan.

Rosen, George. 1974. "Christian Fenger, Medical Immigrant." *Bulletin of the History of Medicine* 48(1): 129–45.

Ross, Ann H., and Shanna E. Williams. 2021. "Ancestry Studies in Forensic Anthropology: Back on the Frontier of Racism." *Biology* 10(602). https://doi.org/10.3390/biology10070602.

Samuel, Sigal. 2018. "China Is Going to Outrageous Lengths to Surveil Its Own Citizens." *The Atlantic.com*, 16 August. Retrieved 28 March 2022 from https://www.theatlantic.com/international/archive/2018/08/china-surveillance-technology-muslims/567443/.

Savitt, Todd L. 1982. "The Use of Blacks for Medical Experimentation and Demonstration in the Old South." *The Journal of Southern History* 48(3): 331–48.

Scarre, Chris, and Geoffrey Scarre, eds. 2006. *The Ethics of Archaeology: Philosophical Perspectives on Archaeological Practice.* Cambridge: Cambridge University Press. https://doi.org/10.1017 /CBO9780511817656.

Schmidhuber, Jürgen. 2015. "Deep Learning in Neural Networks: An Overview." *Neural Networks* 61: 85–117. https://doi.org/10.1016/j.neunet.2014.09.003.

Schmidt, Ben. 2015a. "Vector Space Models for the Digital Humanities." *Ben's Bookworm Blog.* Retrieved 28 March 2022 from http://bookworm.benschmidt.org/posts/2015-10-25-Word-Embeddings.html.

———. 2015b. "Word Vectors: An R Package for Building and Exploring Word Embedding models, v1.3." *Github.* Retrieved 28 March 2022 from https://github.com/bmschmidt/wordVectors/releases.

———. 2015c. "Gendered Language in Teacher Reviews." *benschmidt.org.* Retrieved 28 March 2022 from https://benschmidt.org/profGender.

———. 2015d. "Word Embeddings for the Digital Humanities." Retrieved 28 March 2022 from http://bookworm.benschmidt.org/posts/2015-10-25-Word-Embeddings.html.

———. 2015e. "Rejecting the Gender Binary: T Vector-Space Operation." Retrieved 28 March 2022 from http://bookworm.benschmidt.org/posts/2015-10-30-rejecting-the-gender-binary.html.

Schroeder, Bryon, and Xoxi Nayapiltzin. 2022. "A Complicated History: Collaboration with Collectors to Recover and Repatriate Indigenous Human Remains Removed from Spirit Eye Cave." *Advances in Archaeological Practice* 10(1): 26–37. https://doi .org/10.1017/aap.2021.36.

Schwartz, Matt. 2001. "eBay Will Prohibit Sales of 'Murderabilia.'" *The Houston Chronicle*, 9 May. Retrieved 28 March 2022 from https://www.chron.com/business/article/EBay-will-prohibit-sales-of-murderabilia-2033344.php.

Schwartz, Oscar. 2019. "Instagram's Grisly Human Skull Trade Is Booming." *Wired UK*, 18 July. Retrieved 24 March 2022 from https://www.wired.co.uk/article/insta gram-skull-trade.

Scott, David A. 2013. "Modern Antiquities: The Looted and the Faked." *International Journal of Cultural Property* 20(1): 49–75.

Sehl, Katie. 2021. "Instagram Demographics in 2021: Important User Stats for Marketers." *Hootesuite*. Retrieved 21 March 2022 from https://blog.hootsuite.com/instagram-demographics/.

Seidemann, Ryan M., Christopher M. Stojanowski, and Frederick J Rich. 2009. "The Identification of a Human Skull Recovered from an eBay Sale." *Journal of Forensic Sciences* 54(6): 1247–53. https://doi.org/10.1111/j.1556-4029.2009.01194.x.

Shelar, Jyoti. 2017. "When Unclaimed Bodies Turn Cadavers." *The Hindu*, 27 May. Retrieved 28 March 2022 from https://www.thehindu.com/news/cities/mumbai/when-un claimed-bodies-turn-cadavers/article18589168.ece.

Sheppard, Kathleen. 2010. "Flinders Petrie and Eugenics at UCL." *Bulletin of the History of Archaeology* 20(1): 16–29. https://doi.org/10.5334/bha.20103.

———. 2012. "Between Spectacle and Science: Margaret Murray and the Tomb of the Two Brothers." *Science in Context* 25(4): 525–49. https://doi.org/10.1017/S026988 9712000221.

Shorten, Connor, and Taghi M. Khoshgoftaar. 2019. "A Survey on Image Data Augmentation for Deep Learning." *Journal of Big Data* 6(60). https://doi.org/10.1186/ s40537-019-0197-0.

Siapkas, Johannes. 2016. "Skulls from the Past: Archaeological Negotiations of Scientific Racism." *Bulletin of the History of Archaeology* 26(1): 1–9.

Silayo, Valence, and Valerian Meriki. 2022. "What Are You Doing with My Grandfather's Skull? A Conversation with Isaria Anaeli Meli Bin Mandara." *Jahazi* 10(1): 20–24.

Sinnreich, Aram, Patricia Aufderheide, and Neil W. Perry. 2021. "Performative Media Policy: Section 230's Evolution from Footnote to Loyalty Oath." *AoIR Selected Papers of Internet Research*. https://doi.org/10.5210/spir.v2021i0.12242.

Skeates, Robin. 2010. *An Archaeology of the Senses: Prehistoric Malta*. New York: Oxford University Press.

Skeates, Robin, and Jo Day, eds. 2020. *The Routledge Handbook of Sensory Archaeology*. London: Routledge.

Smith, Julia M. H. 2012. "Portable Christianity: Relics in the Medieval West (c. 700–1200): 2010 Raleigh Lecture on History." In *Proceedings of the British Academy Volume 181, 2010–2011 Lectures*, ed. Ron Johnston. Retrieved 22 November 2022 from https://doi .org/10.5871/bacad/9780197265277.003.0006.

Solsman, Joan E. 2022. "YouTube Adds Its TikTok-Like Shorts to TVs." *CNET.com*, 7 November. Retrieved 19 November 2022 from https://www.cnet.com/news/you tube-adds-its-tiktok-like-shorts-to-tvs/.

Stanish, Charles. 2009. "Forging Ahead. Or, How I Learned to Stop Worrying and Love eBay." *Archaeology* 62(3): 18–66.

Stienne, Angela. 2018. "Encountering Egyptian Mummies, 1753–1858." PhD diss., School of Museum Studies, University of Leicester.

———. 2022. *Mummified: The Stories Behind Egyptian Mummies in Museums*. Manchester: Manchester University Press.

Stiftung Preußischer Kulturbesitz (SPK). 2019. "Chief Mangi Meli's Skull Not in Collections of Stiftung Preußischer Kulturbesitz." *Stiftung Preußischer Kulturbesitz*, 9 September. Retrieved 9 May 2023 from https://www.preussischer-kulturbesitz.de/en/news-detail-page/article/2019/09/20/schaedel-des-mangi-meli-nicht-in-spk-sammlung0.html.

Stokel-Walker, Chris. 2022. "YouTube Wants to Take on TikTok and Put Its Shorts Videos on Your TV." *MIT Technology Review*, 7 November. Retrieved 18 November 2022 from https://www.technologyreview.com/2022/11/07/1062868/youtube-wants-to-take-on-tiktok-with-shorts-videos-for-your-tv/.

Stroud, Ellen. 2018. "Law and the Dead Body: Is a Corpse a Person or a Thing?" *Annual Review of Law and Social Science* 14: 115–25. https://doi.org/10.1146/annurev-lawsocsci-110316-113500.

Stutz, Liv Nilsson. 2016. "To Gaze Upon the Dead: The Exhibition of Human Remains as Cultural Practice and Political Process in Scandinavia." In *Archaeologists and the Dead*, ed. Howard Williams and Melanie Giles, 268–92. Oxford: Oxford University Press.

Suri, Manveena. 2017. "India: Police Arrest 8 in Human Bone Smuggling Ring." *CNN.com*, 23 March. Retrieved 28 March 2022 from https://edition.cnn.com/2017/03/23/asia/india-bone-smuggling/index.html.

Swain, Hedley. 2016. "Museum Practice and the Display of Human Remains." In *Archaeologists and the Dead*, ed. Howard Williams and Melanie Giles, 169–83. Oxford: Oxford University Press.

Swenson, Victoria Marie. 2013. "Ancestral and Sex Estimation Using E.A. Marino's Analysis of the First Cervical Vertebra Applied to Three Modern Groups." Master's thesis, University of Montana. Retrieved 28 March 2022 from https://scholarworks.umt.edu/etd/145/.

Szegedy, Christian, Wei Liu, Yangqing Jia, Pierre Sermanet, Scott Reed, Dragomir Anguelov, Dumitru Erhan, Vincent Vanhoucke, and Andrew Rabinovich. 2014. "Going Deeper with Convolutions." *arXiv*: 1409.4842 [cs.VC]. https://doi.org/10.48550/arXiv.1409.4842.

Tallman, Sean D., and Allysha P. Winburn. 2015. "Forensic Applicability of Femur Subtrochanteric Shape to Ancestry Assessment in Thai and White American Males." *Journal of Forensic Sciences* 60(5): 1283–89. https://doi.org/10.1111/1556-4029.12775.

Tanner, Martin A., and Wing Hung Wong. 1987. "The Calculation of Posterior Distributions by Data Augmentation." *Journal of the American Statistical Association* 82(398): 528–50.

Tarantola, Andrew. 2016. "Interpol Is Using AI to Hunt down Child Predators Online." *Engadget.com*, 2 December. Retrieved 28 March 2022 from https://www.engadget.com/2016/12/01/interpol-is-using-ai-to-hunt-down-child-predators-online/.

Tennant, Jonathan P., François Waldner, Damien C. Jacques, Paulo Masuzzo, Lauren B. Collister, and Chris H. J Hartgerink. 2016. "The Academic, Economic and Societal Impacts of Open Access: An Evidence-Based Review." *F1000 Research* 5: 632.

Tharoor, Ishaan. 2016. "Over 1,000 African Skulls in Berlin Are a Reminder of Europe's Dark Colonial History." *Washington Post.com*, 25 November. Retrieved 28 March 2022 from https://www.washingtonpost.com/news/worldviews/wp/2016/11/25/over-1000-african-skulls-in-berlin-are-a-reminder-of-europes-dark-colonial-history/.

Thomas, Suzie, Oula Seitsonen, and Vesa-Pekka Herva. 2016. "Nazi Memorabilia, Dark Heritage and Treasure Hunting as 'Alternative' Tourism: Understanding the Fascination with the Material Remains of World War II in Northern Finland." *Journal of Field Archaeology* 41(3): 331–43.

Trainor, Kevin M. 1992. "When Is a Theft Not a Theft? Relic Theft and the Cult of the Buddha's Relics in Sri Lanka." *Numen: International Review for the History of Religions* 39(1): 1–26.

Tran, Gina A., and David Strutton. 2014. "Has Reality Television Come of Age as a Promotional Platform? Modeling the Endorsement Effectiveness of Celebrity and Reality Stars." *Psychology & Marketing* 31(4): 294–305.

Tremain, Cara Grace. 2017. "Fifty Years of Collecting: The Sale of Ancient Maya Antiquities at Sotheby's." *International Journal of Cultural Property* 24(2): 187–219.

Tremble, Catherine A. 2017. "Wild Westworld: Section 230 of the CDA and Social Networks' Use of Machine-Learning Algorithms." *Fordham Law Review* 86(2): 825.

Tringham, Ruth. 1991. "Households with Faces: The Challenge of Gender in Prehistoric Architectural Remains." In *Engendering Archaeology: Women in Prehistory*, ed. Joan Gero and Margaret Conkey, 93–131. Oxford, UK: Blackwell.

Tringham, Ruth, and Annie Danis. 2019. "Doing Sensory Archaeology." In *The Routledge Handbook of Sensory Archaeology*, ed. Robin Skeates and Jo Day, 48–75. London: Routledge.

Troian, Martha. 2019a. "Federal Conservative Candidate Gives Boyfriend Human Skull for Birthday." *APTN National News*, 3 July. Retrieved 28 March 2022 from https://www.aptnnews.ca/national-news/federal-conservative-candidate-gives-boyfriend-human-skull-for-birthday/.

———. 2019b. "Human Skull Purchased from Oddity Shop by Conservative Candidate, Likely an Orphaned Skull Says Owner." *APTN National News*, 8 July. Retrieved 28 March 2022 from https://www.aptnnews.ca/national-news/human-skull-purchased-from-oddity-shop-by-conservative-candidate-likely-an-orphan-skull-says-owner/.

Uliwa, Caroline. 2019. "Exhibit Brings Mangi Meli of Old Moshi Back to Life." *The East African.com*, 25 January. Retrieved 28 March 2022 from https://www.theeastafrican.co.ke/tea/magazine/exhibit-brings-mangi-meli-of-old-moshi-back-to-life-1411106.

Ünlütürk, Özge. 2017. "Metric Assessment of Ancestry from the Vertebrae in South Africans." *International Journal of Legal Medicine* 131: 1123–31. https://doi.org/10.1007/s00414-016-1483-4.

United Kingdom Public General Acts. 2004. "Human Tissue Act." Retrieved 28 March 2022 from https://www.legislation.gov.uk/ukpga/2004/30/schedule/1.

United States Congress. 1990. "H.R.5237—101st Congress (1989–1990): Native American Graves Protection and Repatriation Act." *Congress.gov*, Library of Congress, 16 November. Retrieved 28 March 2022 from https://www.congress.gov/bill/101st-congress/house-bill/5237.

Uzuner, Sedef. 2007. "Educationally Valuable Talk: A New Concept for Determining the Quality of Online Conversations." *MERLOT Journal of Online Learning and Teaching* 3(4): 400–10.

Valentine, Carla. 2016. "Flogging a Dead Corpse: The Sale of Human Remains." *Huffington Post UK*, 13 October. Retrieved 28 March 2022 from https://www.huffingtonpost.co.uk/carla-valentine/flogging-a-dead-corpse-th_b_8283974.html.

Valentino-DeVries, Jennifer, Natasha Singer, Michael H. Keller, and Aaron Krolik. 2018. "Your Apps Know Where You Were Last Night, and They're Not Keeping It Secret." *The New York Times*, 10 December. Retrieved 28 March 2022 from https://www.nytimes.com/interactive/2018/12/10/business/location-data-privacy-apps.html.

van der Maaten, Laurens. 2014. "Accelerating t-SNE using Tree-Based Algorithms." *Journal of Machine Learning Research* 15: 3221–45.

van der Maaten, Laurens, and Geoffrey E. Hinton. 2008. "Visualizing High-Dimensional Data Using t-SNE." *Journal of Machine Learning Research* 9: 2579–605.

van Dyk, David, and Ziao-Li Meng. 2001. "The Art of Data Augmentation." *Journal of Computational and Graphical Statistics* 10(1): 1–50.

van Strydonck, Mark, Anton Ervynck, Marit Vandenbruaene, and Mathieu Boudin. 2016. "Anthropology and 14C Analysis of Skeletal Remains from Relic Shrines: An Unexpected Source of Information for Medieval Archaeology." *Radiocarbon* 51(2): 569–77.

Veblen, Thorstein, and Martha Banta. (1899) 2009. *The Theory of the Leisure Class*. Oxford: Oxford University Press.

Venturini, Sofia, and David L. Roberts. 2020. "Disguising Elephant Ivory as Other Materials in the Online Trade." *Tropical Conservation Science* 13(4): 1–8.

Vergano, Dan. 2016. "eBay Just Nixed Its Human Skull Market." *BuzzFeed News*, 12 July. Retrieved 28 March 2022 from https://www.buzzfeednews.com/article/danvergano/skull-sales.

Vidiyala, Ramya. 2020. "What, Why and How of t-SNE." *Towards Data Science*, 19 May. https://towardsdatascience.com/what-why-and-how-of-t-sne-1f78d13e224d.

Villa, Federica. 2021. "Authentically Exotic and Authentically Beautiful." In *Crime and Art—Sociological and Criminological Perspectives of Crimes in the Art World*, ed. Naomi Oosterman and Donna Yates, 135–52. Cham: Springer Press.

Viyandath, Siva. 2018. *Antisocial Media: How Facebook Disconnects Us and Undermines Democracy*. Oxford: Oxford University Press.

Voorzitter Museumvereniging. 2006. "Ethische Code voor Musea." Retrieved 29 June 2021 from https://www.museumvereniging.nl/media/ethischecode_20112006.pdf.

Vraag En Antwoord Tweede Kamer. 2009. 20 May. 2009D24805 (R. van Raak). Retrieved 28 June 2021 https://www.tweedekamer.nl/kamerstukken/kamervragen/detail? id=20 09Z05527&did=2009D24805.

Wadbring, Ingela, and Sara Ödmark. 2016. "Going Viral: News Sharing and Shared News in Social Media." *Observatorio (OBS*)* 10(4): 132–49.

Wallace, Terry, and Claudia Lauer. 2022. "Police: Pennsylvania Man Tried to Buy Stolen Human Remains on Facebook." *NBC Philadelphia.com*, 20 August. Retrieved 18 November 2022 from https://www.nbcphiladelphia.com/news/local/pa-man-tried-to-buy-stolen-human-remains-police-say/3339576/.

Wall Street Journal Staff. 2021. "Inside TikTok's Algorithm: A WSJ Video Investigation." *The Wall Street Journal*, 21 July. Retrieved 28 March 2022 from https://www.wsj.com/articles/tiktok-algorithm-video-investigation-11626877477.

Walsham, Alexandra. 2010. "Skeletons in the Cupboard: Relics after the English Reformation." *Past & Present* 206(5): 121–43.

Waters-Rist, Andrea, Rachel Schats, and Menno L. P. Hoogland. 2016. "Ethical Issues in Human Osteoarchaeology: Recommendations for Practice in the Netherlands." In *The Urban Graveyard: Archaeological Perspectives*, ed. Roos M. R. van Oosten, Rik Schots, Karl Fast, Nico Arts, and Hans M. P. Bouwmeester, 9–27. Leiden: Sidestone Press.

Watkins, Rachel J. 2020. "An Alter(Ed)Native Perspective on Historical Bioarchaeology." *Historical Archaeology* 54(1): 17–33. https://doi.org/10.1007/s41636-019-00224-5.

Watkins, Jennifer K., Samantha H. Blatt, Cynthia A. Bradbury, Gordon A. Alanko, Matthew J. Kohn, Marion L. Lytle, Joanna Taylor, Deborah Lacroix, Maria A. Nieves-Colón, Anne C. Stone, and Darryl P. Butt. 2017. "Determining the Population Affinity of an Unprovenienced Human Skull for Repatriation." *Journal of Archaeological Science: Reports* 12: 384–94. https://doi.org/10.1016/j.jasrep.2017.02.006.

Watson, Michelle, and Amanda Musa. 2022. "Brother of 1985 MOVE Bombing Victims Sues Philadelphia and UPenn for Allegedly Mishandling the Black Teens' Remains." *CNN.com*, 10 November. Retrieved 17 November 2022 from https://edition.cnn.com/2022/11/10/us/philadelphia-move-bombing-lawsuit-remains-reaj/index.html.

Webb, Denver A. 2015. "War, Racism, and the Taking of Heads: Revisiting Military Conflict in the Cape Colony and Western Xhosaland in the Nineteenth Century." *The Journal of African History* 56(1): 37–55.

Weimann, Gabriel, and Natalie Masri. 2020. "Research Note: Spreading Hate on Tik-Tok." *Studies in Conflict and Terrorism.* https://doi.org/10.1080/1057610X.2020.17 80027.

Weisberger, Mindy. 2019. "Stolen Mummy Feet, Arms and More Found Stashed in Speakers at Cairo Airport." *Live Science.com*, 26 February. Retrieved 28 March 2022 from https://www.livescience.com/64851-mummy-parts-recovered-airport.html.

Weiss-Krejci, Estella. 2016. "'Tomb to Give Away': The Significance of Graves and Dead Bodies in Present-Day Austria." In *Archaeologists and the Dead*, ed. Howard Williams and Melanie Giles, 169–83. Oxford: Oxford University Press.

Wescott, Daniel J. 2005. "Population Variation in Femur Subtrochanteric Shape." *Journal of Forensic Sciences* 50(2): 281–88. https://doi.org/10.1520/JFS2004281.

Westmont, V. Camille. 2022. "Dark Heritage in the New South: Remembering Convict Leasing in Southern Middle Tennessee through Community Archaeology." *International Journal of Historical Archaeology* 26: 1–21.

Wet. 6 July 2013. Oudende instemming met het Verdrag ter bescherming van het cultureel erfgoed onder water, aangenomen te Parijs op 2 november 2001 (1) (2). Belgisch Staatsblad 25 October 2013. Retrieved 23 November 2022 from http://www.ejustice.just .fgov.be/eli/wet/2013/07/06/2013015218 /staatsblad.

———. 9 December 2015. Erfgoedwet. 18 December 2015. Retrieved 23 November 2022 from https://wetten.overheid.nl/ BWBR0037521/2020-04-01.

———. 1 August 2018. Lijkbezorging. Retrieved 23 November 2022 from https://wetten .overheid.nl/BWBR0005009/2018-08-01#HoofdstukVII.

———. 1 July 2020. Orgaandonatie. Retrieved 23 November 2022 from https://wetten.over heid.nl/BWBR0008066/2020-07-01.

Wetboek van Strafrecht. 2021. Strafrecht. Retrieved 23 November 2022 from https://wetten .overheid.nl/BWBR0001854/2021-05-01.

Wevers, Melvin, Thomas Smits, and Leonardo Impett. 2018. "ImageTexts: Studying Texts and Images in Conjunction" (Poster), *DH2018*. Retrieved 28 March 2022 from https:// pure.knaw.nl/ws/portalfiles/portal/7670493/Poster_DH18.pdf.

Whitehead, David, Carly Cowell, Anita Lavorgna, and Stuart Middleton. 2021. "Countering Plant Crime Online: Cross-Disciplinary Collaboration in the Floraguard Study." *Forensic Science International: Animals and Environments* 1: 100007. https://doi.org/ 10.1016/j.fsiae.2021.100007.

Williams, Howard A. 2019. "Selling Dead Bodies and Mortuary Artefacts in the UK Today: Welbeck Hill." *ArchaeoDeath*, 9 February. https://howardwilliamsblog.wordpress .com/2019/02/09/selling-dead-bodies-and-mortuary-artefacts-in-the-uk-today-wel beck-hill/.

Williams, Howard, and Melanie Giles, eds. 2016. *Archaeologists and the Dead*. Oxford: Oxford University Press.

Wise, Sarah. 2005. *The Italian Boy: Murder and Grave Robbery in 1830s London*. London: Pimlico Press.

Witten, Ian H., Eibe Frank, Mark A. Hall, and Christopher J. Pal. 2017. *Data Mining: Practical Machine Learning Tools and Techniques*. Cambridge, MA: Elsevier.

Wolfe, Samuel J., and Robert Singerman. 2009. *Mummies in Nineteenth-Century America: Ancient Egyptians as Artifacts.* Jefferson: McFarland & Company.

World Archaeological Congress (WAC). 2010. "WAC November 2010 eNewsletter – Volume 35." Retrieved 28 March 2022 from https://worldarch.org/blog/wac-novem ber-2010-enewsletter-volume-35/.

Wright, Richard. 1992. CRANID. Retrieved 28 March 2022 from https://app.box.com/s/ h0674knjzl.

Xu, Qing, Mingxiang Cai, and Tim K. Mackey. 2020. "The Illegal Wildlife Digital Market: An Analysis of Chinese Wildlife Marketing and Sale on Facebook." *Environmental Conservation* 47(3): 206–12.

Yang, Maya. 2021. "US Widow Horrified as Husband's Body Donated to Science Is Dissected Publicly." *The Guardian.com*, 10 November. Retrieved 17 November 2022 from https://www.theguardian.com/us-news/2021/nov/09/widow-horrified-bo dy-donated-to-science-dissected-publicly.

Yates, Donna. 2013. "Toi moko." *Traffickingculture.org*, 30 October. Retrieved 28 March 2022 from https://traffickingculture.org/encyclopedia/case-studies/toimoko/.

———. 2014a. "Two Looted, Mutilated Maya Monuments for Sale Online." *Anonymous Swiss Collector*, 27 October. Retrieved 28 March 2022 from http://www.anonymous swisscollector.com/2014/10/2-looted-mutilated-maya-monuments-for-sale-online .html.

———. 2014b. "Lies, Damned Lies, and Archaeologists: Antiquities Trafficking Research as Criminology and the Ethics of Identification." *AP Online Journal of Public Archaeology* 4(7): 7–19.

———. 2022. "Violence as a Value Enhancer in the Art Market." *Social Science Research Council*, 2 March. Retrieved 28 March 2022 from https://items.ssrc.org/ where-heritage-meets-violence/violence-as-a-value-enhancer-in-the-art-market/.

Yucha, Josephine M., James T. Pokines, and Eric J. Bartelink. 2017. "A Comparative Taphonomic Analysis of 24 Trophy Skulls from Modern Forensic Cases." *Journal of Forensic Sciences* 62(5): 1266–78. https://doi.org/10.1111/1556-4029.13426.

Zech, John R. 2018. "What Are Radiological Deep Learning Models Actually Learning?" *Medium.com*, 9 July. https://medium.com/@jrzech/what-are-radiological-deep-learning-models-actually-learning-f97a546c5b98.

Zech, John R., Marcus A. Badgeley, Manway Liu, Anthony B. Costa, Joseph J. Titano, and Eric K. Oermann. 2018. "Confounding Variables Can Degrade Generalization Performance of Radiological Deep Learning Models." *arXiv*: 1807.00431.

Zimmer, Adam Netzer. 2018. "More Than the Sum Total of Their Parts: Restoring Identity by Recombining a Skeletal Collection with Its Texts." In *Bioarchaeological Analyses and Bodies: New Ways of Knowing Anatomical and Archaeological Skeletal Collections*, ed. Pamela K. Stone, 49–70. Cham: Springer Press.

Zimmerman, Larry J., Karen D. Vitelli, and Julia J. Hollowell, eds. 2003. *Ethical Issues in Archaeology*. Waltman Creek: Altamira.

Index